THE FIGURE OF THE MIGRANT

THE FIGURE OF THE MIGRANT

Thomas Nail

STANFORD UNIVERSITY PRESS

STANFORD, CALIFORNIA

Stanford University Press
Stanford, California

Printed in the United States of America on acid-free, archival-quality paper

Library of Congress Cataloging-in-Publication Data

Nail, Thomas, author.
    The figure of the migrant / Thomas Nail.
        pages   cm
    Includes bibliographical references and index.
    ISBN 978-0-8047-8717-8 (cloth : alk. paper)
    ISBN 978-0-8047-9658-3 (pbk. : alk. paper)
        1. Marginality, Social—Political aspects. 2. Political science—Philosophy.
I. Title.
HM1136.N35 2015
320.01—dc23

                                                        2015007378

ISBN 978-0-8047-9668-2 (electronic)

For Eliot

Contents

Acknowledgments

I am extremely grateful to the Fulbright Association for providing me with the means to spend a year in Canada working with the migrant justice group No One Is Illegal–Toronto and building the research for this book. This project has benefited greatly from that year and all the connections it made possible. I also thank Concordia University, the University of Toronto, and McMaster University for hosting me as a visiting Fulbright Scholar while in Canada. When I returned to the States, I was fortunate to have the support of the Wayne Morse Center for Law and Politics at the University of Oregon, which provided me with funding as well as a desk from which to continue my research on the politics of migration. The University of Denver provided some financial assistance to help with the costs of editing and indexing.

While I was writing this book, several universities invited me to speak about my research on migration and borders. The feedback and questions that followed these talks ultimately strengthened the work. For this, I thank the University of Toronto, DePaul University, the University of Oregon, the University of Redlands, and the University of Colorado at Denver. My own department at the University of Denver has been overwhelmingly supportive of this project. I am lucky to find myself among such generous colleagues.

I am indebted to a number of people for their support and encouragement of this project: Colin Koopman, Ted Toadvine, Dan Smith, Nicolae Morar, Robert Urquhart, Josh Hanan, Adam Israel, Adam Bobbette, Etienne Turpin, David Craig, Kieran Aarons, Julia Sushytska, and all the folks I worked with at *Upping the Anti: A Journal of Theory and Action.* I also acknowledge No One Is Illegal–Toronto for its tireless passion and hard work toward migrant justice and for welcoming me into the organization as a fellow activist while I lived in Toronto. Thank you especially to Fariah Chowdhury, Faria Kamal, Farrah Miranda, and Syed Hussan. To Peter Nyers, for his generous feedback and continuing support for my work, I am more than grateful. During my time as the director of Post-Doctoral Faculty in Migration and Diaspora at the University of Denver, I benefited from the support of and fascinating work done by the researchers there. In the final production of this manuscript I am thankful for the help of Nicholas Esposito, Michael Lechuga, and Timothy Snediker at the University of Denver, and the help of Emily-Jane Cohen, Friederike Sundaram, and Cynthia Lindlof at Stanford University Press. I am grateful for the reports from my referees and their helpful feedback. Specifically, I thank Tim Cresswell for his extensive and thoughtful commentary throughout the entire manuscript. Above all, I am grateful to my wife, Katie, for her love and support.

THE FIGURE OF THE MIGRANT

Introduction

The twenty-first century will be the century of the migrant. At the turn of the century, there were more regional and international migrants than ever before in recorded history.[1] Today, there are over 1 billion migrants.[2] Each decade, the percentage of migrants as a share of the total population continues to rise, and in the next twenty-five years, the rate of migration is predicted to be higher than during the last twenty-five years.[3] It has become more necessary for people to migrate because of environmental, economic, and political instability. Climate change, in particular, may cause international migration to double over the next forty years.[4] The percentage of total migrants who are non-status or undocumented is increasing, which poses a serious challenge to democracy and political representation.[5]

In other ways, we are all becoming migrants.[6] People today relocate to greater distances more frequently than ever before in human history. While many people may not move across a regional or international border, they tend to change jobs more often, commute longer and farther to work,[7] change their residence repeatedly, and tour internationally more often.[8] Some of these phenomena are directly related to recent events, such as the impoverishment of middle classes in certain rich countries after the financial crisis of 2008, subsequent austerity cuts to social welfare programs, and rising unemployment. The subprime mortgage crisis led to the expulsion of millions of people from their homes worldwide (9 million in the United States alone). Foreign investors and governments have acquired 540 million acres since 2006, resulting in the eviction of millions of small farmers in poor countries, and mining practices have become increasingly destructive around the world—including hydraulic fracturing and tar sands. This general increase in human mobility and expulsion is now widely recognized as a defining feature of the twenty-first century.[9] "A specter haunts the world and it is the specter of migration."[10]

However, not all migrants are alike in their movement.[11] For some, movement offers opportunity, recreation, and profit with only a temporary expulsion. For others, movement is dangerous and constrained, and their social expulsions are much more severe and permanent. Today, most people fall somewhere on this migratory spectrum between the two poles of "inconvenience" and "incapacitation." But what all migrants on this spectrum share, at some point, is the experience that their *movement* results in a certain degree of expulsion from their territorial, political, juridical, or economic status. Even if the end result of migration is a relative increase in money, power, or enjoyment, the *process of migration itself* almost always involves an insecurity of some kind and duration: the removal of territorial ownership or access, the loss of the political right to vote or to receive social welfare, the loss of legal status to work or drive, or the financial loss associated with transportation or change in residence.

The gains of migration are always a risk, while the process itself is always some kind of loss. This is precisely the sense in which Zygmunt Bauman writes that "tourism and vagrancy are two faces of the same coin" of global migration. Both the "tourist" (the traveling academic, business professional, or vacationer) and the "vagabond" (migrant worker or refugee), as Bauman calls them, are "bound to move" by the same social conditions but result in different kinds and degrees of expulsion from the social order. Businesspeople are compelled to travel around the world in the "global chase of profit," "consumers must never be allowed to rest" in the chase of new commodities and desires, and the global poor must move from job to job wherever capital calls. For the tourist this social "compulsion, [this] 'must,' [this] internalized pressure, [this] impossibility of living one's life in any other way," according to Bauman, "reveals itself . . . in the disguise of a free exercise of will."[12] The vagabond sees it more clearly. The social compulsion to move produces certain expulsions for all migrants. Some migrants may decide to move, but they do not get to decide the social conditions of their movement or the degree to which they may be expelled from certain social orders as a consequence. Migration in this sense is neither entirely free nor forced—the two are part of the same *regime of social motion*. The concept of expulsion simply means the degree to which a migrant is deprived or dispossessed of a certain status in this regime.

The tourist and vagabond are always crossing over into one another, as Bauman writes. "None of the insurance policies of the tourists' life-style protects against slipping into vagabondage. . . . [M]ost jobs are temporary, shares may go down as well as up, skills, the assets one is proud of and cherishes now become obsolete in no time."[13] Migration is the spectrum between these two poles, and the figure of the migrant is the one who moves on this spectrum. In this way, migratory figures function as mobile social positions and not fixed identities. One is not born a migrant but becomes one. This book is a philosophical history of the political subject we have become today: *the migrant.* However, there are two central problems to overcome in order to develop such a theory.

Two Problems

The first problem is that the migrant has been predominantly understood from the perspective of *stasis* and perceived as a secondary or derivative figure with respect to place-bound social membership. Place-bound membership in a society is assumed as primary; secondary is the movement back and forth between social points. The "emigrant" is the name given to the migrant as the former member or citizen, and the "immigrant" as the would-be member or citizen. In both cases, a static place and membership are theorized first, and the migrant is the one who lacks both. Thus, more than any other political figure (citizen, foreigner, sovereign, etc.), the migrant is the one least defined by its being and place and more by its becoming and displacement: by its *movement*.

If we want to develop a political theory of the migrant itself and not the migrant *as a failed citizen*, we need to reinterpret the migrant first and foremost according to its own defining feature: its movement. Thus, this book develops a theoretical framework that begins with movement instead of stasis.[14] However, beginning from the theoretical primacy of movement does not mean that one should uncritically celebrate it. Movement is not always good, nor is movement always the same. Movement is always distributed in different concrete social formations or types of circulation.[15] It is not a metaphor. Thus, this book is neither a valorization of movement, or an ontology of movement in general. It is a kinetic and philosophical history of the subject of our time: *the migrant*. It seeks to understand the material, social, and historical conditions under which something like the migrant has come to exist for us today. It is a philosophical history of the present.

In this way, it is not only a theory of the migrant but also a theory of the social motions by which migration takes place. Society is always in motion. From border security and city traffic controls to personal technologies and work schedules, human movement is socially directed. Societies are not static places with fixed characteristics and persons.[16] Societies are dynamic processes engaged in continuously directing and circulating social life. In a movement-oriented philosophy there is no social stasis, only regimes of social circulation. Thus, if we want to understand the figure of the migrant, whose defining social feature is its movement, we must also understand *society itself* according to movement. This, therefore, is the guiding interpretive framework of this book.[17]

The second problem is that the migrant has been predominantly understood from the perspective of *states*.[18] Since the state has all too often written history, the migrant has been understood as a figure without its own history and social force. "In world history," as Hegel says, "we are concerned only with those peoples that have formed states [because] all the value that human beings possess, all of their spiritual reality, they have through the State alone."[19] This is not to say that migrants are always stateless but that the history of migrant social organizations has tended to be subsumed or eradicated by state histories. Often, the most dispossessed migrants have created some of the most interesting non-state social organizations.

In response to this problem, this book offers a counter-history of several important migrant social organizations that have been marginalized by states. The migrant is not only a figure whose movement results in a certain degree of social expulsion. The migrant also has its own type of movement that is quite different from the types that define its expulsion. Accordingly, migrants have created very different forms of social organization that can clearly be seen in the "minor history" of the raids, revolts, rebellions, and resistances of some of the most socially marginalized migrants. This is a challenging history to write because many of these social organizations produced no written documents, or if they did, they were systematically destroyed by those in power. It is not a natural fact that the history of migrants has become ahistorical, as Hegel argues—it is the violence of states that has rendered the migrant ahistorical. This book does not try to render a complete account of this (a)history but rather to provide a *social kinetic interpretation* of several important migrant social formations in Western history that have been buried by the history of states and citizens.

The Consequences

There are three important consequences of developing a political theory of the migrant in this way. First, it allows us to *conceptualize the emergence of the historical conditions* that gave rise to the types of social expulsion that define the migrant. The major forms of kinetic social expulsion that define the twenty-first century did not emerge out of nowhere. They emerged historically. At different points in history, migratory movement was the result of different types and degrees of social expulsion: territorial, political, juridical, and economic. New forms of social organization rose to dominance through history. As states triumphed over villages, and markets triumphed over feudalism, we begin to see an explosion in new techniques for expelling migrants from their previous status. Once these new techniques emerge historically, they tend to persist. Today, we find the contemporary migrant at the intersection of all four major forms of historical social expulsion. However, this book is not a universal history of the migrant that shows the vast intertwining of all the previous forms of social expulsion at every historical point and to every degree for every social figure.[20] This is too large a task. It is also not able to be sensitive to all of the changes that certain key terms like "territory" have undergone over thousands of years of history.[21]

The aim of this book is more modest: to provide an analysis of four major techniques for expelling migrants during their period of historical dominance and to provide a conceptual, movement-based definition of the migratory figures associated with these expulsions.[22] The present study does not provide a history of the relative deprivations of tourists, diplomats, business travelers, explorers, and state functionaries, although such a history would also be interesting. Instead, it focuses on the more marginalized figures of historical migration (nomads, barbarians, vagabonds, and the proletariat) for three reasons. First, because it is primarily their history that has been decimated and is in the most need of recovery and reinterpretation. Second, because it is in their history that the emergence of each new form of social expulsion (of which the tourist experiences only the smallest degree) is most sharply visible. Third, and most important, because it is their history that more closely resembles the situation of most of the people we call migrants today.

The second consequence is that developing a theory of the migrant will allow us to *analyze contemporary migration* because the history of migration is not a linear or progressive history of distinct "ages." Rather, it is a history of coexisting and overlapping social forces of expulsion. The same techniques of territorial, political, juridical, and economic expulsion of the migrants that have emerged and repeated themselves in history are still at work today. For example, territorial expulsion, the dispossession of land,[23] does not occur only once against the nomadic peoples in the Neolithic period but gets taken up again and mobilized in various ways throughout history—up to the present. The invention of territorial social expulsion created *historical* nomadic peoples, but it also invented a *social* type of migrant subjectivity characterized by territorial expulsion that also continues to define other territorially displaced peoples. This is the sense in which migrants may be "nomadic" without being exactly the same as historical nomads.

As an example, in the ancient world, migrants were expelled from their territories by war and kidnapping; in the medieval world, they were expelled by enclosure and the removal of customary laws that bound them to the land; and in the modern world, they have been expelled by the capitalist accumulation of private property. Although each dispossession of land is historically unique, each shares a common social kinetic function. Contemporary migration is part of this legacy.[24] Today, migrant farmworkers are expelled by industrial agriculture; indigenous peoples are expelled from their native lands by war and forced into the mountains, forests, or "waste lands"; and island peoples are expelled from their territory by the rising tides of climate change. There is a certain truth in the fact that the popular press often refers to all these people as "nomads," even though they are not literally the same as early historical nomads. However, what all these migrants share is a specific social kinetic form of territorial expulsion that first rose to prominence in early historical nomadism.[25]

The analysis of contemporary migration presented here is not one of total causal explanation: of push-pull factors, psychological volunteerism, neoclassical or structural economism, and so on. Instead, it offers an original kinetic analysis. The aim of this book is not to explain the causes of all migration but to offer better descriptions of the conditions, forces, and trajectories of its historical emergence and contemporary hybridity.

The third consequence of developing a theory of the migrant is that it allows us to *diagnose the capacity of the migrant to create an alternative* to social expulsion. The figure of the migrant is not merely an effect of different regimes of social expulsion. It also has its own forms of social motion in riots, revolts, rebellions, and resistances. Just as the analysis of the historical techniques for the expulsion of the migrant can be used to understand contemporary migration, so too can the historical techniques of migrant social organizations be used to diagnose the capacity of contemporary migrants to pose an alternative to the present social logic of expulsion that continues to dominate our world.

Today, the figure of the migrant exposes an important truth: social expansion has always been predicated on the social expulsion of migrants. The twenty-first century will be the century of the migrant not only because of the record number of migrants today but also because this is the century in which all the previous forms of social expulsion and migratory resistance have reemerged and become more active than ever before. This contemporary situation allows us to render apparent what had previously been obscured: that the figure of the migrant has always been the true motive force of social history. Only now are we in a position to recognize this.

The argument of this book is developed in four parts. Part 1 defines and lays out the logical structure of social motion. Part 2 argues that the migrant is defined not only by movement in general but by several specific historical conditions and techniques of social expulsion. Part 3 shows how several major migrant figures propose an alternative to this logic, and Part 4 shows how the concepts developed in Parts 2 and 3 help us to better understand the complex dynamics of contemporary migration in US-Mexico politics.

PART I

POLITICAL THEORY OF THE MIGRANT

CHAPTER I

The Figure of the Migrant

The Migrant

Creating a concept of *the migrant* allows us to understand the common social conditions and subject positions of a host of related mobile figures: for example, the floating population, the homeless, the stateless, the lumpenproletariat, the nomad, the immigrant, the emigrant, the refugee, the vagrant, the undocumented, and the barbarian. To be clear, these are all distinct mobile figures in political history and are not always and in every circumstance identical to the figure of the migrant. However, under certain social conditions, they become migratory figures. This book is a history of the common social conditions and agencies that emerge when these mobile figures become migrants. In other words, "the figure of the migrant" is a political concept that identifies the common points where these figures are socially expelled or dispossessed as a result, or as the cause, of their mobility.

In this sense, the migrant is the political figure of movement. But movement has too often been defined as derivative or lacking. In a spatio-temporal sense,[1] movement is defined as beginning from a point of departure (A) and passing, via translation, to a place of arrival (B). Movement, according to this definition, is change of place. Movement is the line AB, which is traversed and, like space, can be infinitely divided. This definition imagines that movement occupies each of the infinite points between A and B in succession and coincides with the immobility of each point in turn. Each point in the series is like a possible point of arrival.

The problem with this logic, according to the Greek philosopher Zeno, is that we would have to traverse an infinite distance of intervals in order to arrive anywhere. Thus, movement would be impossible. The same result occurs, according to Zeno, when we understand movement as a series of temporal now-points or instants. If every unit of time is infinitely divisible, it will take an infinity of time to move from one point to any other. The problem is that movement cannot be divided without destroying it. By thinking that we can divide movement into fixed, immobile stages based on departures and arrivals, we spatialize and immobilize it.[2] Movement, according to such a definition, is just the difference between divisible points of space-time, but there is no real continuity.

The same problem appears in the case of the political figure of movement: *the migrant*. The migrant is often defined as the one who moves from country A to country B—from one fixed social point to another. The fixity of the social points is presupposed as primary, and the migrant is the one who temporarily or permanently lacks this fixity or social membership. This definition has political consequences. In the spatio-temporal definition, movement is presupposed as the line AB, but since this line can be infinitely divided into units of immobile space-time, movement is ultimately unrepresented in the system: the migrant is the political figure who is unrepresented but still exists socially *as unrepresented* in the system.

However, with respect to movement, displacement is not a lack but a positive capacity or trajectory (even if the empirical outcome is not desirable, i.e., involuntary exile). To view migration and movement as lack is also to conceal the conditions of expulsion required by social expansion. It is to treat migration as an "unfortunate phenomenon" rather than the structural necessity of the historical conditions of social reproduction. In other words, to understand migration and movement as lack is to accept the banality of social dispossession. For example, every day our cities must be maintained, remade, built up, torn down, and cleaned. Our office buildings and homes are cleaned and maintained while we are away by an underground and largely invisible reproductive labor force disproportionately composed of migrants. What appears to be the relatively static place we call "society" is constantly being modified through the cleaning and maintenance of labor.

Without this labor, our cities, homes, and streets would be unusable. Yet these sorts of reproductive labor are often paid less and are less valorized than their "productive" counterparts are. The appearance of social stasis in this case is an illusion of the capitalist division between productive and reproductive labor. But the illusion of stasis is not unique to capitalism. Every society has its own social illusions of stasis. Accordingly, the challenge of defining the political figure of the migrant is to positively reconceptualize what has previously been understood as an unrepresentable lack in political philosophies based on stasis. "[T]he world is about to change its foundation. We are nothing, let us be all."[3]

One way to do this is to distinguish between two kinds of movement that define the migrant. The first kind, made up of units of space-time, is extensive and quantitative: movement as change of place, or translation. The second kind of movement is intensive and qualitative: a change in the whole, a transformation. In the example of the line AB, Henri Bergson argues that it is "already motion that has drawn the line" to which A and B have been added afterward as its end points.[4] A and B presuppose the movement of the line, on which they are points. The division into A and B is always a division *of something*: an attempt to impose arbitrary divisions into a continuous movement. Movement is already primary, but we imagine it is not in order to explain it later as derived. According to Bergson, "[I]t is movement which is anterior to immobility."[5] "Reality is mobility itself. . . . If movement is not everything, it is nothing."[6] When an extensive movement occurs from A to B, the whole AB undergoes a qualitative transformation or change.[7]

This second definition also has important political consequences for the political theory of migration. The movement of the migrant is not simply from A to B but is the constitutive condition for the qualitative transformation of society as a whole. The migrant not only undergoes an extensive movement but also affects an intensive or qualitative social movement of the whole of society itself.[8] In this sense, the figure of the migrant is a socially constitutive power. It is the subjective figure that allows society to move and change. However, since the migrant's movement has often been viewed as derivative or lacking sufficient stability (from the extensive perspective), societies have most frequently responded to these qualitative changes of the migrant in two ways. First, they may institute forms of social deprivation that aim at arresting any change that does not accord with the fixed values of those in power: the state, law, profit, and so on. In this case, the migrant does not simply change place but also changes status (becomes apolitical, criminal, unemployable, etc.). Second, when societies desire change or expansion, they may harness the mobility of the migrant in the form of slavery, militarism, incarceration, and waged labor in order to help them expand.[9]

Without a doubt, the migrant moves both extensively and intensively. In the former case, movement and the migrant appear as derivative and lack. In the latter, the movement of the migrant appears as the constitutive force of qualitative social motion, as the condition for the change and growth of society as a whole. What appear to be fixed points are instead points where movement has only slowed down or appears to have stopped relative to other movements. From the perspective of the migrant, these points are simply relays or portions of a continuous trajectory that have been arbitrarily or strategically selected as discrete from the continuum of social motion. According to Bergson, the "stasis" points A and B are simply the "dead and artificial reorganization of movement by the mind."[10] The political theory of the migrant is an analytics of the regimes of social motion that have strategically reorganized movement into the circulation between artificially static social points. But the theory of the migrant is also a theory of movement and migration as the constitutive force of social motion, a theory of the extensive *and* intensive social movement of the migrant. The two are always present together like the latitude and longitude of a social cartography of motion. But insofar as intensive movement remains primary, the migrant remains the constitutive dimension of social motion upon which society divides, organizes, and circulates.

Following this definition, we can see how the migrant forms a common social position between different migratory figures. For example, the emigrant is only an emigrant from the perspective of a socially fixed point *from which* it departs. However, from the perspective of the socially fixed point *to which* the emigrant arrives, it is not an emigrant at all but an immigrant. The distinction between the emigrant and immigrant is a socially relative one, based on certain fixed social points. But the figure called an "emigrant" from one point and called an "immigrant" from another is *the same figure: the migrant.* It is the same figure seen from two sides of the same Möbius strip.

Similarly, what defines the nomad, the barbarian, the vagabond, and the proletariat as migrant subjects is the sense in which each of these figures is displaced and made mobile in its own way and with respect to its own relative points of expulsion. With respect to the territory, the nomad is the one who is expelled from the land; with respect to the political order, the barbarian is the one who is expelled from politics; with respect to the juridical order, the vagabond is the one who is expelled by the law; and with respect to the economic order, it is the proletariat who is expelled from the economic means of production.[11] Each of these migratory figures is defined according to the dominant type of social order from which it is expelled. These are merely relative definitions of the same figure from the perspective of different sites of social expulsion. The migrant is the underlying and common figure of social movement and expulsion.

Accordingly, there is no theory of the migrant "as such." There is no general ontology of the migrant.[12] There are only figures of the migrant that emerge and coexist throughout history relative to specific sites of expulsion and mobility. In this sense, the theory of the migrant offered in this book is a specifically political and historical one. It is political insofar as it is primarily concerned with the social conditions or regimes of motion within which different types of migratory figures emerge and coexist. It is historical insofar as these conditions are not universal or global but regional. Thus, it is neither strictly ontological nor strictly empirical.

So there is not only one migrant, but many. Just as there are different types of societies, so there are different types of migrants, different degrees of mobility, and different forces of expulsion. But in the end, every society produces its migrants. The political theory of the migrant examines each situation according to its types, degrees, and forces.

The movement of the migrant is not always "good," and social regimes of expulsion are not always and in every way "bad." This book does not put forward a theory of what we ought to do. Instead, it lays bare the theoretical, historical, and political conditions for the movement of the migrant that remain obscured today by certain voluntaristic and neoclassical economic accounts. Before we can take political action on contemporary migration policy, we need a better description of the phenomenon and its conditions than we currently have. If there is any kind of normative imperative in this study, it is a conditional one: if you want to struggle against the regimes of social expulsion, here are some tactics and points of intervention that may prove helpful in that struggle.[13]

The Figure

A figure is not a fixed identity or specific person but a mobile social position. One becomes a figure when one occupies this position. One may occupy this position to different degrees, at different times, and in different circumstances. But there is nothing essential about a person that makes the person this figure. The figure of the migrant, for example, is like a social persona that bears many masks (the nomad, barbarian, etc.) depending on the relative social conditions of expulsion.

In this sense, the figure of the migrant is broader than specific groups of migrants defined by crossing national borders. But it is also more regional and historical than a general ontology of migrant subjectivity. A figure is not an unchanging essence lying beyond the concrete, but neither is it merely a specific individual or a group of individuals. A figure is a social vector or tendency. Insofar as specific individuals take up a trajectory, they are figured by it. But it is also possible for individuals to leave this vector and take up a different social position, since it does not define their essence. In other words, the *figure* of the migrant has a "vague essence" in the etymological sense of the word: a vagabond or migratory essence that lies *between* the ideal and the empirical.

For example, in geometry, a circle is an exact ideal essence. This is in contrast to inexact empirical objects that are round (such as bowls, planets, or balls). However, figuration is like "roundness": it is more than an empirical object but less than an ideal exact essence. Roundness can refer equally to bowls and to ideal circles: both are round.[14] Thus, as a figure, the migrant refers both to empirical migrants in the world *and* a more abstract social relation. It is irreducible to either.

In this sense, migration refers both to the millions of actual migrants identified by the United Nations and to the sense in which many more people than these are also migrants to some degree and in some circumstances. As a social position or figure, the migrant is a subjective formation that anyone may become. No one's movement is guaranteed to be safe from some degree of social expulsion. In a political sense, the theory of the migrant, viewed from the primacy of movement, may even present a more inclusive model of international relations than citizenship currently does.[15] The migrant is not only empirical but also prefigures a new model of political membership and subjectivity still in its early stages. Thus, there are empirical migrants, but their meaning and potential extend beyond their empirical features under the current conditions of social expulsion. What would it mean to rethink political theory based on the figure of the migrant rather than on citizenship? This book presents a variety of concepts aimed at answering this question.

PART II

EXPANSION BY EXPULSION

CHAPTER 2

Kinopolitics

The history of the migrant is the history of social motion. In particular, the migrant is defined by two intertwined social motions: expansion and expulsion. This chapter defines and lays out the logical structure of this social motion, and Chapters 3–7 analyze the historical conditions that give rise to it.

Primitive Accumulation

Perhaps another way to conceptualize this thesis is as a radicalization of Marx's concept of "primitive accumulation." Marx develops this concept from a passage in Adam Smith's *Wealth of Nations*: "The accumulation of stock must, in the nature of things, be previous to the division of labour."[1] In other words, before humans can be divided into owners and workers, there must have already been an accumulation such that those in power could enforce the division in the first place. The superior peoples of history naturally accumulate power and stock and then wield it to perpetuate the subordination of their inferiors. For Smith, this process is simply a natural phenomenon: powerful people always already have accumulated stock, as if from nowhere.

For Marx, however, this quote is perfectly emblematic of the historical obfuscation of political economists regarding the violence and expulsion required for those in power to maintain and expand their stock.

Instead of acknowledging this violence, political economy mythologizes and naturalizes it. For Marx, however, the concept of "primitive accumulation" has a material history. It is the precapitalist condition for capitalist production. In particular, Marx identifies this process with the expulsion of peasants and indigenous peoples from their land through enclosure, colonialism, and anti-vagabond laws in sixteenth-century England. Marx's thesis is that the condition of the social expansion of capitalism is the prior expulsion of people from their land and from their juridical status under customary law. Without the expulsion of the people, there is no expansion of private property and thus no capitalism.

While some scholars argue that primitive accumulation was merely a single *historical* event in the sixteenth to eighteenth centuries, others argue that it plays a recurring *logical* function within capitalism itself: in order to expand, capitalism today still relies on noncapitalist methods of social expulsion and violence.[2] However, the thesis in Part 2 of this book is notably different from these in two important ways. First, the process of dispossessing migrants of their social status (expulsion) in order to further develop or advance a given form of social motion (expansion) is not unique to the capitalist regime of social motion. We see the same social process in early human societies whose progressive cultivation of land and animals (territorial expansion) would not have been possible without the expulsion (territorial dispossession) of a part of the human population—including hunter-gatherers, whose territory was transformed into agricultural land, as well as surplus agriculturalists for whom there was no more arable land left to cultivate at a certain point. Thus, social expulsion is the condition of social expansion in two ways: an internal condition that allows for the removal of part of the population when certain internal limits have been reached (carrying capacity of a given territory, for example) and an external condition that allows for the removal of part of the population outside these limits when the territory is able to expand outward into the lands of other groups (hunter-gatherers). In this case territorial expansion was possible only on the condition that part of the population be expelled in the form of migratory nomads, forced into the surrounding mountains and deserts.

Later, we see the same logic in the ancient world, whose dominant political form (the state) would not have been possible without the expulsion (political dispossession) of a large body of barbarian slaves kidnapped from the mountains of the Middle East and Mediterranean and used as workers, soldiers, and servants so that a growing ruling class could live in luxury. The social conditions for the expansion of a growing political order (including warfare, colonialism, and massive public works) were precisely the expulsion of a population of barbarians who had to be depoliticized at the same time. This occurs again and again throughout history.

The second difference between previous theories of primitive accumulation and the more expansive one offered here is that this process of "prior" expulsion or social deprivation noted by Marx is not only territorial or juridical, and its expansion is not only economic. Expulsion does not simply mean forcing people off their land (although in many cases it may include this). It also means depriving people of their political rights through slavery, criminalizing types of persons through vagabondage, or restricting their access to work through unemployment. Accordingly, societies also expand their power in several major ways: through territorial accumulation, political power, juridical order, and economic profit. What is similar between the theory of primitive accumulation and the theory of expansion by expulsion is that most major expansions of social kinetic power also require a "prior" or primitive violence of kinetic social expulsion. The concept of primitive accumulation is merely one historical instance of a more general social logic at work in the emergence and reproduction of previous societies. The migrant is the subjective figure defined by this general logic.

However, Marx also makes several general statements in *Capital* that support something like this thesis. For Marx, the social motion of production *in general* strives to reproduce itself. He calls this "periodicity":

Just as the heavenly bodies always repeat a certain movement, once they have been flung into it, so also does social production, once it has been flung into this movement of alternate expansion and contraction. Effects become causes in their turn, and the various vicissitudes of the whole process, which always reproduces its own conditions, take on the form of periodicity.[3]

According to Marx, every society (not just capitalist ones) engages in some form of social production. Like the movements of the planets, society expands and contracts itself according to a certain logic, which strives to reproduce and expand the conditions that brought it about in the first place. Its effects, in turn, become causes in a feedback loop of social circulation. Social production, for Marx, is thus fundamentally a social motion of circulation.

Part 2 of this book is a radicalization of Marx's concept of primitive accumulation and social periodicity under the concept of "expansion by expulsion."[4] However, before we can elaborate on the consequences of such a concept for the phenomenon of historical and contemporary migration, it needs to be further defined according to the more general method followed here: the analytics of social motion, or what I call "kinopolitics," from the Greek word *kino*, meaning "movement."

Kinopolitics

Kinopolitics is the theory and analysis of social motion: the politics of movement.[5] Instead of analyzing societies as primarily static, spatial, or temporal, kinopolitics or social kinetics understands them primarily as "regimes of motion."[6] Societies are always in motion:[7] directing people and objects, reproducing their social conditions (periodicity), and striving to expand their territorial, political, juridical, and economic power through diverse forms of expulsion. In this sense, it is possible to identify something like a political theory of movement.

However, a political theory of social motion based on movement, not derived from stasis, time, or space, will also require the definition of some conceptual terms important for this analysis. The core concepts in the definition of social motion are "flow," "junction," and "circulation," from which an entire logic of social motion can be defined, in which expansion by expulsion and migration takes place.

Flow

The conceptual basis of kinopolitics is the analysis of social flows.[8] The key characteristic of flows is that they are defined according to their "continuous movement." In this sense, the philosophical concept of flow parallels the historical development of the fluid sciences (aerodynamics and hydrodynamics).[9] In fluid dynamics, a flow is not the movement of fixed solids analyzed as discrete particles, as it is in solid mechanics. The presupposition of the fluid sciences is continuum.[10]

The history of the study of human migration also developed as the study of flows. For early seventeenth-century demographers (and even migration scholars today), measuring the movement of human populations is more like measuring a continuous and variable process than a fixed solid body. This is precisely why migration scholars and the popular press still talk about migration in terms of "flows," "flux," "floods," and other water metaphors.[11] This is the case in part because modern demography and the study of migration emerged alongside the birth of statistics, which made possible the study of large amounts of variable data flows—often over time—based on theories of probability and chance. Statistics is the study of change and chance: of unpredictability. It is the science of making probable the unpredictable. Since a continuous flow cannot be totalized, it had to be measured in an entirely new way.[12] Statistics, faithful to its etymological origins in the root *stat-*, thus emerged as the capture of human migration flows into states.

Beyond the birth of statistics and human flows (migration), we find during this same time in the seventeenth century an explosion of scientific descriptions of flows: flows of food, money, blood, and air. In 1614, the Italian physiologist Sanctorius Sanctorius founded the study of metabolism, the science of transformative biological flows, recorded in *Ars de Statica Medicina*. In his 1628 book, *Exercitatio Anatomica de Motu Cordis et Sanguinis in Animalibus,* William Harvey conducted the first controlled experiments on, and popularized the idea of, pulmonary circulation as originating in the heart, which was previously thought to originate in the liver.[13] In 1686, the English astronomer Edmond Halley published the first map of the trade winds in the Southern Hemisphere. In 1671, Isaac Newton invented a mathematics of flows in *Method of Fluxions*—now called differential calculus. Jean-Baptiste Moheau synthesized many of these studies in 1778 and brought them to bear directly on human mortality in *Recherches et considérations sur la population.* This was the century of the sciences of the variable, of the continuous, of flux.[14] This legacy continues today. Human migration is still studied as *flows*. If the migrant is the political subject of our time, then "flows" should be our conceptual starting point.

However, measuring "a" flow is difficult because a flow, like a river, is indivisible and continually moving. Thus, there is never only one flow, or any total of flows, but a continuous process, a multiplicity. A flow is by definition a non-unity and non-totality whose study can never be completed because it keeps moving along to infinity like a curved line. However, regional stabilities composed of a certain confluence or "flowing together" of two or more moving streams do exist.[15] One flow does not totalize or control the other, but the two remain heterogeneous: like a mixture without unity. Confluent flows are heterogeneous, continuous, but also overlap in a kind of *open* collection without unity.

In this conceptual sense, flows are not only physical, metabolic, or statistical but also social. The political philosophy of migration is precisely the analysis of social flows: flows across borders, flows into detention centers, counter flows (strikes), and so on.

A flow is not a probability. It is a process. A political philosophy of flows is an analysis of their bifurcations, redirections, vectors, or tendencies—not their unities or totalities. The science of probability assumes that a flow is a percentage of 100 (i.e., a totality): $x/100$. A *per-cent-*age presumes a knowledge of the whole such that the *per-* is a part of the known *cent-*, or whole. But a flow is not a part in a whole; it is a "percentage" of infinity: x/∞. For this reason flows include chance, uncertainty, and events. Every "point" already presupposes a process that it marks. A point is simply a relay—both an arrival and departure point for further movement.[16] This also explains why social flows are poorly understood in terms of inclusion and exclusion. Nothing is done once and for all: a flow is only on its way to something else. One is never completely included or excluded but always inclusively excluded or exclusively included: hybrid.[17] Movement, as a continuous flow, is always both/and: it is an inclusive disjunction.

Finally, flows are just as difficult to study as they are to control. They are not controlled by blocking or stopping them but rather by redirecting or slowing them down. The effects of border walls, for example, are not as much about keeping people excluded or included as about redirecting movements and changing the speed and conditions of crossing. The US-Mexico border wall, for example, has more than three thousand documented holes in a constant state of rotation between repair and reopening. The Israeli security fence is filled with underground passageways and supply lines that are similarly destroyed, moved, and rebuilt time and again. Every systemic aim for totality is confronted with the continuity

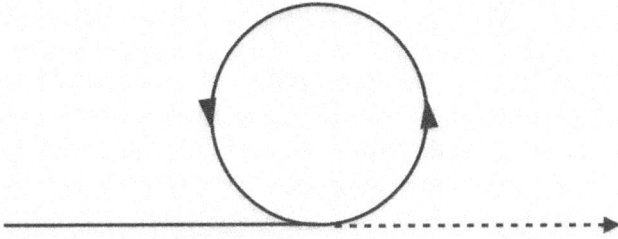

FIGURE I. Junction

and non-totality of flows that leak from its periphery. The control of flows is a question of flexible adaptation and the modulation of limits. Accordingly, the politics of movement is first and foremost defined by the analysis of continuous movement, changes in speed, and the redirection of flows.

Junction

The second basic conceptual term of kinopolitics is the "junction" (see Fig. 1). If all of social reality is comprised of continuous flows, junction explains the phenomenon of relative or perceived stasis. But this relative stasis is always secondary to the primacy of the social flows that compose it. A junction is not something other than a flow. It is the redirection of a flow back onto itself in a loop or fold. In this way, the junction is distinct from a confluence. A confluence is an open whole of overlapping and heterogeneous flows, but a junction occurs when a single flow loops back over *itself.* A junction remains a process, but a vortical process that continues to repeat in approximately the same looping pattern—creating a kind of mobile stability or homeorhesis.[18] A junction is the joining together of a flow with itself. The point at which the flow returns to itself is an arbitrary one, but also one that constitutes a point of self-reference or haptic circularity that yokes the flow to itself.[19]

The junction then acts like a filter or sieve that allows some flows to pass through or around the circle and other flows to be caught in the repeating fold of the circle. The movement of the captured flow can then be connected to the movement of another captured flow and made into all manner of mobile technologies: a vehicle for travel, a tool for moving the ground, or a weapon of war. But the yoking of the flows also augments them, not by moving them faster or slower necessarily, but by putting them under the control of something else: a driver. The driver is not necessarily a person but the given point at which the flow intersects with itself. Although the flow is continually changing and moving around the loop, the driver appears to remain in the same place. In this sense, the driver absorbs the mobility of the yoked flow while remaining relatively immobile itself: a mobile immobility—an immobility that moves by the movements of others.

The concept of the "junction" stands in contrast to the concept of "node," developed in spatial location theory and the geography of movement. For example, Lowe and Moryadas define movement as the "routes" between prior discrete "nodes." Movement is purposive, "and each bit of movement has a specific origin and destination. . . . Our schema is predicated on the existence of nodes prior to the development of networks and movement. . . . Without nodes, why is there movement, and where is it consigned?"[20] In contrast to this view this book offers an alternative to this sort of static and spatialized theory, which has been thoroughly critiqued elsewhere.[21]

In fact, one might easily invert Lowe and Moryadas's question and ask, "Without movement, how did nodes or stable points emerge in the first place?" Placing the fixed nodes first means that movement is always already yoked to an origin and destination, so there is no junction. Bergson argues that we will never understand movement beginning with immobility. My argument is that movement cannot be understood as a route between presupposed origins and destinations and that junctions are not fixed nodes given in advance of movement.[22] Junctions, as the joining of flows, are secondary to the continuous movement of those flows.

As are flows, junctions are social. Every society creates its points of relative stability in a sea of turbulence. The house is a territorial junction, the city is a political junction, and the commodity is an economic junction, and so forth. With respect to migration, a border wall is a junction of rocks, metal, and wood harnessed together into a relatively fixed vehicle whose drivers are mounted at its check points, fixed on its survey towers, or surveying its perimeters in a patrol vehicle. The border is also a yoke or filter that allows some migrants to pass through with only minor inconvenience, others to obtain work under illegal and exploitive conditions, and

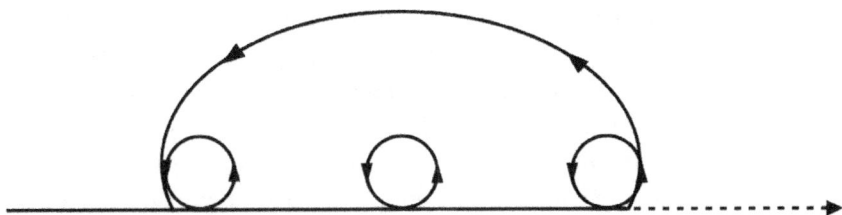

FIGURE 2. Circulation

others still to be caught and held for years in detention centers without charges. On the other side of the border, migrant labor flows are then harnessed through work junctions into a vehicle for production, profit, and social subordination. The flows that do not pass the border junction can end up in the detention junction harnessed into a vehicle of profit for private prison contractors and private security forces responsible for deporting them. Many kinds of political junctions yoke and direct social motion. Kinopolitics is a study of the function and typology of these junctions.

Circulation

The third basic conceptual term of kinopolitics is "circulation," which connects a series of junctions into a larger curved path (see Fig. 2). This curved path continually folds back onto itself, wrapping up all the junctions together. Circulation is the regulation of flows into an ordered network of junctions. But flows are indivisible, so circulation does not divide them but rather bifurcates and folds them back onto themselves in a series of complex knots. Since flows are continuously variable and the junctions are vortical, circulation is dynamic. It acts less like a single ring than like an origami object that brings together multiple folds: changing the neighborhoods of the junctions each time it folds. Even to "remain the same," circulation has to keep changing at a relatively stable rate. And since flows have no absolute origin or destination, neither does circulation. It always begins in the middle of things.

Circulation, just like flows, is not well understood by using the concepts of exclusion and inclusion. The conceptual basis of circulation is that something goes out and then comes back in again, and again. It is a continuum. In this sense, circulation is both inside and outside at once. It is a multifolded structure creating a complex system of relative insides and outsides without absolute inclusions and exclusions. But the insides and outsides are all folds of the same continuous process or flow. Each time circulation creates a fold or pleat, both a new inclusion and new exclusion are created. But circulation itself is not reducible to just these two categories.

The aim of circulation is not only to redirect flows through a network of multiple junctions but also to expand them. Just as flows are yoked into vehicles through junction, so are junctions folded together through circulation. The junctions remain distinct, but flows tie them together. Through circulation, some junctions act together (by connecting flows) and become larger; others separate and become weaker. Circulation turns some junctions away and merges other junctions together in an expanding network. As a circulatory system increases the power and range of its junctions, it increases its capacity to act in more and more ways. It becomes more powerful.

Circulation is more complex than "movement in general" or even "harnessed movement" (junction); it is the controlled reproduction and redirection of movement. Just as Marx locates the circulation of capital in the three basic circuits of money, production, and commodities in *Capital*, other forms of social circulation also have their circuit subsets. A circuit is the repeated, and often expansive, connection between two or more connected junctions.

Capitalism is a form of economic circulation, and there are also forms of territorial, political, and juridical circulation. For example, in migration studies, "circulatory migration" refers to the repeated or seasonal going out and coming back of migrants.[23] The migrant is always in motion. The migrant only appears to have "permanently" settled from the perspective of its *extensive* movement between presumed static social points (sites, states, regions, etc.). However, from the perspective of its *intensive* movement, a migrant is continually changing the supposedly static points from which it departed or to which it arrives. For example, by leaving, migrants may depopulate a labor force, break up a family, deplete the intellectual or cultural climate, be deported, or be deprived of social status in a variety of ways. This changes the qualitative character of the whole society. Even from a purely extensive point of view, the daily life of most migrants includes the continual social motions of commuting, traveling, working, and actively maintaining the material conditions of extensive motions in general (such as construction workers, janitors, or maids). In this sense, migration is always circulatory.[24] It will be harnessed, redirected, and circulated at every level, but it will not stop.

However, within these larger circulations are smaller subcirculations, or circuits that constitute circulation. Border politics is also a circulation in which we can locate at least three circuits. The first is the border circuit, which itself is composed of three movements: (1) Migrants *cross* the border. But the border is a junction: a vehicle of harnessed flows. The border acts as a sieve or filter, as it allows capital and the global elite to move freely but, like a yoke, catches the global poor. (2) A flow of migrants crosses the border (legally or illegally), and if the migrants have lost their status, they are *apprehended* by the drivers of the border junction—the Border Patrol. The flow of migrants might also cross and then be caught far from the border later on. The space/proximity is not the primary issue. The militarized, legalized, and political border creates the criminal act itself. It interpellates the mobility of the migrant as illegal. All immigration enforcement becomes "border enforcement." (3) The captured flow of migrants is harnessed to the enforcement apparatus and then turned or sent back across the border via *deportation*. The deported migrants are released and begin the cycle again. The border circuit is thus cross, apprehend, deport, cross (C-A-D-C). Each cycle in the circuit generates money, power, and prestige for immigration enforcement and justifies its reproduction and expansion.

The second circuit is the detention circuit, which can begin from the crossing of migrants, but it can also begin as a relay from the border circuit during apprehension. The detention circuit is also composed of three basic parts: (1) Migrants cross the border and are apprehended. (2) Instead of being quickly deported, they are harnessed into a different junction—the prison, detention, or camp junction. The flow of migrants is expanded into the detention center. The detention center, as a junction, is also a vehicle that harnesses or extracts mobility from the migrants through their labor,[25] their occupancy, and consumption of their own incarceration: food, water, clothing, medical care, and so on (this generates private profits that are heavily subsidized by the government). In the United States, for example, "of the detainee population of 32,000,

18,690 immigrants have no criminal conviction. More than 400 of those with no criminal record have been incarcerated for at least a year."[26] (3) Once the maximum degree of mobility has been extracted from this flow (sometimes many years of detention), migrants are then deported. Once they are deported, the circuit can begin again or pick up like a relay into the next circuit. The detention circuit is thus apprehend, detain, deport, apprehend (A-DT-D-A).

The third is the labor circuit. Again, this circuit is also composed of three parts: (1) A flow of migrants crosses the border either legally or illegally. This could be after detention-deportation (DT-D), or apprehension-deportation (A-D), or the initial crossing (C). (2) The migrants are then harnessed by a labor junction, which aims to extract as much movement from the migrants as possible. If the migrants have no status, employers and the economy can extract even more than if the migrants were legal (through the suppression of unions, threat of deportation, reduced wages, and dangerous work conditions). In this case, the capitalist is the driver of the work vehicle: moved without moving. The movement of the migrant's labor pulls the vehicle along under the yoke of the capitalist. (3) From the labor junction, the migrant may return across the border, then return again to work, and so on until one of the other circuits begins through capture, detention, or deportation.

The labor circuit, however, aims to indefinitely extend the extraction of movement from the migrant flow and harness it into the many junctions of the economy. Instead of folding back into the detention center, the flow is extended in the largest loop of the three: the indefinite labor circuit. The aim of this circuit is to reproduce an economy of disempowered migrant labor that props up the empowered labor and wages of citizens. The labor circuit is thus: cross, work, cross, work . . . deport, cross (C-W-C-W . . . D-C). The movement within and between these circuits is the circulation of border politics.

These are only three circuits of one type of circulation. However, the border circuit does not help us understand how migrant flows occur in the first place. With the knowledge of what social motion is (flows, junctions, and circulations), it is now easier to outline the kinetic components of the specific form of social circulation under consideration, expansion by expulsion.

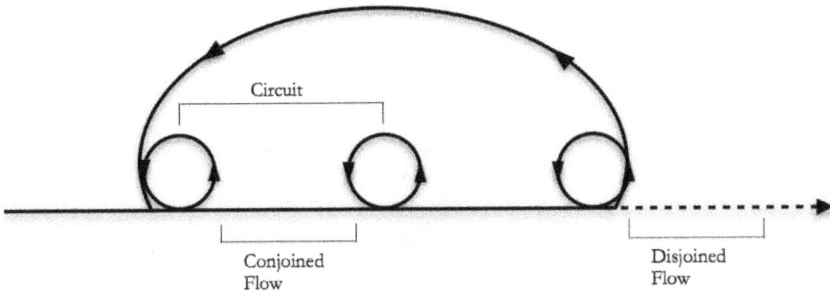

FIGURE 3. Conjoined and Disjoined Flows

Expansion by Expulsion

Expansion by expulsion is a logic of social circulation and is crucial for understanding the different ways in which migratory movement is socially conditioned. But the dual nature of this logic of expansion by expulsion also requires a dual exposition of our previous three social kinetic concepts: flow, junction, and circulation.

Conjoined and Disjoined Flows

A distinction exists between two types of flows: conjoined flows and disjoined flows (see Fig. 3). A flow, as previously defined, is not a single static thing but a process of fluid, indivisible movement. A conjoined flow is always harnessed or directed in a *limited* circuit of movement. It is still a continuous movement, but it is also redirected according to the aims of a larger vehicle and driver that have curved the flow for some particular task. The conjoined flow is the flow in-between two or more junctions that connects them into a circuit. A disjoined flow is not part of any larger vehicle, or if it is, it still remains open to redirection and connection to other flows without junction. In short: conjoined flows form closed and limited circuits between junctions, and disjoined flows are open to new connections.

Limit and Non-Limit Junctions

There are also two types of junctions: limit junctions and non-limit junctions (see Fig. 4). Limit junctions are the final junction in a

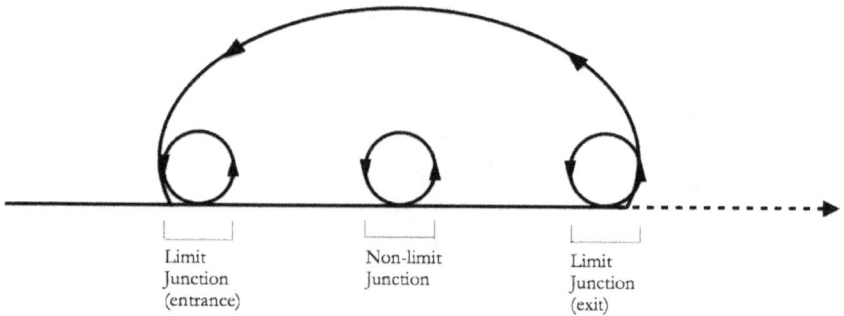

FIGURE 4. Limit and Non-Limit Junctions

circulatory system (previously described as social borders). The limit junction or border is the junction after which flows are unbound or enter into a new social circulation. The limit junction is a filter and redirector of flows. Once a flow moves through a series of circuits and reaches the limit, it is either expelled or recirculated back across the previous circuits. But there are also two kinds of limit junctions: exit junctions and entrance junctions. The task of the exit junction is to actively expel, destroy, or unbind flows. It both removes flows from circulation and detaches or disjoins flows from other noncirculating junctions. It also redirects circulation back to previous circuits. Entrance junctions are filters that allow some flows to enter into circulation and others to be blocked or redirected. But limit junctions are not always located at the spatial limit of societies. They can appear inside or outside a social area because, as kinetic social techniques, they are responsible for the junctions that define "society" in the first place, the kinetic conditions for social interiority and exteriority. Accordingly, entrance and exit junctions can also coexist in the same material phenomena: boundary markers, city gates, military operations, border patrol, customs offices, and so forth. The non-limit junction, or simply "junction," is part of a circuit within circulation. At the end of each circuit, a flow can either start over or move on to another circuit until it reaches a limit junction. These junctions do not filter what comes in or out of a circulatory system.

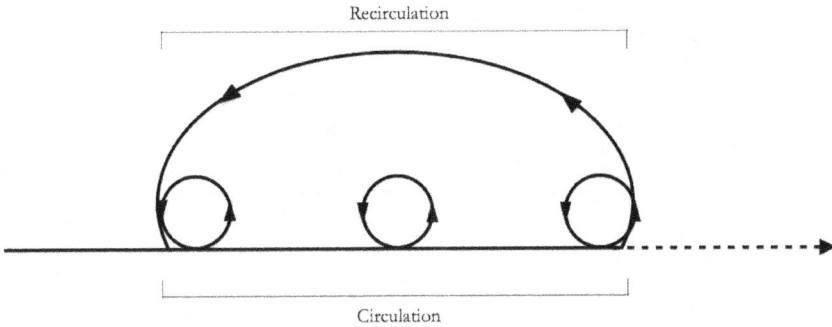

Recirculation

Circulation

FIGURE 5. Circulation and Recirculation

Circulation and Recirculation

There are two types of circulation: circulation and recirculation (see Fig. 5). Circulation is a regulated system of flows and junctions, including one or more internal circuits. Circulation has two poles, or limit junctions, one at either end: an entrance junction that allows flows to enter and an exit junction that allows or forces flows to leave. Circulation moves from entrance junction to exit junction, passing through one or more series of conjoined circuits. In this way, circulation expands itself by allowing in more and more new flows and harnessing them to more junctions within the circulatory system. Once these new flows reach their limit, they are either expelled or recirculated. Accordingly, recirculation moves from exit junction to entrance junction across all the previous circuits. Recirculation then secures and orders what has already been harnessed.

Expansion by Expulsion

Expulsion is a social movement that drives out, the deprivation of social status.[27] Social expulsion is not simply the deprivation of territorial status (i.e., removal from the land); it includes three other major types of social deprivation: political, juridical, and economic. It is not a spatial or temporal concept but a kinetic concept insofar as we understand movement extensively *and* intensively (see Fig. 6).

Social expulsion is the qualitative transformation of deprivation in status, resulting in, or as a result of, extensive movement. Furthermore,

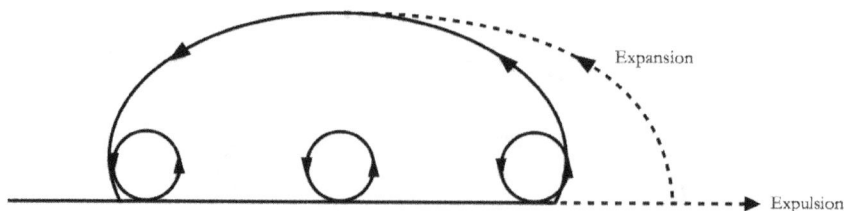

FIGURE 6. Expansion by Expulsion

the social expulsion of the migrant is neither essentially free nor forced. In certain cases, some migrants may decide to move, but they are not free to determine the social conditions of their movement or the degree to which they may be expelled from certain social orders. Nonetheless, expulsion is still a "driving" out insofar as it is not freely or individually chosen but socially instituted and compelled. If a junction is the yoke of flows into a vehicle, including a driver, then the expulsion of certain flows is a direct result of the limit-junction vehicle. It is this last exit junction that utilizes its vehicle of harnessed flows to drive out other flows, or to abandon part of the vehicle itself. Expulsion is a fundamentally social and collective process because it is a loss of a *socially* determined status (even if only temporarily and to a small degree).[28]

Expansion, on the other hand, is the process of opening up that allows something to pass through. This opening up also entails a simultaneous extension or spreading out. Expansion is thus an enlargement or extension through a selective opening. Like the process of social expulsion, the process of social expansion is not strictly territorial or primarily spatial; it is also an intensive or qualitative growth in territorial, political, juridical, and economic kinopower. It is both an intensive and extensive increase in the conjunction of new flows and a broadening of social circulation.

Kinopower is defined by circulation, but this circulation functions according to a dual logic. At one end, social circulation is a motion that drives out, or disjoins flows within or outside its circulatory system: expulsion. This is accomplished by the exit junction—the last junction, which is one of the circuits of the circulatory system but also outside this system, in charge of redirecting and driving out certain flows through exile, slavery, criminalization, or unemployment. At the other end of circulation is the entrance junction—an opening out and passing in of newly conjoined flows through a growth of territorial, political, juridical, and economic power. Expansion by expulsion is the social logic by which some members of society are dispossessed of their status so that social power can be expanded elsewhere. The migrant is the subjective figure whose movement is defined by this logic.

For circulation to open up to more flows and become more powerful than it was, it has historically relied on the disjunction or expulsion of migrant flows. In other words, the expansion of power has historically relied on a migrant surplus.[29] The following chapters in Part 2 present a kinopolitical historical analysis of the dominant ways in which human movement has been socially expanded through expulsion.

A Kinopolitical History of Migration

The quality, quantity, and type of expansion by expulsion vary greatly. The conceptual framework drawn up thus far is still too general for us to understand the different types of migrants and their social conditions. It is difficult to understand contemporary migration or movement through any single domain. Contemporary migration is a mixture of all of these. An understanding of each, according to its proper historical emergence, is necessary before delving into their contemporary admixtures. Accordingly, the historico-political elaboration of this logic is discussed at length.

The four types of kinopower presented are not meant to be exhaustive or exclusive but rather coexistent to varying degrees throughout history. However, each type of power does have a historical period in which it emerges most strongly or is expressed most dominantly. For example, even in the earliest forms of human organization there is already the formation of territorial stock, a degree of political centrality (the village, the shrine/ temple), juridical norms and techniques of punishment, and economic exchange. To be clear, the transformation and advent of the forms of kinopower considered are not linear, evolutionary, or progressive: not linear because kinopower is always a mix of its different types: emerging, receding, and reemerging in history; not evolutionary because the new form does not abandon the previous one; and not progressive because there is no end or goal for which kinopower strives. Societies simultaneously circulate movement in multiple ways.[30] This book examines only four types of kinopower, and only during their major periods of dominance. Future work remains to explore all of their diverse admixtures and figures.

CHAPTER 3

Centripetal Force

If kinopower is the social compulsion to move,[1] the history of kinopower and migration begin together with the emergence of society.[2] Although it may sound strange, settling down is the first kinopolitical event. Without a settled social area or territory, there is little or no need for regimes of social compulsion to redirect movement back upon itself into fixed social junctions.[3] Without permanent settlement, early human social life largely followed the flows of wild game and changes in the weather. Sedentarism, however, is misunderstood as the lack of movement. Sedentarism is not immobility. It is the redirection of social flows, the creation of junctions, and the maintenance of a social circulation. Thus, kinopower emerged with the first sedentary human societies.

Historically, the first dominant form of kinopower is the movement to delimit an area of the earth as socially distinct: to create a territory. The earth is composed of continuous flows of water, soil, rock, and organic life, but the territory is the social delimitation of these flows back onto themselves into junctions. Territorialization is the process of turning the earth back on itself to create a relative stability in its flows.[4] Territorialization turns the soil back over itself in the creation of human graves, it turns the rock over itself into houses, and it turns organic life back over itself in the selective breeding of plant and animal agriculture. The surface of the earth has no center, but the territory creates one. The center does not preexist but must be socially made by gathering the earth's continuous flows and turning them back over themselves into a fold, loop, or junction. In this sense, it is defined by a kind of gathering inward or centripetal social force.

Social Force

As discussed earlier, the social circulation of the migrant is defined by the logic of expansion by expulsion. This general logic is also expressed historically in four distinct but coexisting types of "social force": centripetal, centrifugal, tensional, and elastic. By social force, I mean that which *describes* the motion of society. I do not mean the vital or metaphysical *cause* of motion. As Bergson argues, force "is known and estimated only by the movements which it is supposed to produce in space . . . [but it is] one with these movements."[5] There is no secret cause or "action at a distance" behind different types of movement. There are simply different types or tendencies in social movement. The theory of social forces describes them.

A social force is not the same as a physical force. In physics, the concept of force does not describe social actors, their relations, or causes. It deals only with material bodies *as material.* But political philosophy deals with material bodies as territorial, political, juridical, economic, and so on. Human beings do not necessarily desire, believe, or collectively act in the ways that particles do in physics. Social forces are thus not modeled on physical forces but describe entirely different types of forces.[6]

In a specifically kinopolitical analysis, the dominant types of social motion, their direction, and relation are what are of interest. In kinopolitics, some types of social movement are more or less directed inward toward a dominant social center, or outward away from one, or in a legal tension with others, and so on. For example, a "social center" does not have to be geometrically or exactly in the center of a territory, city, or village. A social center relates to the relatively high degree of power, influence, or prestige of a social institution—power exerted by individuals at the top of a social hierarchy. The type and degree of social motion directed by this power center exert a social "force" insofar as the social motion collectively mobilizes people politically, legally, economically, and so on.[7]

Territorial Expansion by Expulsion

The first historically dominant type of expansion by expulsion is a centripetal social force because its dominant motion is inward—toward the creation of the first stable social centers on the earth's center-less surface. From Africa, the flow of *Homo sapiens* resulted in some of the first settlements in the Fertile Crescent and the beginning of farming around 10,000 BCE (Pre-Pottery Neolithic A [PPNA]).[8] Social junctions and circulations are defined as curves or loops in continuous flows. Territorial circulation is the first curve introduced into the continual flow of the earth's movement. After migrating thousands of miles over thousands of years, early *Homo sapiens* slowed down and bent their northern trajectory to the southeast to the Fertile Crescent. The crescent shape should thus be understood as both geographic and socially kinetic. We find a predominantly centripetal force of gathering and stockpiling of the earth into a vast reservoir of vessels in both the geographic curve and function of entire societies. "The Neolithic period," as Lewis Mumford argues, "is preeminently one of containers: it is an age of stone pottery utensils, of vases, jars, vats, cisterns, bins, barns, granaries, houses, not least great collective containers like irrigation ditches and villages."[9]

During the course of the Neolithic period (10,000–5000 BCE), human beings initiated the largest harnessing and circulation of the earth's flows in history up to that time. For the first time, they redirected the flow of seeds and plants from the wind and rivers into their own circuits: planting, tending, harvesting, processing, consuming. The curved junction of the sickle was created to harvest the flow of cereal grains. The curved millstone was created to grind them. For the first time, the endless and unpredictable flow of wild animals was harnessed by curved U-shaped yokes.[10] The care and raising of animals were added to the circuit of human activity. Animals were stored in pens for meat, clothing, and milk and used to plow crops. The flow of water and milk was contained in a curved piece of wood or clay: in bowl junctions. The creation of clay containers first emerged to harness and store the flow of grain, liquid, and meat. A simple curved piece of clay or wood now made surplus, stock, and distribution possible. In the convex curve of the vessel, everything rolls down the sides toward the center: centripetally. But raising plants and animals and storing their surplus also meant that one could not move as much. Human movement slowed down and tended to its harnessed flows.

The curved junction also catches the flow of *human* movement itself. Territorial circulation produces the dwelling: the upside-down bowl. One lives in a bowl and is buried in one as well: the *tumulus*, or rounded burial mound. These grave junctions, as Lewis Mumford states, were the first cities, the cities of the dead: necropolises.[11] They were also among the first points to which human movement began to return regularly in honor of the dead. The flow of human life from those who lived before (the ancestors) to those alive now is connected through the curve between two parallel filial lines: the marriage between two different clans—flows of descent. Territorial circulation adds several new circuits to human life: the plant-raising circuit, the animal-raising circuit, and the storage circuit. The plants are raised to feed the animals (and humans); the animals are raised to work the fields and fill the vessels with milk, grain, and meat; the milk, grain, and meat feed humans and create a surplus to store in more vessels. Territorial circulation is a multicircuited, curved segmentation of social motion inward toward the first social centers or villages.

However, territory is not first a space and then only later movement across this space. The territory is not the condition for movement, but the inverse. Before there is anything like territory, there is movement. Movement creates a territory; the social territory does not come ready-made. Before there is the territory, there is a process of *territorialization*. The same is true for politics (politicization), law (legalization), and economics (monetization). The movement of creation precedes the thing created. Historically, there are first the proto-territorial movement flows of migrating humans, animals, and rivers (Tigris and Euphrates), which are then harnessed into junctions, and finally into a form of social circulation. Only then is there the "birth of territory" and its later measurement in space and time (early sun/solstice markers).[12]

Just because territorial circulation is "sedentary" does not mean that it is not in a continual motion of harnessing the earth's flows into junctions and then circulating them back among themselves in a curve or fold (e.g., bowls, vessels, dwellings, burial mounds). Territorial curves fold inward with a centripetal force and accumulate a stock. But as a collection of curvilinear motions, they are still too diffuse to amass a center point of accumulation (the temple, the palace, etc.). They tend toward a center but do not necessarily find one, or if they do, the center has little or no power of its own.

Rather than live at the mercy of the chaotic movements of the earth, or try to follow the unending flows of rain, animals, plants, and so on, Neolithic peoples harnessed and circulated these flows into a territory. The mobility of plants and animals was captured so that humans could drive these flows like a great living vehicle: the earth vehicle. Individuals in territorial societies entered into this vehicle together, not as slaves or workers but as relatively equal drivers of the community. For territorial societies, as Marx says,

[T]he earth is the great workshop, the arsenal which furnishes both means and material of labour, as well as the seat, the *base* of the community. They relate naïvely to it as the *property of the community*, of the community producing and reproducing itself in living labour. Each individual conducts himself only as a link, as a member of this community as *proprietor* or *possessor*.[13]

The limited surplus of the earth is used in small exchange, sacrifice, war, and relatively equalized redistribution, since the destination of this vehicle is the sustenance of the community. Individuals are links or junctions between flows in the whole circulatory system of the community. The community is a collective movement or compulsion. But this social compulsion also creates a migrant expulsion.

Centripetal Force

The social motion of territorial societies is predominantly an inward centripetal force. It harnesses the flows of the earth in various junctions—it fences them in and stores their surplus in an ever-increasing series of vessels: pen vessels, house vessels, food vessels, burial vessels. In this way, territorial kinopower *collectively* brings the outside in. Thus, neither expansion nor expulsion is the effect of a single or central ruler, law, or power. Centripetal force does not emerge from the center; it emerges from a decentered periphery. It is the kinetic conditions for a social center. A single center can be created only by slowly accumulating from a heterogeneous periphery of individual farmers and even multiple territories.

However, the condition of redirecting and gathering the outside to the inside also entails an expansion and an expulsion.

The centripetal logic of territorial expansion by expulsion is as follows. At one end of territorial circulation there is a process of conjunction, and at the other, a process of disjunction. Territorial circulation expands by conjoining flows and expels by disjoining others. But there are two types of disjunction or territorial expulsion: internal and external. Internal expulsions are those disjoined with the aim of conjoining them under new conditions elsewhere. External expulsions are those expelled from social conjunction altogether.

In internal territorial expulsion, plants and animals are disjoined from their natural growth and conjoined into circulation as crops, then disjoined by death, only to be conjoined again as food or as exchange later on. The same occurs in regard to animal flows. Animals are disjoined from their natural food source as human cropland destroys their environment. Their flows are then conjoined as domestic animals, then disjoined in death, and then again conjoined as food. This is also the case with humans. Hunter-gathering humans are disjoined from following the flows of moving animals and are then harnessed to the junctions of sedentary farming and husbandry. As their hunting grounds and prey are captured by domestication, so are hunter-gatherers. Now they must farm to survive. As arable land is increasingly exhausted, a portion of this population is pushed outward in search of more land and resources to bring back to the center. Human movement is harnessed into the community as a community of members. But as the segmentation of flows occur, labor is also increasingly specialized. Humans are disjoined from general labor and conjoined as social specialists. Already in the Late Neolithic, there is evidence of specialization in, for example, tool making, jewelry making, animal raising, and farming.[14]

The second type of disjoined flows (external expulsions) are the plants, animals, and humans that are simply expelled from the territory or destroyed. Territorial expansion does not have to directly harness these disjoined flows to benefit from their expulsion from the periphery. Territorial kinopower can expand by external expulsion. Through the destruction or removal of external flows that were "in the way," territorialization makes way for future expansion. The plants deselected for human use and the predatory animals who can no longer find food or land (as a result of farming) are not expelled for what they are but for what they are *not*. Their extinction is literally peripheral to the needs of territorial accumulation. Landless humans and hunter-gatherers without access to increasingly scarce farmland and wild game are not needed for territorial circulation. It is simply enough that these peripheral figures be increasingly expelled from the outside of the territory to make way for its future expansion.

These early forms of territorial expansion by expulsion are confirmed by recent archeological discoveries. While archeologists and historians in the past have attributed the migration of humans from the Fertile Crescent into the steppe largely to climatic rises in temperature during the end of the Neolithic period, recent archeological research proves "there were hunter-herder-gatherers [nomads] in the North Arabian steppe before climate change."[15] This means that climate was not the first cause of this migration (although it certainly played a role later on). More convincingly, scholars now suggest

that expansion and colonization by settled village populations within the fertile Mediterranean climatic zone in the PPNB [Pre-Pottery Neolithic B] pushed indigenous hunter-gather groups out into the steppe where, in order to survive on reduced resources, they responded by diversifying and exploiting available food sources more intensively [becoming nomads].[16]

Scholars have also surmised that "environmental degradation caused by extensive deforestation and overgrazing [is a] strong contributing [factor]" to the migration of peoples into the steppe.[17] It also seems highly likely, archeologists contend, that the emergence of a new form of social life (sedentary agrarianism), widespread deforestation, and overgrazing would also have given rise to social conflict that would have included the forced or voluntary flight of peoples to the steppe.[18] Recent archeological research confirms that well before climate change, steppe nomadism was the result of territorial expulsion based on agricultural expansion.

Since centripetal social force is primarily concerned with accumulation, territorial expulsion remains an *indirect* phenomenon. Hunter-gatherers were not first expelled because they were foreigners or social inferiors. These categories do not emerge as dominant justifications until much later in history.[19] Rather, the type of expulsion related to territorial kinopower creates a centripetal remainder: leftovers—that which is not territorially accumulated. Hunter-gatherers are simply expelled because there are not enough territorial flows left over for them or they are in the way.

This archeological evidence suggests that the first historical nomads were created under the conditions of a social and ecological expulsion necessary for territorial and agricultural expansion. This is the sense in which the nomad is the first figure of the migrant.[20] But nomadism is also a product of the migrant's positive desire to leave and to live in a different way: transhumance. The nomads invented a new form of social motion based on a continuous movement within a system of relays between seasonal pastures and desert oases.[21] This positive dimension of the migrant's movement will be discussed in more detail later, but here the name given to the Neolithic migrant is "the nomad" because it is the name of the social figure whose emergence and movement are defined by its social expulsion from the territory.

This early form of territorial expansion by expulsion is also attested to in Syriac mythology:

Adam knew Eve his wife; and she conceived, and bare Cain. . . . And she again bare his brother Abel. And Abel was a keeper of sheep, but Cain was a tiller of the ground. And in process of time it came to pass that Cain brought the fruit of the ground as an offering unto the Lord. And Abel, he also brought of the firstlings of his flock and the fat thereof. And the Lord had respect unto Abel and to his offering; but unto Cain and to his offering he had not respect.[22]

Cain, like agriculture, the older art, came first, and Abel, the nomad, came second. Yahweh respects the art of animal raising and not the tilling of the earth because, as historian Arnold Toynbee suggests, the superiority of the nomad lies in the fact that while the agriculturalist directly consumes a raw material (simple production), nomads have to deliberately work through the medium of the animal by following its migration to seasonal pastures to produce food (complex production). The added stage requires greater "wit and will."[23] Also, since animal raising comes after plant raising in technological development, animal raising remains the more recent and superior art.

Either as a consequence of Yahweh's preference or its technological superiority, "it came to pass, when they were in the field, that Cain rose up against Abel his brother, and slew him."[24] It is Abel's primary expulsion (as a nomad) that brings him back to Cain's field (perhaps in search for grazing land). It is no coincidence that the Hebrew word for "attack," *grh-*, has as its root *gr-*, meaning "to travel and fear strangers." From this same root comes the Hebrew word *gēr,* meaning "stranger, alien, or migrant."[25] Once Abel returns to the agricultural field, he is treated as a migrant (*gēr*) and is attacked (*grh-*).

If we follow the Indo-European translation of the Hebrew word *hârag* as "slay," which is rooted in the word **gwhen-,* "fence," Abel is thus "fenced" out of the territory by agricultural fencing. Killing, fencing, and migration are all etymologically connected to the first social expulsion in this myth. Yahweh then punishes Cain, saying, "[W]hen thou tillest the ground, it shall not henceforth yield unto thee her strength; a fugitive and a wanderer shalt thou be in the earth."[26]

This myth tells us of an exiled territorial society whose expansive circulation expelled migrants into steppe nomadism. This territorial kinopower (Cain) is then condemned to keep itinerantly wandering into Europe because of the structural deforestation, overgrazing, and general exhaustion of the earth's strength required by territorial agriculture. Territorial kinopower is condemned to an itinerant social periodicity of expansion by expulsion. It expands to a new place, expels its inhabitants, and moves along while the nomads remain in the same place so as to move continuously between pastures. Archeological evidence also confirms this eventual movement of territorial societies into western Europe and the extinction of its inhabitants, the Neanderthals.[27] Due to the declining rates of soil fertility, early humans were always on the move in search of new land, but the real migrants were the ones expelled from territorial sedentarism and created a different way of life: nomadism.

The method of territorial expansion by expulsion is thus to accumulate through the destruction of the periphery. Once enough of the periphery has been destroyed or displaced, humans must move on: itinerantly expanding and expelling.

CHAPTER 4

Centrifugal Force

From approximately 10,000 BCE to 5000 BCE, territorial kin-opower remains the dominant form of social force by expanding and multiplying human territories and expelling nomads through the centripetal accumulation of the earth's flows (plant, animal, and human). However, from around 5000 BCE to the fifth century CE, a second social force emerges as dominant: political kinopower. Political kinopower includes more than just territorial accumulation. Once a sufficient threshold of conjoined motion has been pulled into the social center by the centripetal force of territorial accumulation, a center point can be established.

With the dominant emergence of this central point, a new social motion becomes possible: a rotational circulation around this point. As this central point increases, so does the potential for a new *social force* that emanates from the center: a centrifugal force. In addition to yoking the flows of the earth into various territorial circuits (plant, animal, and human junctions), ancient societies become coordinated around an increasingly large and centralized political junction: a mega-junction.[1]

Centrifugal social force is "political" in the kinetic sense in which it emerges alongside the central political cities of the ancient world—the cities of Mesopotamia, Egypt, Greece, and the Roman Empire.[2] Alongside the birth of a distinctly political form of social life in these cities is also the invention of the technology of the wall. The first nondomestic walls appear alongside the first strongly hierarchical and centrally organized cities: Jericho, Ur, Lagash, Eridu, Uruk, and others in Mesopotamia. Together, they form a new trinity of centrifugal social force: political-city-wall. The militarily walled city becomes the hierarchical, vertical, and central point unifying and ruling existing territories. In this sense, political kinopower acts as a socially centrifugal force ruling the territorial periphery from the city center—the newly dominant social power of the ancient world.[3]

Political kinopower expands the curved movements of territorial control into a completely enclosed circle, brings all its stock into a shared resonance around a central axis, and radiates outward. It adds to the system of curved, centripetal expansion a system of concentric, centrifugal expansion and produces a new figure of the migrant: *the barbarian.*

Political Expansion by Expulsion

The expansion and expulsion of political kinopower and of territorial kinopower are different. Territorial kinopower expands by creating a stockpile of flows and expels only certain plants, animals, and people (nomads) as an indirect consequence: as an unaccumulated, aterritorial remainder. However, once a central point of accumulation (temple, palace, city, etc.) is established, this point begins to react to the accumulated social junctions. Society begins to circulate predominantly according to the will and direction of a central point (i.e., king, emperor, despot).

While the primary, although not exclusive, social motion of territorial societies is a social force of centripetal containment corresponding to the invention of vessels, bowls, permanent dwellings, and such, the social motion of political cities like those in Mesopotamia, Egypt, Greece, and Rome are the inverse. Once social containment has been established, the conjoined flows can be centrally controlled and used as a force for or against the rest of society.

The history of Western political kinopower begins roughly with the emergence of urban societies in Mesopotamia during the Ubaid period around 5300 BCE and includes many ancient empires within Mesopotamia (the Sumer, Akkadian, Babylonian, and Assyrian) and centralized state powers elsewhere: Egypt, Greece, and Rome.[4] The social circle is a curve that curves again and ends up back at itself—producing an encircled and enclosed interiority. Political kinopower emerges when this interiority creates a central junction to which all other curves are subordinated.

Instead of the asymmetrical social curves of territorial kinopower (roundish bowls, rounded mounds, coil pottery, domed houses), political kinopower creates symmetrical and concentric movements. To the inward curve of territorial kinopower political kinopower adds an equally powerful outward curve that distributes or recirculates from a center point: a centrifugal motion. This outward and expansive force is made possible by the storage and release of social kinetic force. The great releases of war, public works, taxation, and transportation are all made possible by a central administration that expands outward. Social stratification follows the movement of concentric circles in the form of a social and political hierarchy based on increasingly "superior" inner circles of the city plan: temple, courtyard, inner city, outer city, countryside, and so on.

If centrifugal social force becomes dominant during this time, it does not mean that centripetal force is no longer active. Centripetal expansion and expulsion continue to be the twin conditions for the establishment of the center that directs the accumulation. With the invention of the palace, temple, and public building, however, there is the possibility of an even greater kinetic storage (of people, food, money, etc.). With greater storage, there is an even greater capacity for kinetic release. The ancient empires are like gigantic coiled springs wound tightly around one mega-junction and released on the world as a political torsion.

Ancient urban planning demonstrably follows this rotational and centrifugal model. Cities in Mesopotamia, Egypt, Greece, and the Roman Empire were almost all planned around the centralized storage of social kinetic force. Temples stored spiritual force, palaces stored political force, and treasuries stored economic force.[5] Even though many ancient cities were internally divided by grid patterns, the center preceded the grid.[6] The ancient city and country grid is subordinate to the relationship between the center and periphery. First, the center is determined as the axis and center of the universe; then the lines radiating outward are measured and subdivided in the form of a grid. The cardinal directions, on which the grid is based, all begin at the *axis mundi* of the city, which was often modeled on the cosmos.[7] Just as the heavens moved, so did the city: in cosmopolitical periodicity. In the center of Babylon, for example, were the temple and/or palace, outside the center was the housing for public officials and then for merchants; beyond the wall were the neighborhoods outside the city, then agricultural areas, and so on into the periphery: a vast centrifugal hierarchy of power and prestige radiating outward from the city. The territorial countryside winds up the spring with centripetal force (a kinetic stock of plants, animals, and labor); the central city stores it and then releases and recirculates this torsional energy back across the towns and territories in concentric circles like a great resonating earthquake. The kings of Mesopotamia and Egypt radiated power outward and downward in the form of taxes, laws, military command, public works, canals, and roadways leading in and out of the central city, while the city-states of Greece radiate outward and horizontally across a network of cities.

With the invention of the wheeled vehicle around 3000 BCE, the centrifugal force of the center becomes exponentially more expansive.[8] The wheel is the circle that turns and returns around a central axis. The chariot ties this wheel to an animal-engine. With this combination, the territory is forever changed into a series of paths, ports, and bridges: the territory becomes nothing but points of arrival/departure for social flows (the flow of armies, slaves, water, orders, goods, etc.).[9] After the appearance of the chariot and wagon, the territory changes from the inward curve of relatively immobile stock into a trans-port-(st)ation or circuit through which flows between the center and periphery travel. The territory becomes transport: the ports across which society turns. The sedentary territorial community and its vessels are now mobilized into a fluid (but centrally regulated) state of movement.

Political kinopower combines the centripetal force of accumulation and the centrifugal force of administration into a continual circulation between inside and outside. This social motion allows for a resonance of the whole. Orders and laws from inside (from kings, pharaohs, emperors, princes) go out across the towns; things and people return and resonate in accordance. This is attested to from Mesopotamia to Rome. All ancient empires built massive transportation systems of roads and canals that led back to the central city. The power of centrifugal empires is thus precisely the power to come and go between center and periphery as they wish, when they wish.[10]

Centrifugal Force

In contrast to the nomad, who is defined by territorial expulsion and social exteriority (aterritoriality) from the community of relative equals, the figure of the barbarian designates above all a political status of "inferiority" that exists both within and outside the social territory. While centripetal force simply "leaves out" the nomad from territorial accumulation, centrifugal force brings the inside and the outside into a hierarchical resonance around a center. Thus, barbarians are not simply nomads in the mountains "left out" of society; neither are they merely foreigners from different territories or cities or even people who have been enslaved. The barbarian designates a specifically *depoliticized* inferiority (political expulsion) inside and outside a central state that is created by ancient political kinopower.

"The barbarian" is the ancient migrant defined by the motions of political expulsion. For Aristotle, barbarism, above all, designates this political inferiority: a natural incapacity for proper speech and reason that disallows political life. If people do not have a city-state, then they cannot possibly have political rationality.[11] Barbarians are those whose temporary encampments, mobility, and even geographic distance from the polis create a natural inferiority. "Instead of establishing towns or walls, they are all mounted archers who carry their homes along with them and derive their sustenance not from cultivated fields but from their herds."[12] The barbarian is the social figure whose inferior motion is conjoined in the form of slavery (or disjoined in the form of extermination) in order to expand the rising political and military power of the state.

The idea of natural political inferiority and the figures associated with it, like the barbarian, were invented in the ancient world largely to conceptualize political slavery. The problem was that the migrant was no longer simply "out there" but also "in here" in the form of the slave or foreigner. In this way, the political status of the migrant is in between that of the human and the animal: in the city but not belonging to the city. The ancient figure of the migrant is called the "barbarian" or "inferior subject," not the "slave," because the concept of barbarism or natural inferiority is first required to legitimate slavery. One cannot truly be a slave, according to Aristotle, unless one is first and naturally a barbarian. Whether or not the barbarian is actually enslaved does not change the fact that one is predisposed to slavery wherever one is. The barbarian is the true and natural slave regardless of empirical enslavement.

Aristotle understood the concept of ancient political inferiority well. In *Politics*, he argues that a slave cannot be defined simply by being enslaved. The practical condition of slavery does not necessarily tell us anything about the kind of being that the slave is. If it is possible, Aristotle says, for someone to be unjustly enslaved, then "no one would say that someone is a slave if he did not deserve to be one."[13] In Aristotle's political writings, we can distinguish between two kinds of slaves: the slave by fortune and the slave by nature. The slave by fortune is not a true slave, since he or she may have been enslaved unjustly or by accident—for example, civic slavery. The natural slave, however, is the one who has nothing in himself or herself that rules by nature. The name of this type of natural or true slave is what Aristotle calls the βάρβαρον, *barbaron*, barbarian. Insofar as "slave" means "slave by nature" and not by fortune, "the barbarian and the slave are in nature the same [ταὐτὸ φύσει βάρβαρον καὶ δοῦλον ὄν]." "Wherefore Hellens do not like to call Hellens slaves but confine the term to barbarians. Yet, in using this language, they really mean the natural slave of whom we spoke first."[14] Thus, the barbarian is not merely enslaved but the human being whose very nature is to be inferior to the political center: the polis or city-state.

The Greek word βάρβαρος, *barbaros*, originates from the onomatopoetic sound of the babbling of the foreigner who does not speak Greek.[15] Thus, the determination of the "nature" of the barbarian is already relative to a geographic and political center—in this case, the Greek polis. Barbarism is already a political determination. The periphery of the center is barbarian, mobile, diffuse, inferior, and unintelligible. Accordingly, the antonym for the Greek word *barbaros* is *civis* or *polis*—both words that applied to cities.[16] The barbarian is the "non-Greek, non-city-dweller."[17]

What makes barbarians inferior is both their non-Greek status (although most non-Greeks also did not speak Greek) and their inability to use political speech and reason (*logos*) that were politically bound to the specifically Greek *logos*. Thus, the figure of the barbarian unites three concepts all tied to the centrifugal political apparatus: (1) the inability to speak the language of the political center (Greek); (2) the inability to use the reason of the political center (*logos*); and (3) an excessive geographic mobility in relation to the political center (polis).

Although the word *barbaron* originates with the Greeks and is directly carried on by the Romans, migratory expulsions in the Egyptian and Sumerian Empires were justified by the same theory of natural political inferiority. For example, many of the ancient names for "slave" are based on the *natural geographic status* and *mobility* of migrants, not on the mere contingency or description of their actually being enslaved. The oldest known tablets that survive today (the Sumerian Code of Ur-Nammu, ca. 2100 BCE–2050 BCE, and the Code of Hammurabi, ca. 1792–1750 BCE) contain codes of law that clearly indicate that *geographic* foreigners and *mountain* peoples were among the first slaves.[18] The earliest names for "slave"—*nita*, male, + *kur*, mountain—appear in ancient Sumer and are equivalent to "foreign people who live in the mountains." The later Akkadian word for slave is *arad* and is also derived from the word *wardum*, meaning "mountain."[19] In Egypt, the majority of foreign slaves who were taken captive were described according to their geographic mobility as *shasu*, or "wanderers," regardless of whether they were actually wandering or not. These ancient terms are all kinopolitical designations since they naturalized the link between the geography, mobility, and political inferiority of the migrant. Since *nitakur*, *wardum*, and *shasu* are also synonymous with the concept of "natural slaves," regardless of where they live or whether or not they are actually enslaved, these terms are the political precursors to the Greek and Roman concept of barbarism.

With the rise of ancient slavery, the mountains became a reservoir of slave labor to be brought into the cities. The movement of the migrant became the living motor of the ancient state. Accordingly, the migrant could no longer be designated by a merely aterritorial status (the nomad) but had to be designated according to some other characteristic that could follow the migrant wherever he or she went: a natural/political inferiority and potential slavery—always relative to the political center.

Just as nomadism is produced by two types of territorial expansion by expulsion (internal and external), so barbarism and political inferiority are also produced by two simultaneous types of expansions by expulsion. Internally, political kinopower expels peasants and debtors from their homes as internal inferiors and expands by using them as forced laborers and debt slaves. Externally, political kinopower expels barbarians from the mountains through war, colonialism, and kidnapping and expands by slavery. The political state is far from immobile or static. Rather, according to Virilio, "The State apparatus is in fact simply an apparatus of displacement [*déplacement*], its stability appears to be assured by a series of temporary gyroscopic processes of delocalization and relocalization."[20]

Internal Expansion by Expulsion

Internal expansion by expulsion creates migration by forced labor and debt slavery. For ancient states, public expansion was made possible largely through forced labor, or *corvée*.[21] *Corvée* is not the same as chattel slavery (owning a human being), but it is a form of unpaid/unfree labor that often designated an inferior social status. The massive public works of statecraft like canals, roads, temples, walls, mining operations, and military service were all made possible by disjoining peasants from their homes in the countryside and conjoining them into a labor circuit for months, sometimes years, until the project was completed. Peasants were given provisions, housed in camps, and circulated among projects. Egyptian *corvée* migrants were taken from their farms near the Nile and sheltered temporarily in camp junctions near the construction sites. In Mesopotamia, migrant workers were also set up in temporary camps and kept only for the winter season so they could be recirculated back to agricultural work in the summer.[22] The creation and expansion of public works were largely made possible by the internal expulsion of the state's own people at the temporary expense of their political status as free farmers.[23] Hence, public centrifugal expansion was based on peasant expulsion in the figure of the *corvée* slave: temporarily reduced to an inferior status.

Internal displacement was not only for public expansion. Private expansion and wealth were also amassed through an internal expulsion of debt slaves. The debt slave is the figure who becomes apolitical or inferior by failing to repay his or her debts. Debtors forfeited their political status and frequently ended up running away to live in the mountains with the rest of the barbarians.

Ancient debt and debt slavery are made possible by the centrifugal force of the early political state. The centripetal action of territorial societies created the conditions for the first centralized public buildings (temples). But once these centers became larger, the palace (based on the temple) emerges and begins to request donations/offerings from the territory.[24] The priests in Mesopotamia began to use this surplus to provide

loans. Some of the very first written documents of Mesopotamian civilization are tablets reporting credits and debts, rations issued by temples, and
money owed for rent of temple lands. The value of these loans was measured by silver shekels (one shekel = one bushel of barley = thirty days of
rations).[25] Priests would then use this surplus/offering to provide loans to
merchants trading grain and foodstuffs for stone, wood, and more silver
from outside the valley.

Although it is not known exactly when interest-bearing loans
originated, anthropologist David Graeber suggests that they were likely
invented to support the merchant caravan trade so the temples could be
compensated for their accounting labor.[26] "By 2400 BC, it already appears
to have been common practice on the part of local officials, or wealthy
merchants, to advance loans to peasants who were in financial trouble on
collateral and began to appropriate their possessions if they were unable
to pay."[27] If there was a bad harvest and the debtors failed to pay, lenders
would begin taking their animals, houses, fields, then children, wives, and
finally the debtor himself as a debt slave. The debt peon was expelled from
his political status, his home and family, and made to work against his will
in the home of the creditor. In this way, the institution of debt slavery is
important for the centrifugal expansion of both public and private accumulation, even if it is not based on a purely natural slavery. Debt begins as
owed to the center (the temple, the palace) and then radiates outward in
the form of slavery owed to wealthy private persons.

Another consequence of debt slavery is that during droughts or a
poor farming season, farmers, in fear of slavery, abandoned their farms en
masse and joined barbarian bands in the mountains or desert fringes.[28]
Debt expulsion is thus double-sided: it may result in an increase in slaves
for private merchants and officials, or once the peasants flee to the mountains as apolitical barbarians, they can be captured by the military or slave
hunters and used as public slaves—or sold for private profit as "natural"
slaves. Of course, if their defection is large or strong enough, it may also
undermine political kinopower altogether. This is precisely why Sumerian, and later Babylonian, kings periodically announced debt forgiveness
for all debt slaves (although not for all slaves), called "declarations of freedom," or *amargi* (literally "return to mother")—since the *amargi* reunited
families separated by slavery.[29] The *amargi* is an important kinetic tool for

regulating the circulation between politics and barbarism. Its aim was to create the proper kinetic ratio between the expulsion of barbarians from their homes and the expansion of the state or private persons.

External Expansion by Expulsion

In addition to *internal* expansion by expulsion, political kinopower produces barbarian migrants through an *external* expansion by expulsion in war, colonialism, and kidnapping. Ancient city and state militaries were made possible by the conjunction of barbarian motion. One of the main objectives of ancient militaries was to take prisoner slaves. Prisoner slaves could be any type of political inferior and hence potential slaves: artisans kidnapped from their homes by an occupying army; defeated or captured combatant soldiers; nomadic herders living in the mountains or deserts and kidnapped by the military; noncombatant women and children of a conquered territory; or a combination of these, including debt slaves or food slaves (children sold by their parents for food).

For example, in the Egyptian New Kingdom (1558–1080 BC), expeditions were sent explicitly to buy and/or kidnap "workers" from the Nile delta and nomads from Asia.[30] The Greeks brought back barbarians from their territories in the Mediterranean, in particular the mountainous regions of Phoenicia.[31] And the Romans took slaves from all over the Mediterranean, especially from the barbarian northern territories, such as Scythia.

Slavery was by far the largest cause of human expulsion and migration in the ancient world.[32] In ancient Athens, slaves constituted about one-third of the population between the fifth and third centuries BCE.[33] In Roman Italy, slaves also constituted a third of the population between the second and fourth centuries BCE.[34] In Egypt and Sumer, it is more complicated to estimate the number of slaves, but if we consider the number of humans displaced as a structural requirement of state warfare and public works (including *corvée*, prisoners, and debt slaves), then these ratios easily match those of Greece and Rome.[35]

Mountains, deserts, and foreign lands served as a continuous supply of migrant slaves. "The mountains," according to Fernand Braudel, "have always been a reservoir of men for other people's use."[36] Whenever expansion was needed, a centrifugal force was deployed to the periphery to capture barbarians. Once captured, they were returned to the center and used for all manner of political expansions.[37] Barbarian slaves were forced into public military service and then sent out to gather even more slaves or to conquer more territory for the ruler in an ever-expanding social circulation from center to periphery and back.[38] In short, internal and external expansion by expulsion was made possible only by a new kind of dominant kinopower that could be harnessed, stored, and projected outward at great distances through centrifugal force.

CHAPTER 5

Tensional Force

Political kinopower harnesses the centripetal stockpile of territorial flows (bowls, mounds, domes), connects them (forming a circle and a center), and centrifugally forces them outward from a central mega-junction in an ever-expanding circulation. But once the centrifugal force of political kinopower has united the territorial junctions into a whole between the center and periphery, it becomes possible for certain junctions at the periphery to begin to break away from the whole and generate their own social motions. When this occurs, other political centers may multiply. These centers can then link up with one another under limited (not global or imperial) conditions. This social kinetic link binds two or more junctions together by channeling specific flows between them, but without merging the two junctions. The legal contract is such a kinetic link between social junctions that aims to keep the junctions bound together but also held apart in relative autonomy.

The "parcelized sovereignty," as Perry Anderson calls it, which characterizes European society from around the fifth to the seventeenth centuries, creates precisely this sort of social motion. Feudal power is one of multiple warring kingdoms, each with its own center, bound together largely by the linkage of legal contracts between and within them. The kinopower of feudalism and early-modern states is no longer that of the central empire centrifugally unifying heterogeneous territories. Its form of expansion and expulsion are less defined by a single political center than by a thousand tiny centers linked through a web of juridical connections based on a *glebae adscripti*: a binding or writing into the earth that legally binds serfs, vassals, and lords to a piece of land and its cultivation.[1]

This type of kinopower is juridical in the kinetic sense in which law binds the movement of social beings to one another and to a certain social condition or territory. This is also the etymological meaning of the word "feudalism" as "soil-bound value." This meaning derives from the Latin *feudum*,[2] from the Latin *fee,* pertaining to both a heritable piece of revenue-producing land (from the PIE root **fehu-,* "cattle") and the juridical relation of the overlord to the vassal bound to the property "in fee."

Although the concept and practice of law are, in some sense, as old as human society, feudal law includes a much larger range of social activities than ancient and even modern justice does. As Perry Anderson explores at length in *Passages from Antiquity to Feudalism,*

Justice was the central modality of political power—specified as such by the very nature of the feudal polity. . . . It is thus necessary always to remember that mediaeval "justice" factually included a much wider range of activities than modern justice, because it structurally occupied a far more pivotal position within the total political system. It was the ordinary name of power.[3]

Thus, the dominant, though not exclusive, form of kinopolitical expansion by expulsion in the Middle Ages is juridical. During antiquity, most migration was caused by political slavery, but in the Middle Ages it is caused by the transformation of legal codes. The medieval force of expansion and expulsion is no longer merely centripetal or centrifugal. It becomes a tensional force held between legally bound persons. The contraction and release of these legal bonds of tensional force produce a third major type of migrant: *the criminal migrant or vagabond.*

Juridical Expansion by Expulsion

The history of the dominance of juridical expansion and expulsion begins with the collapse and fragmentation of the Roman Empire and the subsequent emergence of a vast number of warring kingdoms. Over time, the new kingdoms, churches, and universities, all with their own juridical links, gradually consolidated into the kingdoms of France, Spain, England, Russia, Hungary, and others around the seventeenth century.

However, among the medieval kingdoms and early-modern states that existed up until that time, a huge multicentered and contractually linked social motion emerged and dominated.

In the Middle Ages, social motion no longer radiated from a single center (Rome) but from multiple centers. Law and contracts were socially expanded and redefined as binding relations between individuals. This differs from the law of ancient empires, which was determined by only a few central individuals (Greek or Roman property-owning men, Egyptian pharaohs, and Mesopotamian kings) and then centrifugally enforced on the majority of society (slaves, women, foreigners, craftsmen, etc.).

In medieval Europe, however, law breaks free from the center and multiplies at the vast periphery where non-enslaved individuals enter into mutual juridical relations. With the absence of centralized law, medieval Europe experienced an enormous proliferation of heterogeneous, non-unified legislation: for example, kingdom, town, customary, canon, and university law. As a consequence, the Middle Ages invented a new system of decentered contract law among multiple sovereign junctions that mediated almost every social relationship.

This transformation emerged as barbarian migrations captured or destroyed Roman estates—launching slaves, Romans, and other barbarians into a dangerous and uncertain world increasingly dominated by powerful warrior-leaders with cavalry. From this mass expulsion emerged a new kinetic form of social circulation: juridical linkage. This does not mean, however, that slavery disappeared in Europe completely. Rather, "the concrete social formations of mediaeval Europe were always composite systems, in which other modes of production survived and intertwined with feudalism proper."[4] By the seventh century, the rural slave-labor force of Carolingian Europe was still around 10 to 20 percent,[5] and by 1086 in England only 9 percent of the labor force were slaves.[6]

What emerged as the newly dominant social relation, in place of and in addition to slavery, however, was serfdom. Previous slaves, farmers whose crops had failed, shepherds, and anyone threatened or displaced by barbarian raids sought out the protection of those with military power. In their earliest forms (tenth and eleventh centuries), these loose alliances between near equals were not called "fiefs" but *precaria*; in the twelfth century they became more hierarchical and legally codified.[7] In exchange for protection in their precarious situation, these individuals offered their services. In particular, supporting a landed military cavalry required significant agricultural, textile, and metallurgical production.

Feudal relations are no longer predominantly centrifugal as in the ancient world, but juridically linked and predominantly tensional. Serfs were linked to the land, and the lords were linked to the juridical administration of the serfs. But the lords did not own the land and were, in turn, linked, as vassals, to the land "in fee" by a superior lord, to whom lords owed military knight service. This contract was formalized by an oath of complete fealty (conjunction) to the lord, who ceremonially held the vassal's head in his hands and handed him a clod of dirt representing the fief to which he was now bound.[8] But this granting lord was also the vassal of one or more feudal superiors, and so on, all the way in a vast chain of multiple alliances to a monarch. The monarch

was a feudal suzerain of his vassals, to whom he was bound by reciprocal ties of fealty, not a supreme sovereign set above his subjects. His economic resources would lie virtually exclusively in his personal domains as a lord, while his calls on his vassals would be essentially military in nature. He would have no direct political access to the population as a whole, for jurisdiction over it would be mediatized through innumerable layers of subinfeudation. He would, in effect, be master only on his own estates, otherwise to great extent a ceremonial figurehead.[9]

The social kinetics of feudalism is not defined primarily by the rotational and centrifugal power of the ancient sovereign but by the linked rotation and tensional power of the feudal suzerain among innumerable layers of subinfeudation. "The consequence of such a system," according to Anderson, "was that political sovereignty was never focused in a single centre. The functions of the State were disintegrated in a vertical allocation downwards, at each level of which political and economic relations were, on the other hand, integrated."[10] This new form of social circulation, therefore, produced a new dominant force of motion: "*a dynamic tension . . .* within the centrifugal State."[11] It is precisely the "disintegration in a vertical allocation downwards" that defines this form of social motion as predominantly juridical: "a laying *down* of law."

Tensional Force

This kinetic model of linked centers produces a new dominant mode of social expansion and expulsion: tensional force, created by at least two junctions bound together by a rigid link, which keeps them together and apart. It decenters their motion while also strengthening it. Kinetically, both junctions are relatively autonomous centers with their own form of motion, but since their movements are held together by the tension of the link, the motion of one is always restricted by the motion of the other.

Tensional motion occurs when there are two or more points whose movement is inelastically relativized by the others, for example, the movement of the human arm.[12] The human arm is composed of several radial joints connected by several bone linkages. Each ball joint rotates in its own orbit with its own degrees of freedom, while the rigid linkage between them both decenters and strengthens their movement.

Socially, tensional force is expressed in the juridically conjoined flows between individuals. Each individual retains a certain degree of freedom, but relative to a vertical and horizontal network of legal ties. Each feudal vassal has a lord above and a serf below, in addition to agreements with other vassals to the side. Each lord above is also another vassal with similar connections. Further, one might be a vassal or lord in multiple kingdoms at the same time. Political hierarchy is nothing new, but in feudalism the top is decentered and the middle multiplies. Only a complex mesh of legally binding agreements holds each to the other.

In contrast to the centripetal expulsion of the nomad, who is simply left out of an inward territorial accumulation, and to the centrifugal expulsion of the barbarian, whose capture and enslavement are directed by a centralized administration, the tensional expulsion of the vagabond is created by the dissolution of old juridical linkages and the creation of new ones. However, the release of juridical tensions only appears to be freedom. The abolition of customary rights, for example, frees the peasant from being tied to the land and reduces excessive taxation, but it also robs the peasant of the right to stay on the land.

Legal linkages and contracts bind social junctions into a multiplicity of interconnected centers without margins.[13] This creates a vast social and juridical tension holding everything together—like a multicentered spider web. But these links can also be broken and reassembled from just as many different points in the spider's web. The churches, lords, vassals, workshops, and prisons all have their own forms of justice. Together, they form a mesh of nonunified but overlapping and conflicting laws and codes, which are "dense, entangled, conflicting powers, powers tied to the direct or indirect dominion over the land, to the possession of arms, to serfdom, to bonds of suzerainty and vassalage . . . a myriad of clashing forces."[14]

Tensional migratory expulsion occurs when these juridical linkages are severed and release a social flow: vagabondage. However, just as easily as these juridical linkages can be dissolved, so they can be reassembled into new circuits. Without the coordination of a central apparatus like the emperor or monarch, this is much easier, albeit more prone to conflict. Over the course of the Middle Ages, however, numerous older laws were slowly replaced with an increasingly centralized form of law: the juridical state. The state that emerged from feudal Europe around the seventeenth century was a definitively juridical state insofar as it presented itself as the arbitrator of conflicting legal tensions between multiple conflicting powers. It offered to release the mounting juridical tension of a thousand tiny justices in favor of a single great justice: a point of maximum tension. "Law was not simply a weapon skillfully wielded by monarchs; it was the monarchic system's mode of manifestation and the form of its acceptability,"[15] because of its emergence from the tensional network of juridically clashing forces. Accordingly, "since the Middle Ages," Foucault states, "the exercise of power has always been formulated in terms of law."[16]

Just like territorial and political kinopower, juridical kinopower also expands its form of circulation by disjoining and conjoining social flows. Internally, juridical kinopower expels peasants and debtors from their legal right to the land and expands legal power by criminalizing them as vagabonds. Externally, juridical kinopower expels foreign peoples through war, colonialism, and kidnapping and expands its legal power by colonial legislation: the *encomienda*.

Between the fifth and fifteenth centuries, tensional expulsion produced a group of migratory figures defined by their deviant juridical status as criminals. Although there are many names for the criminalized migrant during this time (such as the rogue, debtor, beggar, pauper, vagrant, heretic, witch, Jew, foreigner, and homeless), the most dominant name of the criminalized migrant is "the vagabond," the migrant whose movement is juridically expelled as "illegal."

However, the figures of the nomad and the barbarian do not disappear but persist throughout the Middle Ages and are increasingly refigured as subjects of feudal contracts, criminality, and incarceration. The word "serf" comes from the Latin *servus*, meaning "slave or servant"; and the word "vagabond," meaning "wanderer," parallels the ancient Egyptian designation "wanderer" (*shasu*) for the pastoral nomadic herders of the Levant enslaved by the Egyptians. The medieval name "vagabond" takes up these figures and reinterprets the wandering slave as a predominantly *criminal* offender.

Internal Expansion by Expulsion

Internal expansion by expulsion expels peasants from the legal right to the land and expands legal authority over their evicted mobility. There are, however, two sets of internal strategies corresponding to three periods of juridical expulsion: before commutation (conversion to land rent) in the thirteenth century, during commutation, and after.

Before Commutation

Before commutation the first internal strategy is the expansion of a system of legally contracted or "landed" labor through the disjunction of slaves from Roman estates. This was accomplished in two ways.

The first method occurred in the fourth century when Roman landlords began granting plots of land to slaves to keep them from running away and joining Maroon communities (like Bacaude in Gaul), which were growing at the periphery of the empire.[17] However, defecting or living on independent plots of land and competing with slave labor often put these communities at a disadvantage economically and militarily. New landlords took advantage of this situation by offering protection in exchange for services. In this way, the expelled slaves often came under the protection of an expanding landlord system.

The second method was accomplished through hundreds of years of barbarian revolt that eventually destroyed the Roman estate system.

Frankish and Lombard rulers, for example, confiscated local *latifundia* (large Roman estates) and distributed them to their noble retinues, who conjoined them into village-style communities that eventually became a prominent feature of medieval feudalism.[18] The Anglo-Saxons instituted a system of Celtic-style hamlets that gave way to nucleated villages "in which individual property of peasant households was combined with collective co-aration of open fields."[19] By the seventh century, England had in place a legal-contract system of local lords who had consolidated power and hereditary control of the land.[20] While the Visigoths, Burgundians, and Ostrogoths mainly continued slavery in their appropriation of seized Roman estates (under the *hospitditas* agreements), the slave system was eventually merged with the barbarian code of personal homage and honor with the rise of Charlemagne and the Carolingian Empire. As Perry Anderson writes,

In the course of the later 8th century, "vassalage" (personal homage) and "benefice" (grant of land) slowly fused, while in the course of the 9th century "benefice" in its turn became increasingly assimilated to "honour" (public office and jurisdiction). Grants of land by rulers thereby ceased to be gifts, to become conditional tenures, held in exchange for sworn services.[21]

While slavery had by no means ended, previous slaves and barbarian villages were slowly synthesized and expanded into this new system of exchange of sworn (legal) services. Thus, it is through hundreds of years of mass expulsion, migration, and kidnapping that the barbarians are able to weaken the ancient estate system and expand a new system of barbarian "honor and services," which formed the basis of feudal contractual society.[22]

Commutation and After

The second strategy, during and after commutation, was an increasingly unified independent legal apparatus that expanded through the expulsion of serfs from the land, made possible by the commutation process outlined in detail in the following section. In part, this made possible the rise of an increasingly centralized juridical apparatus to control a new population of landless and masterless vagabonds. The rise of this system occurred through a massive expansion and unification of the Christian and secular legal codes and enforcement against what were called "vagabonds" (including heretics, witches, the poor, beggars, and others). As Guy Geltner argues in *The Medieval Prison,*

Centralization went hand in hand with a quest for administrative efficiency and financial security, goals that the prison served in its capacity as a place of custody and coercion. Prison administration took its cue from the know-how accumulated in other areas of urban government such as nomination proceeds, remuneration, record-keeping, and supervision, all devised to address the demands of a mercantile culture. The endeavor was often costly, and urban magistrates took some care to revise incarceration fees and offer certain services to the inmates by which they hoped to increase the cities' income from this new facility. [However,] by the time this [unprofitable venture] was becoming apparent, the administration of justice in many cities had come to rely on prisons, not only as places of custody and coercion, but also as punitive facilities.[23]

The increasing centralization of church, merchant, and state administration in the institution of the prison is accomplished by a dramatic expansion of legal code and its enforcement across Europe from the thirteenth to seventeenth centuries. More laws produce more criminals, and more criminals produce a greater need (and justification) for an expanded legal/carceral apparatus in the form of the early-modern state. This period of juridical expansion rises to dominance through six major types of juridical expulsion created during this time: commutation, enclosure, vagabond laws, plague laws, workhouse and poor laws, and witch hunts.

Commutation.   Commutation, money rent, or (as its etymology suggests from the root *mei-) "the right of mobility," was the result of hundreds of years of peasant resistance against aristocratic lords. Paradoxically, however, it was also the basis on which the vagabond laws acted to expand juridical power. The serfs wanted mobility and freedom from the tensional forces of juridical *adscription* (legal binding to the land) and taxation, but what the lords proposed (commutation) benefited only a few peasants who could pay money rent—the rest were evicted from the land.

Commutation was therefore the result of a steadily increasing antagonism between serfs and lords from the fifth to twelfth centuries. As contracted serfs collectively worked feudal lands, they gained a sense of entitlement to the products of their labor and felt the arbitrariness of feudal power relations. Taxation, in particular, was a major source of this manorial antagonism that led to commutation. These taxes included

the *manomorta* (a tax which the lord levied when a serf died), the *mercheta* (a tax on marriage that increased when a serf married someone from another manor), the *heriot* (an inheritance tax paid by the heir of a deceased serf for the right to gain entry to his holding, usually consisting of the best beast of the deceased), and, worst of all, the *tallage*, a sum of money arbitrarily decided, that the lords could exact at will. Last but not least the *tithe*, a tenth of the peasant income, that was exacted by the clergy, but usually collected by the lords in the clergy's name.[24]

Peasant revolt was constant between the fifth and twelfth centuries but reached a fever pitch in the thirteenth and fourteenth and could no longer be ignored. Armed insurrection, the murder of tax collectors, the refusal to work, theft, tardiness, sabotage, military defection, and attacks on the lord's castle were common.[25] Even more common were the endless legal disputes initiated by serfs against the abuses and services requested by the lords and for the free access to noncultivated lands (such as forests, rivers, lakes, and hills). Serfs carried out their threat to flee to nearby towns to escape manorial taxation. "Men are reported to be fugitives, and dwelling in the neighboring towns; and although order is given that they be brought back, the town continues to shelter them."[26] Defection and formation of Maroon societies were criminal acts, punishable by the forced return of the peasant to the landlord.

While commutation laws allowed some peasants with larger tracts of land to pay their rent and hire other peasants, the majority of poorer peasants with very few acres could barely survive, fell into chronic debt, and were eventually evicted from the land. Peasant expulsion after commutation thus occurs in two ways: either peasants were expelled through debt (as a result of commutation), or they were directly expelled through the system of land privatization, or enclosure legislation, which also began its first phase in the thirteenth century and spread slowly throughout Europe over the next several hundred years. As a consequence, displacement was rampant.

Thirteenth-century documents contain increasing amounts of information about "landless" peasants who manage to eke out a living on the margins of village life by tending to flocks. . . . In Southern France the "*brassien*" lived entirely by "selling" the strength of their arms (*bras*) and hiring themselves out to richer peasants or landed gentry. From the beginning of the fourteenth century the tax registers show a marked increase in the number of impoverished peasants, who appear in these documents as "indigents," "poor men" or even "beggards."[27]

Thus, commutation laws initiated a specifically juridical form of expulsion: the expulsion from the laws of adscription that bound serfs to the land by right. Once serfs were disjoined from their legal right to the land, they then became subject to a new set of laws that served to expand the new juridical institutions of the prison, the workhouse, the state, the inquisitional court, and the church.

Enclosure.   The practice of legally privatizing feudal open-field systems and common-use areas, abolishing customary land-use laws, and evicting peasant tenants produced an enormous vagabond population that expanded the prevalence of tenant farming and sent migrant farmers to urban areas. The primary motivation for many of these enclosure laws was that a number of large landholders in Europe (mainly in England) wanted to convert subsistence farmland into sheep-grazing land to sell the wool for manufacture in Flanders. A large landowner could make much more money in this way than from subsistence peasantry or small-scale agriculture. Although this meant an increase in profit for the few, it meant mass unemployment for most.

Adding to this unemployment was a rising population throughout Europe with fewer jobs available. In England alone, the population nearly doubled from 2.7 million in 1541 to 5.2 million in 1651.[28] Economic depression also contributed to vagabondage. In England, any manufacturing gains barely kept up with the population and were insufficient to check rising food prices.[29] Real wages fell by 50 percent, and inflation rose for 150 years.[30] Historians once thought that the process of legal dispossession in England began in the eighteenth century, but according to A. L. Beier, "now they see the process beginning in the Middle Ages."[31] Thus, the three main intertwined causes of vagabondage during these years were population growth, poverty, and enclosures.

There are two periods of enclosure. The first (1235–1760) has a predominantly tensional form of expulsion in that it is mainly defined by an enormous legal battle lasting hundreds of years with the aim of breaking the legal links of tenant rights and customary laws in favor of private land for sheep grazing and the rights of landlords.[32] This process created tens of thousands of vagabonds whose juridical expulsion then constituted the basis for a legal expansion that relinks them into another set of contracts through the dominant juridical forms of the inquisition, the prison, land rent, the monastery/poorhouse, and the early-modern state. Once the legal battle was largely won, the second period of enclosure (1761–1844) became a more economic form of expulsion.

However, this first phase of enclosure that began to sever customary laws also threatened the tensional stability of other juridical linkages. When the enclosure process gathered speed in Britain during the fifteenth and sixteenth centuries, both the church and state actively tried to outlaw the practice. The English government, for example, was concerned that enclosure would produce a homeless population, which would lead to lower tax revenues. As whole towns were depopulated and destroyed, there would be fewer potential military conscripts for the Crown and an increase in dangerous vagabonds. The Depopulation Act of 1489 was the first in a series of eleven acts of Parliament over the next 150 years aimed at stopping the enclosure process.[33] The state used a two-pronged approach to maintaining the tensional linkage of customary law: it bound landlords to an increasingly centralized tensional point by criminalizing enclosures through state-controlled property laws and bound vagabonds to an expanding juridical tension of police, prison, and courts, thus criminalizing vagabondage. Both processes were often unsuccessful but were the subject of legal battles that dragged on for hundreds of years.

The church was opposed to enclosure because the depopulation of the towns meant a reduction in local tithes and an increase in the costs of providing aid for the mass of paupers that resulted. In addition to these practical concerns, there was moral outrage. Notable objections to using enclosures to raise sheep include Sir Thomas More's criticisms in *Utopia* (1516).

[The process of enclosure] by which your sheep, which are naturally mild, and easily kept in order, may be said now to devour men and unpeople, not only villages, but towns. . . . [The enclosure process is stopping] the course of agriculture, destroying houses and towns, reserving only the churches, and enclose[ing] grounds that they may lodge their sheep in them.[34]

More's criticisms of enclosure were shared by many, including the cardinal of England. In one 1460 account, a Warwick priest named John Rous counted sixty-two townships, manors, and parishes that had been partly or wholly depopulated in his county.[35] These depopulations expelled hundreds of families, now reduced to vagabondage. In this way the battle for legal expulsion through the use of enclosures won out in the end.

Vagabond Laws. After commutation and the first phase of enclosures, these roaming, angry hordes of displaced paupers were the primary target of a massive juridical expansion over peasant mobility: the vagabond laws, or what Marx calls "the bloody legislation."

The vagabond laws refer to a variety of laws that criminalized the peasants who were expelled by commutation and enclosure beginning in the thirteenth century. These vagabonds, or "masterless men," could not be allowed to wander across Europe freely. This process of criminalization required a massive expansion of the legal code and a new institutional apparatus of enforcement (prisons, record keepers, guards, Inquisition officials, courts, etc.). Some of the first prisons in Europe were built to deal specifically with the need to hold thousands of people accused of "masterlessness" and heresy by various religious inquisitions. In 1245, the first inquisitorial prison was built in Toulouse. Around 1300, one of the first public prisons in Europe was built in Italy: Le Stinche.[36] An entire administrative apparatus began to emerge around these new institutions. In Le Stinche, for example, "there were four wardens, four to six guards, a notary, a chamberlain, a physician, a chaplain, a caretaker, and two friars who attended to the prisoners' needs; as well as three different supervisory boards to monitor the officials' conduct and the inmates' welfare."[37]

The years 1250–1350 are thus, according to Guy Geltner, "a watershed period in the history of the prison."[38] This is in great part due to "the widescale imprisonment of heretics by papal inquisitors in the thirteenth century."[39] European inquisitions imprisoned hundreds of thousands of peasants—more peasants than there were cells to hold or had ever been imprisoned. It was common practice to keep a defendant in prison for years before the trial even began to obtain new information. Even after confession, defendants were sent back to prison if the Inquisition felt that they had not "fully" confessed.

The vagabond laws often could not be separated from heresy laws.[40] Vagabonded peasants, for example, posed a constant threat of rebellion against the landlord and church system of property ownership and the growing money economy. The ideology of vagabond peasant resistance often took the form of millenarian beliefs in alternative social, religious, and sexual norms, which the landlords and churches denounced as heresy. The purpose of the vagabond laws and the Inquisition was to reduce vagabond resistance by criminalizing and confining anyone who was homeless, poor, or begging. The tensional force of the law was thus used first to disjoin the serfs from their legal right to the land and then to conjoin them to the tensions of growing religious and state-controlled juridical administration.

Among the vagabond laws responsible for the incarceration of an historically record number of juridically expelled peoples is the Statute of Cambridge (1388), which placed restrictions on the movements of laborers and beggars by requiring written approval from the local leaders. Without such approval, vagabonds would be placed in the stocks. At best, statues like these restricted vagabond movement to an absolute minimum. At worst, they put vagabonds in a paradoxical position: to request permission to beg, one must already announce oneself to the authorities as a beggar, which was discouraged. To request permission to travel for work, one must already have secured that work. But it was difficult to secure work without traveling in the first place.

Later on, the vagabond laws became increasingly punitive and mandated forced labor. The Vagabonds and Beggars Act (1494), for instance, declared that

vagabonds, idle and suspected persons shall be set in the stocks for three days and three nights and have none other sustenance but bread and water and then shall be put out of Town. Every beggar suitable to work shall resort to the Hundred where he last dwelled, is best known, or was born and there remain upon the pain aforesaid.[41]

Those who had nothing and had nowhere to go would beg. And when they begged and got nothing, desperation led them to rebuke individuals who did not give them money. In London in 1517, beggars were legally not allowed to rebuke the people who gave them nothing.

Authorities even went as far as to create laws that allowed designated beggars with badges to expel other vagabonds and beggars without badges. If they did not expel the other vagabonds, they would lose their right to beg, or they would be punished according to laws like those established in 1530 in England that mandated beggars and vagabonds

to be tied to the cart-tail and whipped until the blood streams from their bodies, then they are to swear on oath to go back to their birthplace or to where they have lived the last three years and to "put them-selves to labour." For the second arrest for vagabondage the whipping is to be repeated and half the ear sliced off; but for the third relapse the offender is to be executed as a hardened criminal and enemy of the commonwealth.[42]

As commutations, enclosures, and religious inquisitions increased, so did the number of homeless vagabonds. As the vagabonds increased, so did the jails and the intensity of punishments for vagabondage. In 1547, the Act for the Punishing of Vagabonds even went as far as to institute chattel slavery, announcing that

if anyone refuses to work, he shall be condemned as a slave to the person who has denounced him as an idler. The master shall feed his slave on bread and water, weak broth and such, refuse meat as he thinks fit. He has the right to force him to do any work, no matter how disgusting, with whip and chains. If the slave is absent for a fortnight, he is condemned to slavery for life and is to be branded on forehead or back with the letter S; if he runs away three times, he is to be executed as a felon.[43]

As vagabondage grew, the types of people considered vagabonds increased. The law needed to unravel the many names of the vagabond and make sure that they were all accounted for (and punished/confined). For example, in 1572, the Poor Law further enumerated the increasing names of the vagabond:

All fencers, bearwards [bear trainers], common players of interludes, and minstrels (not belonging to any baron of this realm, or to any other honourable person of greater degree) . . . all jugglers, peddlers, tinkers, and petty chapmen, common labourers refusing to work for such reasonable wages . . . and all scholars of the universities . . . that go about begging, not being authorized under the seal of the said universities, and all shipmen pretending losses by sea, and all persons . . . not having licence from two Justices of the Peace shall be taken,

adjudged, and deemed rogues, vagabonds, and sturdy beggars . . . to be griev-
ously whipped and burnt through the gristle of the right ear with a hot iron.[44]

The Poor Law also required the deportation of those without proper
papers "to the place where he or she was born or most conversant by the
space of three years next before" and the kidnapping of vagabond children. If the children of vagabonds between the ages of five and fourteen
"shall be liked of by any subject of honest calling who shall be willing to
take the said child into service, the said subject shall have the said child
bound with him." These kinds of laws existed not only in England but
were enacted in France, the Netherlands, and United Provinces.[45]

The aim of all these laws was to expand a specifically juridical control over the undesirable movement of peasants, beggars, paupers, heretics, minstrels, Jews, witches, and rebellious travelers of all kinds grouped
under the criminal name "the vagabond." Tensional kinopower expands
its network of juridical linkages first by breaking the old laws that inhibit
expansion (land tenure, customary law, etc.) and then by expanding a
host of new laws with even wider coordinated impact between linked
institutions (the church, lords, prisons, and enforcement). Eventually, as
Guy Geltner argues at length, it is this increasing juridical coordination
required to apprehend and manage vagabonds/heretics that gives rise to
the early-modern state as a complex network of legally interconnected
institutions.[46]

Plague Laws.   Plague laws are another way in which vagabonds were
expelled, and an increasingly powerful juridical apparatus was expanded
to control social mobility. Throughout its spread the bubonic plague was
associated with figures of the migrant: "strangers—Gypsies, Jews, vagabonds—who also found themselves expelled when the plague threatened." In September 1539, the Venetian Council of Ten noted that Milan
had expelled "poor persons suspected of carrying the plague" and ordered
them barred from entering Venice. "Venice then acted in kind, banishing
4,000 to 5,000 beggars and other recent immigrants, many of them to
service on the city's galleys."[47]

Along with the expulsion of the poor and vagabonds was the legalized expulsion of those who were sick. Even as early as 1348, "Uzerche,
France, expelled unfortunate victims, and Pistoia's plague ordinances

called for 'the sick' to be removed from the city: destination unclear."[48] If the vagabonds and beggars were not sick at the time, their expulsion along with the sick often put them in the same hostels and homes with sick persons. Further, the mass expulsion of "the sick," foreigners, and vagabonds also required a heightened fortification of the juridical apparatus: increased guards, police, strict laws, and the emergence of an increasingly independent administration over town functions, because many people were often locked in their homes. The vagabond is thus not the politically enslaved "barbarian" but the migrant subjected to a juridical order of expulsion: expulsion of the legal right of residence, work, visitation, travel, and so on. This could potentially be anyone under plague conditions. The plague laws were social kinetic laws pertaining to the control and criminalization of forbidden mobilities within and between towns.

Beyond the control of movement *within* the city, many European cities established posts outside their gates. Whether they were called pilgrims, armies, merchants, vagabonds, refugees, gypsies, or itinerant craftspeople, during plague outbreaks "people on the move" in general were considered a threat to the safety of cities and entire regions.[49] Such people had to be kept out. Hordes of expelled migrants and the sick roamed the European countryside searching for food and shelter. Everywhere they turned, they were beaten, criminalized, and expelled. In Paris, Jean de Venette describes the epidemic and the resulting anti-Semitism and fear of mobile others (kinophobia) that resulted in France and Germany:

Some said that the pestilence was the result of infected air and water . . . and as a result of this idea, many began suddenly and passionately to accuse the Jews of infecting the wells, fouling the air, and generally being the source of the plague. Everyone rose up against them most cruelly. In Germany and elsewhere—wherever Jews lived—they were massacred and slaughtered by Christian crowds and many thousands were burned indiscriminately.[50]

Plague laws criminalized many forms of mobility (such as leaving one's house, exiting the city, and traveling between certain areas without a passport) and all forms of unauthorized migration and strongly associated migrants with disease and death.[51] Disease became associated with the fluid dynamics of air and water, as well as the social figure of hydrodynamics: the migrant. By expelling migrants and the sick together, forcing them to roam the countryside together or reside in the same sick camps (which were converted migrant hostels), the link between disease and migrancy was effectively produced and retroactively confirmed.

The plague laws also gave birth to some of the first early-modern refugee camps in Europe. Camps were created for those expelled from the city for being either sick or vagabonds. The two terms became increasingly similar under the plague law. If migrants or vagabonds were not sick before entering the camps, they surely would become sick while staying in them. Sickness would then confirm the kinophobia that put the migrants there in the first place. The sick were also expelled to "pest houses" or "lazarettos" (named after Lazarus, from the Gospel of John). The pest house was the site of expulsion for the sick and the vagabond. Pest houses were often converted poorhouses, inns, pilgrim hospices, agricultural workers' huts, or lean-tos in the fields and forests. "All too often, pest houses consisted of groups of cheap, temporary huts—'hovels,' 'cabins,' 'tents,' 'booths,' even 'cages'—erected when the plague struck and destroyed or disassembled and stored for the next epidemic."[52] Thus, plague laws were a key juridical control over movement that both expelled the sick/vagabonds and further expanded an increasingly independent and criminal enforcement apparatus. The plague town was "shut in," and the vagabond was "shut out."

Workhouse Laws.   In addition to the expansion of juridical kinopower through plague laws, expelled vagabonds of all sorts were used to expand juridical kinopower through workhouse laws. Vagabonds were criminalized first as rebel heretics, then as diseased migrants. After the plague, the prisons and pest houses were full, and labor shortages were high. But the purpose of the early workhouse laws was not primarily one of productivity, since workhouses were unprofitable and terribly inefficient, but the capture and suppression of roaming vagabonds to place vagabonds back under the law. This was effected in a series of laws starting in the fourteenth century. During this time, kinopower expanded in early workhouses through largely juridical, not economic, means.

The origins of the workhouse can be traced to the Poor Law Act of 1388, which attempted to address the labor shortages following the plague by restricting the mobility of laborers to a given area, instead of allowing them to seek higher wages elsewhere. But the institution of the workhouse itself emerges from an act passed in 1564 to suppress the "roaming beggar" by granting parish officers the power to capture beggars and "appoint meet and convenient places for the habitations and abidings."[53] This was followed by the 1576 Act for Setting the Poor on Work that provided raw materials (wool, hemp, and flax) to the able-bodied poor.

In 1601, the Act for the Relief of the Poor made parishes responsible for the care of the poor, who were divided into three groups: the able-bodied poor, who should be sent to houses of correction (workhouses); persistent idlers, who should be punished; and the impotent poor; and for children, orphanages were created. All these institutions for the poor would be funded by a tax on the wealthy. This taxation required the expansion of an increasingly powerful and juridically central welfare state—less a single authority than a dense knot of kinetically interconnected linkages. Children were taken from their vagabond parents and made into apprentices in the workhouses. As efficient and productive worksites the workhouses failed, but as juridical institutions they succeeded in increasing the power of an administrative and police power that reconjoined vagabonds to the tensional force of law.

Thus, the effect of the workhouse laws was not only to restrict regional and daily mobility but to multiply the sites of juridical power through incarceration, enforcement, and expanding legislation. In many cases, workhouses or poorhouses could not be distinguished from prisons.

Witch Hunts. Finally, witch hunts added another set of laws that expanded the juridical control over peasant mobility through the expulsion of "witches." The figure of the witch is a type of vagabond: *a heretical criminalized migrant.*

Many women accused and tried for witchcraft were old and poor. Often they depended upon public charity for survival. Witchcraft—we are told—is the weapon of the powerless. But old women were also those in the community most likely to resist the destruction of communal relations. . . . They were the ones who embodied the community's knowledge and memory. The witch-hunt turned the image of the old woman upside down: traditionally considered a wise woman, she became a symbol of sterility and hostility to life.[54]

The aim of criminalizing witches, as Silvia Federici points out, was to undermine peasant resistance to the landlords, the rich, and the church. European witch hunts were expansions of a tensional legal force (the

Inquisition) to conjoin and incarcerate poor women to the juridical apparatus of the prison or the home. The fear of accusation sent a message to all women to stay immobilized in the home and raise children.

Peasant expulsion from the land (through commutation or enclosure) disproportionately affected women, since they were not legally allowed to work as day laborers. Hence, it was almost entirely women (and children) who would dig up enclosure fences in the middle of the night to gain access to pasturage. It was also predominantly older or single women who lived off public assistance and begging and defaulted on their rent.[55] When they were refused alms, they would give the "evil eye" or make curses. The acts that initiated a witch accusation were almost always the crimes of the vagabond who took revenge, stole, begged, or roamed without license. Federici also notes that it is quite significant that "in England, most of the witch trials occurred in Essex where, by the 16th century, the bulk of the land had been enclosed, while in those regions of the British Isles where land privatization had neither occurred nor was on the agenda have no record of witch-hunting."[56]

The criminalization of the witch's Sabbat is also linked to the criminalization of those other kinetic heretics, the Jews (and their Sabbath), and to the secret meetings of rebellious peasants held at night on lonely hills and forests.[57] Witches were also often persecuted for *flight* or *travel*, so Luciano Parinetto argues that the criminalization of the "witches flight" and travel should also be interpreted as a criminalization of the mobility of immigrant workers and the fear of vagabonds that also pervaded the legal code during this time.[58]

External Expansion by Expulsion

Added to the rapid development of an internal juridical kinopower through the criminalization of vagabonds was an external expansion of juridical kinopower through the colonization of the Americas. In western Europe, expansion by expulsion was predominantly effected through legal institutions such as those just described. Some centripetal and centrifugal forms of kinopower during colonization (such as stockpiling raw materials from the territory, murder and kidnapping of people in Africa and the Americas, and slavery) were resurrected, but a more juridical form of colonial kinopower was also invented: the *encomienda*.

The encomienda, from the Spanish verb *encomendar*, "to entrust," was a legal system employed by the Spanish Crown during the colonization of the Americas to regulate Native American labor. The encomienda was the

delegation of royal power to collect the tribute from, *and to use the personal services of,* the King's vassals (the Indians). The encomendero undertook to look after the welfare of his charges and to educate them in proper (Spanish) norms of conduct, as well as to discharge the usual feudal obligation of bearing arms in the King's defense.[59]

In 1503, the Crown began to legally grant encomiendas to soldiers, conquistadors, and officials, and the system lasted until the seventeenth century. Encomienda is distinct from previous forms of direct political exploitation like slavery and extermination insofar as it focuses on expanding a quasi-feudal juridical structure. Instead of direct slavery or territorial capture, it acts directly on the legislated mobility of the peasants themselves, just as feudalism did in Europe. The encomienda is a tensional force of exchanged services. Encomenderos and Indians each owed something to the other on the king's land. Although this was obviously an asymmetrical power relationship, it was not the same as slavery. Indians were not chattel slaves, owned by encomenderos. They could not be bought, sold, or rented or relocated from their territory. Encomenderos had the right only to labor, not the land. Furthermore, encomenderos did not inherit what they were entrusted with and could not pass it on to future generations.[60]

The external expansion of juridical kinopower in the encomienda system also, in the case of the Americas, produced a massive expulsion of the Indians (between 80 and 90 percent died of disease and war). The massive reduction of the Indian population made Indians vulnerable to colonial rule but also, over the course of the sixteenth century, "doomed the encomienda as a device for procuring cheap labor." Despite its modifications over time, the juridical expansion of the encomienda "became the basis of Spanish colonial society, and, in general, it is that of rural Mexico today," according to encomienda scholar Lesley Simpson.[61]

There was also an external juridical expulsion of Europeans to the colonies. The Vagabonds Act of 1597 in England, for example, introduced penal transportation as a punishment for the first time. Vagabonds could choose to be transported to a colony rather than be executed and entered into bond service as workers. These were some of the first colonial migrants to the Americas. The penal system required convicts to do public works: build roads, houses, or mines. Women were expected to work as domestic servants and farm laborers. Thus, America was, and in many ways continues to be, built by criminalized migrant labor.

In Spain, vagabonds were punished corporeally by serving in the galleys to row ships for colonial, slave, or war purposes. If vagabonds were not criminally compelled to migrate to North America, many would voluntarily exchange five to seven years of bonded servitude for passage just for the chance of escaping their criminalized displacement in Europe. In the seventeenth century, indentured servants made up 75 percent of all European immigrants to the Chesapeake region. Most of these indentured servants were English vagabonds who had been expelled from their homes by the enclosure system. In this way, the internal system of European juridical displacement also fueled the external colonial displacement of the indigenous population.

CHAPTER 6

Elastic Force I

The tensional force of juridical kinopower expands by dissolving old legal links and assembling new ones into increasingly dense and powerful networks. However, by dissolving too much or too quickly, feudal tensional force also ends up destabilizing social motion through legal expulsion and enforcement, culminating in what Eric Hobsbawm calls the "Crisis of the Seventeenth Century,"[1] characterized by widespread vagabondage and social turmoil (most notably defined by the Thirty Years' War, 1618–48).[2] The massive expulsion of vagabonds by the dissolution of customary laws created an unstoppable and unconfinable flow of criminalized movement. Thus, a new dominant social kinetic force was needed to manage these vagabond social flows. This new force began to manage unlinked social flows not by stopping their movement by law (tension) but by redistributing them into a more flexible state of equilibrium, or "elasticity."

Elasticity

The sociohistorical period between the eighteenth and twentieth centuries can be kinopolitically defined by the emergence of a newly dominant force of social motion: elasticity. Social elasticity is the capacity for a network of junctions to return to its normal shape after contraction or expansion. Social elasticity is the force that quickly redistributes people to fill a deficit or displace an excess to avoid social decline or collapse.

It is the redistribution of a stretchable social surplus that acts like a buffer against unpredictable expansions and contractions that might disrupt social motion.

More so than previous historical periods, the modern period can be characterized by increasingly rapid forms of social expansion and contraction: expansions and contractions of demand and supply in the market, of births and deaths in the population, of abundance and famine in the food supply, and of space and time in communication and transportation. Because of the increasing oscillation in these social fields they are always producing a relative social surplus or deficit according to the stage of expansion and contraction. And with the increase of social oscillations (expansions and contractions) also comes the centrality of a new social kinetic problem: equilibrium—how to generate new junctions just as fast as (or faster than) they are being expelled. The question of modern kinopower is no longer "How do we juridically bind oscillating flows?" but "How will it be possible to redistribute oscillations to avoid too much or too little of certain kinds of movements?" Elasticity is more than the random oscillation of the social field; it requires a *driving* force to redistribute (expand and expel) a surplus of motion in order to maintain an equilibrium of circulation.

In this sense, social kinetic surplus is motion above and beyond the requirements for basic social reproduction. It is a motion that can be reserved when not needed and can be deployed when needed.[3] The elastic structure of surplus is therefore triadic, composed of three kinds of surplus: a base, a floating, and a future surplus.

The base surplus is the social motion perceived as socially necessary. Despite its social necessity, it is nothing other than a previously accumulated surplus that has been normalized as "acceptable" (i.e., a level of profit, a minimum wage, reasonable commute distance, acceptable traffic or living conditions). However, the problem with the base surplus is its instability with respect to the future. In a world of increasing social oscillations, contractions, and expansions of a seemingly unconfinable population, how can this base surplus ensure social equilibrium with respect to an uncertain future movement?

From this base surplus, a floating surplus is produced—either internally by making part of its own population redundant or externally by taking from another population elsewhere. The floating population is the relatively redundant part of the population that is made to act as a buffer against the future expansions and contractions of social motion. This surplus population is then stored, or "floats," in prisons, workhouses, forests, camps, and so on and awaits its redeployment in the future.

Finally, the future surplus is the surplus anticipated to be required in the future to maintain equilibrium or prepare the conditions of further expansion. While the floating surplus is the actual surplus, the future surplus is the least potential surplus needed to maintain equilibrium or better: expansion.

The aim of this socially elastic triad is not to keep society static (homeostasis) but to maintain a dynamic equilibrium (homeorhesis) and, when possible, to expand this equilibrium. If social motion contracts, the floating surplus is reabsorbed into the base surplus; if social motion expands, the floating surplus is expanded as part of a future surplus. Enclosures, workhouses, prisons, camps, and factories all start to follow this social elasticity in the modern period.

Surplus is distributed both intensively and extensively. Intensively, surplus can be produced and held in place above and beyond the needs of a certain limit of reproduction. Reserving a social surplus tends to intensify competition, such as for jobs, food, and housing. It lowers wages and raises prices. Extensively, a surplus produced in one area can be relocated to another area to offset a deficit, scarcity, famine, or depopulation. The extensive redistribution of surplus can be used both to balance out a deficit or create a surplus elsewhere. As long as a society is capable of producing and mobilizing its surplus and deficits, it will be able to strive toward an equilibrium or expansion.

Thus, elasticity expands and expels, not from the outside to the center (centripetally), nor from the center to the outside (centrifugally), nor by rigid links between centers (tension), but rather by the expansive redistribution of a surplus wherever it is needed.

Economic Kinopower

This elastic force is a specifically "economic" type of kinopower in the sense that economics strives for the free arrangement and movement of things with a minimum of territorial, political, or juridical restrictions and with a maximum of equilibrium. Economics, more broadly construed, is not simply "the science of wealth." It is an entire regime for the direction of social motion. In this way, economics functions more like the management of a household (*oikonomia*) than it does like the management of a state (*polis*). This is precisely why Aristotle, for example, argues that the *techne oikonomike* differs from politics just as the house (*oikia*) differs from the city (*polis*).[4] While the state is concerned with the goal of the public good, the household is simply concerned with the desirable arrangement or balance of the individual's private property. The house is neither the village of centripetally accumulated flows, nor the unified mega-junction of the ancient city from whence power radiates centrifugally, nor the linked junctions of the feudal and monastic institutions in juridical bind with one another. Management of a household and economics are not centric or unifying kinetic processes.

The economy is more like a network of decentered private households that do not, on their own, constitute a city. The city requires a center. But households can be added together indefinitely, without ever establishing a single social center or totality. Instead, the assembly of private households forms an indefinite *series* with a shifting point of equilibrium. The series is not a centripetal curve, a centrifugal circle, or a tensional link. The series is a flow between relay junctions—oscillating between constant contractions and expansions aiming toward social equilibrium.

However, no household is entirely self-sufficient. Every household needs to purchase additional goods to supplement what cannot be made on-site. Economics is, thus, composed of a minimum of two sites necessary for the management of the household: the household to be arranged and the marketplace where surplus can be exchanged and purchased to supplement household production. Market prices are driven by many factors (for example, scarcity, currency, and interest rates). For thousands of years, however, households and markets have been subject to the dominant motions of territorial, political, and legal power that have limited the arrangement of private goods. What occurred in the eighteenth century, however, was that for the first time serial and elastic motion (surplus and competition) became the increasingly dominant social kinetic forces. Their aim was to create the proper equilibrium of social forces through the continual redistribution of surplus mobility—like the addition and subtraction of weights on a shifting balance scale. Again, this does not mean that political, legal, and other forces are not active and intertwined but only that they are more often subordinated to kino-economic forces during this period.

The Figure of the Proletariat

The figure of the migrant produced by the elasticity of economic expansion by expulsion is *the proletariat*. The figure of the proletariat, however, is complex and includes a variety of integral subtypes, including both the actively employed worker and the unemployed floating population. In this sense, not all of the proletariat is always and in every case a figure of the migrant but rather intersects with it in certain circumstances and to different degrees. For instance, if the proletariat is considered an actively employed and relatively stable class identity, it is not a figure of the migrant.[5] If the proletariat is considered according to its economic expulsion from the means of production or employment and its mobility, it overlaps with the history of the migrant being traced in this book. The latter is the sense in which Deleuze and Guattari maintain that "the proletariat . . . appears as the heir to the nomad in the Western world."[6] The figure of the proletariat emerges as the dominant migratory figure of economic kinopower, but the previous migratory figures of the nomad, the barbarian, and the vagabond (and their subtypes) do not disappear. They coexist as added dimensions of the territorial, political, and legal expulsion of the proletariat.

Proletarius, "the one who produces offspring" (from the Latin *proli,* "offspring"), derives from the Roman census designation for those citizens whose property was valued at eleven thousand asses (Roman coins) or less. Their children, *proles* (offspring), were listed on the census instead of their property. The only value of these propertyless citizens for the Romans was the ability to produce children for the empire. These citizens played a very different historical role than did the barbarians, for example, who were the predominant migrants of the ancient world. If barbarians were the "mobile motor" of the ancient world, the *proles* were the "biological motor." The word "proletariat" falls out of use by 2 CE,[7] and it emerges again in the fourteenth century to be used as a derogatory term akin to "rabble" and "knave" up until the nineteenth century. For example, an eighteenth-century dictionary defines the proletariat as "mean, wretched, vile, or vulgar."[8] After studying Roman law at the University of Berlin, Marx began to popularize a modern conception of this figure as the working class as a whole.[9] In doing so, he contributes to the conceptual merger of the mobile and biological motors into the common figure of the modern proletariat.

Marx also introduces a constitutive division into the concept of the proletariat between the proletariat and the lumpenproletariat: between the actively employed and the floating unemployed (or economically expelled). But these two figures are not fixed class or group identities for Marx.[10] They are two poles of the same proletarian spectrum of economic expulsion. One side is constantly being transformed into the other through a continual production of a "relative surplus population."[11] While the working proletariat is absolutely necessary for the reproduction of economic motion, the unemployed or lumpenproletariat is equally necessary. Marx goes so far as to say that the unemployed "relative surplus population" is "the lever of capitalist accumulation, indeed it becomes a condition for the existence of the capitalist mode of production. It forms a disposable industrial reserve army, which belongs to capital just as absolutely as if the latter had bred it at its own cost."[12]

There are at least three major types of this surplus population, according to Marx. Each type follows a unique aspect of social elasticity: the floating, latent, and stagnant populations. The floating population is the part of the surplus population that is "sometimes repelled, sometimes attracted again in greater masses, so that the number of those employed increases on the whole, although in a constantly decreasing proportion to the scale of production."[13] The floating population is the most active and mobile part of the reserve labor army. During periods of contraction or an intensification of production, these workers are laid off but are still elastic enough to follow the emigration of capital elsewhere or to a lower level of production. Large-scale industry, in particular, produces an increasingly larger surplus population in proportion to the expansion of capitalist production. As it expands, it increases the proportion of expelled workers—specifically the old, skilled, and male—in favor of the young, unskilled, and female.

As capital takes possession of agriculture, it produces a slightly less mobile form of surplus population: the latent population. As agricultural production is mechanized, the demand for workers falls dramatically in proportion to the population. Thus, there exists a massive latent population of potential manufacturing workers mostly waiting in rural poverty for manufacturing jobs to open up. When jobs do open up, these workers migrate to the cities from the countryside.

The third category is the least mobile surplus population: stagnant workers. These are workers who are the most irregularly employed and are, for the most part, simply providing the basic acts of biological reproduction for a future surplus population. Marx compares this final type of surplus population to weakened animals simply reproducing so that they may be "constantly hunted down."[14] Their populations increase in an inverse proportion to the level of wages. This population is further divided into three types of paupers: those who can work, orphans and poor children, and those who cannot work. While unemployed, they form a massive weight that the active workers must take care of. These stagnant workers also constantly keep a pressure on the level of wages of active workers because they are still mobile.

The relative mass of the industrial reserve army thus increases with the potential energy of wealth. But the greater this reserve army in proportion to the active labour army, the greater is the mass of a consolidated surplus population, whose misery is in inverse ratio to the amount of torture it has to undergo in the form of labour.[15]

At any point, the proletariat may be fired, forced to migrate elsewhere, or made unemployable (through injury, age, or circumstance). Accordingly, these three types are not fixed but fluid moments of the same proletarian subjectivity with their own degree of expulsion and migration. What they all share in common under capitalist social relations is that each becomes the conditions of the other's impoverishment.

As capitalist markets expand, contract, and multiply "by fits and starts," Marx says, capital requires the possibility of suddenly adding and subtracting "great masses of men into decisive areas without doing any damage to the scale of production. The surplus population supplies these masses."[16] If there were 100 percent employment in all markets, new and expanding markets would not have any source of new labor. Furthermore, if there were total employment, then workers would not be easily replaced and their strikes would have substantial force over production.

Capitalist production, according to Marx, requires and produces a mass of workers that is superfluous to its requirements for two reasons: (1) when expansion or multiplication of markets occurs, there will be a surplus of workers ready at hand; and (2) this surplus of unemployed workers will make the current workers highly replaceable and overworkable, thus requiring fewer active workers (increasing surplus population further) and making active workers available at a cheaper wage. "Modern industry's whole form of motion," Marx claims, "therefore depends on the constant transformation of a part of the working population into unemployed or semi-employed 'hands.'"[17]

However, the unemployed proletariat may not always be a *migrant* proletariat. It becomes so only insofar as its economic expulsion is linked to its extensive mobility. In this category, Marx gives several examples of such lumpenproletarian migrants: "discharged soldiers, discharged jailbirds, escaped galley slaves, ragpickers . . . in short, the whole of the nebulous, disintegrated mass, scattered hither and thither."[18] In this sense, the proletariat is a complex figure because it is always slipping in and out of its migratory status as it is compelled to relocate according to the demands of capitalist valorization or roam the streets without shelter or work. This mobility is *the condition of modern industry's whole form of motion*. Without the migration of surplus population to new markets, from the rural country to the city, from city to city, from country to country (what Marx calls the "floating population"), capitalist accumulation would *not be possible at all*. Even when the proletariat is unemployed or lumpen, its migratory status still exerts a downward pressure on the wages of the working.[19]

Thus, the migrant is that part of the spectrum of the proletariat that is currently economically expelled as a mobile social surplus. This chapter and the next analyze the specific social technologies of expulsion and mobilization that give rise to a variety of such migrant proletarian subjects and expand economic kinopower.

Internal Expansion by Expulsion: Intensive Surplus

Economic kinopower expands elastically by expelling an internal surplus population. This internal surplus is *intensively* expelled as a way to increase competition and production through land enclosures, capitalist valorization, and workhouses.

Enclosures

The first way a migrant proletariat is produced is by its expulsion from the countryside and into the city: from subsistence agriculture to urban industrialism. The first phase of enclosure laws (1235–1760) is kinetically different from the second phase (1761–1844). The first phase was defined by a predominantly juridical or tensional battle that resulted in both the legal privatization of land and the criminalization of vagabondage. The second phase is predominantly about elastically *redistributing* an enormous oscillatory surplus population from the country to the city.

During the fifteenth and sixteenth centuries in Britain, both the church and state actively tried to outlaw the enclosure laws. However, once Britain had established a single competitive market and began to determine land value based on its potential productive capacity in a competitive market, landlords could raise rent prices according to the oscillation of market values. The state then saw a way to recover its economic losses. By requiring increases in renter productivity, landlords, who were forbidden by the state to arbitrarily tax peasant tenants, were able to extract a profit by purely economic means: the intensification of production. The church and state were then able to extract a tax from these profits even if the landlords had entirely eliminated tenants in favor of grazing sheep and selling the wool to expanding markets in northern Europe. Thus, according to the English historian W. E. Tate, the second phase of enclosures was a response to the previous "rigid and inelastic" tensional contracts of customary laws and peasant land tenure.[20]

Even though the elasticity of early enclosure laws during the Tudor period were limited by the juridical tensions that directly opposed enclosures, these laws were eventually overcome and gave birth to a new phase of church- and state-supported enclosures. During the latter part of the first phase of enclosures (1700 and 1760), only 208 acts enclosing 318,000 acres were passed.[21] Compared to this, the second period (1761–1844) is by far the age of enclosure par excellence. During this period, roughly corresponding to the reign of King George III (1760–1820), 3,883 acts enclosed 5.63 million acres, a dramatic increase.[22] Hundreds of thousands of people were expelled from the land in England and migrated into increasingly industrial manufacturing towns like Manchester. The processing of cotton, coal, and iron became the new migrant occupations and the basis of the Industrial Revolution.[23]

For hundreds of years, anti-enclosure and anti-vagabond legislation from the Tudor and Stuart rule upheld the mercantilist/populist belief that the population was the greatest national resource. Now, a desire to encourage British predominance in finance and industry pushed the state in a different direction. The power of royalty was becoming increasingly limited by a growing landowning and commercial class who favored enclosures. Laws against depopulation and enclosures were repealed. As the value of land was no longer fixed but oscillated on a rent market, the value of land increased with the demand for wool and agricultural productivity. Since the value of land rent (rather than the population) became the new index of national prosperity, the state began to see enclosure as a national benefit. As property values and incomes rose, so did the value of the church's tithes. Thus, the leaders of the Anglican Church, looking to collect their share of the profits, also came to identify with the interests of the property-owning classes in supporting enclosure in the late eighteenth and nineteenth centuries.

Accordingly, there was a radical shift in the conditions of social motion and in the figure of the migrant during this time. The first period of enclosure laws coincided with the "bloody" anti-vagabond laws in England and Europe from the sixteenth to early eighteenth centuries and established a new kinetic social tension in the prison, state, and church.[24] The second period, however, coincides with the decline of anti-vagabond and anti-enclosure laws and the rise of an enormous surplus population of migrant proletarians moving to urban centers. While the first period of enclosure is defined by a generalized cellular confinement (tensional mobility) aimed at increasing the population, the second is defined by a generalized elasticity aimed at conjoining or redistributing the surplus population into the cities.

The power of a nation no longer hinged on the size of its population but on its capacity to mobilize its surplus to rising sectors of growth (mills, mines, and manufacturing). Thus, the social kinetic problem of the late eighteenth to twentieth centuries was no longer how to increase the population and confine vagabonds but how to circulate a mobile surplus population in the most productive fashion via railroads, roadways, and factories.[25]

However, the oscillation (expansion and contraction) of the economic market gave rise to wealth as well as risk. The kinopolitical resolution to this problem, supported by the second period of enclosure, was to create an elasticity of social motion through a surplus population that functioned as a backup reserve or buffer in case of market contractions. The mobility of the surplus population allows social motion to expand and contract without breaking.

Thus, we are able to distinguish two important differences between the two periods of enclosure: a difference in the motion of expansion by expulsion (tension vs. elasticity) and a difference in the type of migrant produced (vagabond vs. proletariat).

Capitalist Valorization

The second major way a migrant proletariat is produced is by mobilizing it according to the specific needs of capitalist valorization through unemployment and emigration. Although the process of eighteenth- and nineteenth-century enclosure, or what Marx calls "primitive accumulation," goes hand in hand with the capitalist valorization process, the two produce and manage surplus in importantly different ways.[26] Enclosure focuses on expelling proletarian migrants from their previous economic livelihoods in the countryside. The capitalist mode of production expels them again in the city through a cyclical or periodized unemployment phase according to its oscillatory needs for human labor. Even after the proletariat has been completely enclosed and lives propertyless in the city, capital finds new ways to create surplus. Enclosure and capital are two dimensions of the same kinopolitical elasticity.

The Oscillation of Capital.   Capitalist markets are driven by the imperatives of competition and the intensification of production. These imperatives, according to Marx, create "periodic phases which, as accumulation advances, are complicated by irregular oscillations following each other more and more quickly." The "law of motion" of modern industry is the law of the regulation of the demand and supply of labour by the alternate expansion and contraction of capital, i.e., by the level of capital's valorization requirements at the relevant moment, the labour-market sometimes appearing relatively undersupplied because capital is expanding, and sometimes relatively oversupplied because it is contracting.[27]

Since prices on a capitalist market are not fixed but expand and contract according to demand and supply, so does capital's need for labor. As demand for commodities contracts, so does the demand for workers. Workers are then laid off. As demand for commodities expands, so does the need for workers. Workers are then hired. As long as economic markets are driven by the imperatives of competition and the intensification of production, they will continue to produce this oscillatory movement. "Just as the heavenly bodies always repeat a certain movement," Marx says, "so also does social production."[28]

Hand in hand with the expulsion of the peasants from the countryside, capital creates its own proper form of expulsion as labor demands contract. Additionally, technological development and the intensification of production result in a greater efficiency of the workers, making it possible to cut labor costs by laying off (expelling) part of the workers through unemployment. "Thus the law of supply and demand as applied to labour is kept on the right lines," Marx states. "[T]he oscillation of wages is confined within limits satisfactory to capitalist exploitation, and, lastly, the social dependence of the worker on the capitalist, which is indispensable, is secured."[29] In this way, capitalism both mobilizes the surplus population expelled through enclosures and produces its *own form of expulsion* through the intensification of production and laying off of workers. In other words, there is a production of a mobile surplus population proper to capitalist valorization that is distinct from that of enclosure or any so-called natural population increase.

The Oscillation of Labor.   Just as capitalist valorization produces an oscillation of prices, so it compels an oscillation of labor:

The higher wages draw a larger part of the working population into the more favoured sphere until it is glutted with labour-power, and wages at length fall again to their average level or below it, if the pressure is too great. At that point, the influx of workers into the branch of industry in question not only ceases, but gives place to an outflow of workers.[30]

The oscillation (influx and outflow) of workers thus corresponds to the oscillating (demand and supply) requirements of capitalist production. During contractions in the capitalist demand for workers, the unemployed portion of the working class, or what Marx refers to as the "industrial reserve labor army," "weigh down" the active army of workers by driving down wages—as desperate workers are willing to work for less. During periods of capitalist expansion and feverish activity, there still remains a reserve army capable of breaking up a strike if the employed workers decide to organize.

The over-work of the employed part of the working class swells the ranks of its reserve, while, conversely, the greater pressure that the reserve by its competition exerts on the employed workers forces them to submit to over-work and subjects them to the dictates of capital. The condemnation of one part of the working class to enforced idleness by the over-work of the other part, and vice versa, becomes a means of enriching the individual capitalists.[31]

The harder the workers work, the fewer workers are needed and the greater the size of the industrial reserve labor army, which drives down the wages of the workers. In other words, the workers are made to work toward their own poverty and expulsion.

Accordingly, when capital emigrates, the workers follow.[32] If there were total employment, there would be no surplus or reserve labor army to rapidly follow and fill the labor demands of the emerging new market. Thus, the condition of capitalist emigration and market expansion is the emigration of part of the proletariat: a structural surplus of mobilizable workers waiting in the wings. It is in this sense that part of the proletariat, for Marx, is always migrant. The workers follow capitalist production into the great urban centers and "concentrate the historical motive power of society."[33]

The Elasticity of Capitalism.   The dual oscillation of capital and labor is managed according to the *elasticity* of capitalist valorization.[34] Given the rapid oscillations of demand and supply, capital must be elastic enough to move itself and its labor power without risking collapse or deficit. This elasticity of capitalism is made possible precisely by ensuring that, whatever the situation, there will always be a surplus population of unemployed workers that can be mobilized to stretch production forward in cases of expansion or intensify competition among workers during contraction. The migrant proletariat is thus both "the necessary product of accumulation or of the development of wealth on a capitalist basis" and "the lever of capitalist accumulation."[35]

A one-time surplus population produced by enclosure is not, in itself, sufficient to provide for the continued surplus required for capitalist valorization. The capitalist mode of production requires the continual production of a migrant proletariat through the intensification of labor and technological development. "Independently of the limits of the actual increase of population, it creates a mass of human material always ready for exploitation by capital in the interests of capital's own changing valorization requirements."[36] Nevertheless, the latter certainly contributes to the elasticity of capital. If there were not a mobile surplus from enclosure or from natural population increase elsewhere, capital would have to "breed it at its own cost."[37] When capital encounters natural population surplus or enclosure surplus, it is able to absorb it as if it were part of its own process of surplus production.

Thus, Marx rejects Thomas Malthus's explanation in *Essays on Population* (1798) of the emergence of surplus populations strictly according to the natural difference between the arithmetic growth of material production and the exponential growth of human reproduction. For Malthus, human populations by their very nature will breed faster than they are able to provide material subsistence for themselves. A poor and starving surplus population does not result because capitalist production requires a structural unemployment of a portion of the working class but simply because production cannot keep up with how fast humans are reproducing. Since the phenomena of poverty and unemployment are an effect of the natural increase of population independent of the capitalist mode of production, Malthus proposes two types of social expulsions: positive and preventive. In positive expulsion, the superior power of population must be "repressed, and the actual population kept equal to the means of subsistence, by misery and vice." Hunger, disease, emigration, and war are such positive expulsions, and abortion, birth control, prostitution, postponement of marriage, and celibacy are the preventive expulsions. For example, Malthus was against the English Poor Laws, which provided welfare and housing for the poor, because they tend to "create the poor which they maintain."[38]

Marx does not deny that there are many causes of a net increase in population, but what he rejects is that so-called natural population growth can be the sole explanation for the maintenance of a chronically unemployed and impoverished surplus population. Malthus and other political economists are guilty of naturalizing the capitalist mode of production and the widespread poverty of the surplus population. What is worse is that Malthus provides a moral argument that justifies the expulsion, death, and direct neglect of the poor. The popularity of Malthus's argument, according to Marx, has less to do with the originality of his ideas (which he plagiarized from Sir James Steuart and others) than with the timely support for such ideas by the ruling class.[39]

Capitalism does not limit its production to the natural expansion of the population. Rather, it expands production through the intensification of labor and technological development—which both tend to increase the redundancy and expulsion of the proletariat. Marx states that "capitalist production can by no means content itself with the quantity of disposable labour-power which the natural increase of population yields. It requires for its unrestricted activity an industrial reserve army which is independent of these natural limits."[40] In other words, no matter what the size or growth of the population, capital requires the maintenance of an elastic and mobile surplus population to cushion its expansions and contractions.

The Workhouse

The third major way a migrant proletariat is produced is by its expulsion from the workhouses and into waged labor. The workhouses of the fourteenth to seventeenth centuries were defined primarily by the relinking of vagabonds to an increasingly centralized juridical state apparatus through incarceration, central administration, and public taxation. However, an important kinetic innovation took place around the eighteenth century. Increasingly, workhouses functioned less as tensional confinements for vagabonds and began to expel disjoined vagabond flows from workhouses into productive labor junctions. The kinetic form of expansion by expulsion changes from the linked tension of juridical confinement and cellular power to the elasticity of driven oscillations. The problem is no longer that of confining vagabonds but of properly relocating a surplus population of workers to expand economic power. Historically, this was accomplished by expelling children from the workhouses and setting them to work, by expelling the poor and putting them to work, and by expelling the workhouse administration in favor of the privatization of the workhouse.

There is a qualitative difference between the first age of workhouse laws (fourteenth to seventeenth centuries) and the second (eighteenth to nineteenth centuries), and there is a quantitative explosion in the number of workhouses established in the eighteenth century. According to a survey conducted in 1776, there were more than eighteen hundred workhouses (approximately one-seventh of all parishes) with a capacity of more than ninety thousand places located in England and Wales.[41] This rapid growth of workhouses was prompted by the Workhouse Test Act of 1723, which obligated all paupers to enter a workhouse and undertake a set amount of work without pay.

The first technique of expansion by expulsion relating to the workhouse was the removal of children from the workhouses. This was accomplished in several ways. Throughout Great Britain, women would adopt children from the workhouses and then sell them as chimney sweeps. Even though machines were available to do this work, at least two thousand children still engaged in this labor.[42] The work was extremely dangerous, and incidence of cancer, lung disease, and scabrous skin conditions was high. Pauper children who refused the work assigned to them could be denied parish relief and even sent to prison.[43]

Capitalists also kidnapped children (ages seven to thirteen) from the workhouses and orphanages and put them to work in the cotton factory system. Although the kidnapping of children from workhouses was technically illegal, manufacturers were still able to achieve their aims as a result of complaisance of the local poor law boards.[44] According to John Fielden, in the counties of Derbyshire, Nottinghamshire, and Lancashire, large factories, remote from towns and built on the sides of streams, required thousands of hands, which were immediately available in the form of children. The children's small, nimble fingers were highly desirable in the cotton mills, so the custom of procuring apprentices from London, Birmingham, and elsewhere emerged:

The custom was for the master to clothe his apprentices and to feed and lodge them in an "apprentice house" near the factory; overseers were appointed to see to the works, whose interest it was to work the children to the utmost, because their pay was in proportion to the quantity of work that they could exact. Cruelty was, of course, the consequence. . . . [The children] were harassed to the brink of death by excess of labour . . . were flogged, fettered and tortured in the most exquisite refinement of cruelty; . . . they were in many cases starved to the bone while flogged to their work and . . . even in some instances . . . were driven to commit suicide.[45]

The factory masters also began a practice of what Fielden calls "night-working." After they work one set of tired hands all day (twelve to fourteen hours), they move on to work the next set of children all night.[46]

In addition to those being overworked, underfed, and beaten in the cotton mills, other children were kidnapped from the workhouses and made to work in mines. Pauper children were used to move trucks from the miners to the foot of the mineshaft. "Other children worked as trappers, that is, they sat in pitch dark holes for twelve hours opening and closing the doors that directed the draughts of air through the mines. The children were generally from five to eight years of age." Until the reforms of 1767 known as Hanway's Act, pauper children, especially infants, were considered expendable. The death rate of pauper infants was between 60 and 70 percent. Their high mortality rate was perceived as beneficial since it reduced the costs of poor relief: there were fewer mouths to feed. Infant morality rates in workhouses were, thus, especially high.[47]

The second technique of expansion by expulsion relating to the workhouse was the expulsion of the poor and putting them to work. The economic cost of workhouses had always been high and the profits extremely low, but around the eighteenth century, cost efficiency became a driving motive for expelling/redistributing a surplus of these "unproductive" paupers. In some cases, the surplus was dealt with by allowing pauper children to do dangerous work for a few years before they died or by cutting them off from support if they refused to work and so kill them in that way. In short, there was a new imperative to make the workhouses truly productive by forcing the migratory expulsion of its inhabitants.

This second technique was accomplished by converting the workhouse into a "House of Terror," for only the truly needy would be willing to confine themselves and their families to the misery of the workhouse. The rest would be expelled. Sir Edwin Chadwick, a disciple of and former literary secretary for Jeremy Bentham, followed Bentham's principle of "less eligibility" in supporting the 1834 Poor Law Reform that would force paupers to receive aid only in residence at the workhouse.[48] Similarly, Marx cites Jacob Vanderlint's description of this conversion. Such an ideal workhouse must be made a "House of Terror," he says, and not an asylum for the poor "where they are to be plentifully fed, warmly and decently clothed, and where they do but little work."[49] In this "ideal workhouse, the poor shall work 14 hours in a day, allowing proper time for meals, in such manner that there shall remain 12 hours of neat labour." Following this conversion Marx says, the "'House of Terror' for paupers, only dreamed of by the capitalist mind in 1770, was brought into being a few years later in the shape of a gigantic 'workhouse' for the industrial worker himself. It was called the factory."[50]

Besides being expelled to save money (creating a model of the capitalist factory), the poor were expelled from workhouses to generate profit. Workhouses in Great Britain after 1795 invented the "Roundsmen" system by which able-bodied inmates were sent to work for householders around the parish. Children ten years and older were often put on the rounds.[51] Wages were set incredibly low, and the workhouse covered the reproductive costs of the labor (food and shelter). Thus, farmers often found it more profitable to employ workhouse inmates than their normal hands—driving down wages for all workers.

The third technique of expansion was the expulsion of the public administration from the workhouse in favor of private administrators following an act in 1722 that legalized this practice. This relieved parish authorities of the burden of poorhouse/workhouse management, but since contractors were not able to anticipate how much of the surplus population would arrive at once, it was in their best interest to keep as many paupers out of the workhouse as possible, spend as little as possible on the few paupers who were there, and work the inmates as much as possible. In short, private contractors acted as capitalists in their management of workhouses. Hence, the poor were again expelled from the workhouse by its private managers to expand the wealth of a new group of workhouse capitalists. The workhouse began to follow the same elastic logic of capitalism. Some speculators even attempted to expand their "business" by offering their services to a number of parishes within a twenty- or thirty-mile radius: setting up workhouse management franchises.[52] However, these were never very successful.

The most ambitious for-profit workhouse plan came from none other than Jeremy Bentham, who proposed the construction of 250 "Houses of Industry" separated by two-thirds mile, each with two thousand inmates, and run by a profit-making joint-stock corporation. The workhouses would be run by a national charity company and would have the legal power to confine captured beggars and vagabonds in the workhouse. Able-bodied paupers would be denied outside relief. Bentham imagined an institution that would train pauper children to assume the positions of management of the workhouses as they grew to maturity. This new "pauper kingdom," as he called it, would coexist alongside the larger society of private enterprise and would solve all the problems of inefficiency that the workhouse had been guilty of.[53] Had Bentham's plan been executed as he imagined, we would have seen the largest mass expulsion of able-bodied vagabonds from the workhouses in history. Bentham's plan would also have resulted in the expansion of a "poor system" almost indistinguishable from the capitalist factory system itself.

Modern kinopower has generated some of the most diverse and numerous forms of migratory expulsion in history. This chapter has described only the *intensive* surplus created by an internal expansion by expulsion. Chapter 7 continues with the internal and external forms of elastic expansion by expulsion through penal transportation, emigration, and denationalization.

CHAPTER 7

Elastic Force II

Internal Expansion by Expulsion: Extensive Surplus

Not only is a migrant proletariat created through an intensive expulsion—enclosures, capitalist valorization, and workhouses—in order to increase competition and production, but it is also produced through an *extensive* expulsion (economic expulsion outside the territory) via penal transportation, emigration, and denationalization.

Penal Transportation

The technology of penal transportation marks a kinetic shift from the previous forms of prison management. Tensional force expanded the administrative power of the courts, police, taxation, and so forth through the mass confinement of vagabonds expelled from their legal right to the land. The predominant aim of the prison up to the seventeenth century was to confine and fix a migrant population of vagabonds/heretics. The aim of tensional kinopower was to arrest the process of depopulation and migrant mobility through confinement.

However, around the eighteenth century, carceral technologies were focused less on tensional confinement than on elastic redistribution. The major penal problem shifts from stopping depopulation to capitalizing on a surplus of mobility. Just as the eighteenth-century workhouse began to expel its "surplus" vagabonds in the form of a more profitable migrant proletariat, so the prison began to expel its population. However, in contrast to the intensive expulsion of a locally distributed surplus from the workhouse, penal transportation expels an extensive surplus *outside* the country.

At first, [prisons] were expected to neutralize dangers, to fix useless or disturbed populations, to avoid the inconveniences of over-large assemblies; now they were being asked to play a positive role, for they were becoming able to do so, to increase the possible utility of individuals.[1]

Similar to the workhouse, the prison had never been a profitable institution. However, around the eighteenth century, the prison and the migrant both came to be reinterpreted according to the logic of economic utility and the elasticity of increasingly mobile surplus populations. Thus, the aim of the prison shifted from punishment to economically productive redistribution.

Penal transportation has both a negative and a positive function. Negatively, it works as a way to solve the problem of rising prison costs due to rapid increases in the surplus prison population. The expulsion of prisoners, writes Roger Ekirch, "became Britain's primary remedy for rising crime." By the 1770s, the number of convicted persons, overcrowded prisons, and imprisoned debtors was rising dramatically (due to unemployment and continued rural expulsions). Instead of paying for the costs of more incarceration facilities, administration, whipping, and branding (following the vagabond laws), transportation provided a cheaper long-term solution. In Britain alone, "50,000 convicts were transported, including over two-thirds of all felons convicted at the Old Bailey, London's chief criminal court."[2] Transportation also worked to expel working-class dissidents from Britain and support the economic development of America.

Positively, penal transportation works as a way to provide cheap/ free migrant labor to private colonial enterprise. Systematic prison transportation began when the Transportation Act passed in Britain in 1718. It allowed courts, for the first time, to sentence convicts to seven years' transportation to America. In 1720, the state was authorized to pay private merchants to transport the convict migrants, which also expanded privatization of the prison system. Penal transportation, thus, supported a growing industry of private contractors who were paid to transport criminals, as well as a growing private colonial industry in America, built by purchased criminals. In fact, "apart from the Puritan migration to the northeastern colonies, something between a half and two-thirds of all white emigrants to the Colonies were convicts, indentured servants or redemptions."[3]

In 1776, transportation was halted by the outbreak of war with America. The temporary solution to this crisis was to sentence male convicts to hard labor in large, disease-ridden old ships docked on the Thames, called "hulks." Then, in 1787, transportation resumed but with a new destination: Australia. Overall, 187,000 convicts were sent to Australia, nearly all of them after 1815.[4]

These convicts were, for the most part, migrant proletarians: "first offenders found guilty of petty theft. Most had been employed as free workers in British or Irish labour markets prior to their conviction."[5] Since the transported convicts (both men and women) were basically a cross section of the British working class, they brought with them a wide diversity of useful skills to Australia. It should not be surprising then that they were so capable of a high degree of self-governance in their convict-labor communities and were quick to become autonomous workers again.

Since administration was costly and in short supply in Australia, convicts were increasingly employed by British officers and even private companies launched by entrepreneurial officers, ex-convicts, and their free children. By 1794, the majority of convicts worked for private employers. By 1810, convicts were allowed to work in private service and be paid a wage by employers.[6] When there was a surplus population of workers, the surplus was granted "tickets of leave" (a rudimentary inspiration for the invention of parole), which allowed the convict/workers to make their own living while remaining convicts.

Convicts ran the officers shops and upon gaining freedom, some of these convicts used their newly minted skills to set up businesses themselves, some even eclipsed their patrons. Within twenty years, the richest people in the colony were ex-convict merchants and bankers. Beneath them in the colonial economy was a wide array of ex-convict shopkeepers, publicans and tradesmen.[7]

The figure of the criminalized vagabond migrant is thus expelled from the prison and refigured as the working proletarian migrant. In the case of Australia, this expulsion even produced a new hybrid form of migrant: *the convict shepherd*. Convict shepherds were convicts who were expelled from Britain and then expelled from the Australian prison itself as shepherds who were, at the same time, prisoners in the care of a warden, private workers who could be paid a wage for their wool, and nomadic pastoral-ists who, for the most part, wandered the countryside "living and working away from their masters, and subject to only intermittent surveillance."[8] The expulsion of vagabonds from their lands, from their workhouses, and from the prisons made possible new migrant combinations.

Jeremy Bentham was vehemently opposed to these new migrant hybrids created by extensive expulsion. In 1802, Bentham wrote a short pamphlet, *Panopticon vs. New South Wales*, in which he argued that the convict colony of New South Wales allowed the convicts too much liberty and was not sufficiently reforming their conduct through punishment and enforced moral community—something that the panopticon would accomplish. The convicts, he objects, are even allowed to make profit for themselves and for the administrators—who have turned into merchants. "I question," he says, "whether the world ever saw anything under the name of punishment bearing the least resemblance to it."[9] However, it is hard to see Bentham's criticisms outside his personal investment in his own for-profit prison enterprise: the panopticon.

Unfortunately for Bentham, Britain offered little support for the construction of a prison panopticon company, in part because it required significant financial investment, which was unavailable at the time. Given the financial and cultural success of the Australian colony, it is hard not to view Bentham's criticisms as inflected with a bit of jealousy that he was not the one profiting from the migrant convicts' labor.

The prisoner–turned–nomad proletarian is a kinetically different model from that of the panoptic prison-workhouse. Or, to put it another way, the conflict between the panopticon and New South Wales was a conflict between two forms of internal expansion by expulsion: the expan-sion of private prisons through the intensive expulsion of local vagabonds into confined workers and the expansion of colonial power through the extensive expulsion of prisoners as elastic unconfined workers.

Penal transportation was not simply an English phenomenon. Countries all over the world transported their proletarian migrants else-where to save money on prison administration and expand their social forces elsewhere.

After 1820, a quarter of a million convicts were shipped across the world's oceans to colonize Australia New Caledonia, Singapore and French Guiana, and to meet labor demand in Gibraltar, Bermuda, Penang, Malacca and Mauritius. If forced migration of Russians to Siberia is included, the figure swells to 2.25 million, and the addition of the bounded Indians and Pacific Islanders doubles the number to 5 million.[10]

After witnessing the success of the British, the French began their own extensive expulsions. In the 1790s, France deported 5,000 political prisoners to Cayenne in French Guiana.[11] Following the 1848 revolution, 13,500 unemployed French workers were sent to the colony of Algeria.[12] In 1854, Cayenne became France's first penal colony. By 1911, there were 6,465 transported convicts in Guiana representing 13.2 percent of the population. And by 1915, the penal settlement of 8,568 comprised 50 percent transportés (bound transportees), 34 percent relégués (relegated political migrants), and 16 percent libérés (free migrants), who were able to enjoy freedom so long as they remained within the colony.[13]

Russia followed suit. Between 1820 and 1900, Russia expelled an estimated 187,000 criminals, 513,000 political exiles, and 216,000 followers of these exiles.[14] Other countries also participated in penal expulsions: India, Germany, and the Netherlands, for example.[15] Penal expulsion thus allowed for a massive elastic expansion of a mobile surplus population. Within the country, penal transportation allowed for a reduction of prison costs and the expulsion of various proletarian figures—the poor, ragpickers, beggars, political dissidents—all of which made possible the further growth of economic circulation. Outside the country, it fueled colonialism and expanded the privatization of penal transportation and management. The eighteenth and nineteenth centuries showed that the prison could be profitable following the social kinetic logic of elasticity. It is unfortunate that the migrants of global prison labor and bonded labor are often entirely elided from the traditional history of migration.[16]

Emigration

Emigration between the eighteenth and nineteenth centuries is by far the largest and most thoroughly studied type of extensive expulsion. This attention is due to the quantity and quality of the expulsion. Quantitatively, emigration accounts for the largest extensive movement of people from the eighteenth to twentieth centuries (more than 55 million emigrants).[17] Qualitatively, emigration is a privileged descriptive term because it follows the economically dominant kinetic description of the migrant as a "free" worker.

Within the dominant regime of economic kinopower, the figure of the proletariat is defined by the primacy of its "free" mobility. The task of directing social motion under this regime of motion is not simply to redistribute migrant workers like passive objects (as they were under ancient or feudal power) but to influence their "voluntary" submission to the kinetic imperatives of redirected expansion and contraction: elasticity. "Direct extra-economic force is still of course used, but only in exceptional cases," as Marx notes. For the most part, economic kinopower functions according to "the *silent compulsion* of economic relations [that] sets the seal on the domination of the capitalist over the worker." With very little direct physical violence, "the constant generation of a relative surplus population keeps the law of the supply and demand of labour, and therefore wages, within narrow limits which correspond to capital's valorization requirements."[18] Thus, the workers find themselves in poverty and starvation and then "choose" to emigrate.

It is according to this "silent kinetic compulsion" to mobility that migration scholars often unreflectively consider this time period to be the "age of free migration."[19] The causes of migration are frequently studied according to the purely psychological and economic motivations of the migrants themselves as rational actors—*Homo economicus*.[20] They migrate because of "opportunities" (pull factors) and "hardships" (push factors).

The danger in analyzing emigration as either "free" or "unfree" according to these psychologistic parameters is that it disguises the larger kinopolitical forms of expansion by expulsion required by social motion. It reduces the phenomena of migration to "voluntarism" and obscures the real material and historical forms of human expulsion: such as the enclosures, capitalism, workhouses, and penal transportation. It offers a nonkinetic, idealist, and ahistorical interpretation of the figure of the migrant, who, as an active proletarian worker, is a specific kinetic and historical figure that has not always existed. To analyze the migrant worker simply as human capital is a specific political intervention that risks naturalizing and universalizing this form of the migrant and elastic force. It explains nothing, but itself needs to be explained. Thus, we should not presume that the migrant is essentially *Homo economicus* but try to understand the conditions under which such a figure is produced in the first place.

The key to understanding modern emigration in the eighteenth through twentieth centuries is the kinopolitical concept of a mobile surplus population or migrant proletariat. The surplus population is an excess of social motion that needs to be redirected. Appropriately, this concept emerges alongside the largest demographic explosion in European history. Between 1800 and 1913, Europe's population grew from 188 to 458 million people, a 250 percent increase.[21]

There were several contributors to this growth. Over the course of the nineteenth century, the availability of food resources became more predictable and medical knowledge and defense against infectious diseases improved. Beginning around 1700, the agricultural revolution increased the availability of food resources. The productivity of the countryside began to increase: "shortened fallow times, land reclamation, new crops, better tools, artificial selection of seed strains and livestock and eventually the introduction of agricultural machinery."[22] All of this, according to Paul Bairoch, increased labor productivity from about 0.6 percent per year in 1800 to 1.2 percent between 1880 and 1900.[23] The combination of population increase and labor productivity produced two distinct surplus populations because the more efficient labor became, the fewer workers were needed to do the same job: what Marx called the reserve surplus army and the potential surplus army (active workers).

This dual surplus population caused real wages to fall and caused families to have to split their landholdings among more children. The more the land was fragmented among more people, the less could be produced from a landholding. This led to an increase in poverty and landless families. Further, while cultivatable land in Europe grew by only 7 million hectares between 1860 and 1910,[24] it grew by 100 million in Canada, America, and Argentina. This foreign growth, coupled with low transportation costs, caused Europe to be flooded with cheap grain and other commodities from the Americas, which produced an economic crisis in Europe in the 1870s and motivated many migrants to "decide" to flee.

Population growth and agricultural productivity also fed industrialization. Emigrants not only moved to the Americas but also to cities within Europe. Three-quarters of the European labor force had been employed in agriculture in 1800, but that figure declined to one-third by the early twentieth century. "Urbanization was intense: the population of the 39 European cities with populations over 100,000 in 1850 grew from 6 million in 1800 to 34 million in 1910, an almost sixfold increase."[25]

Another mechanism that made emigration possible, and literally drove increased oscillation, was the lowered costs of transportation. Railroads made it cheaper and easier for emigrants to travel to major seaports. Once emigrants reached a seaport, the introduction of the steamship and the reduced cost and duration of the voyage made emigration significantly easier. At the turn of the eighteenth century, a trip from Liverpool to New York took around five or six weeks. By the 1880s, the trip took about one week and cost only twenty dollars—compared to forty-four dollars in the 1850s.[26]

A final mechanism was the political and legal changes that increasingly permitted and often encouraged emigration as a way for countries to "get rid" of their surplus population. In England and Scandinavian countries, emigration controls were lifted by the 1830s. Before the end of the century, they were lifted in Germany, Austria, Hungary, Russia, and eventually Italy. In America, the US Homestead Act of 1862 granted free land to heads of families twenty-one years of age who planned to start a farm or applied to become US citizens. In 1873, immigration to Argentina was actively encouraged by providing financial support of transportation and employment. In 1888, Brazil did the same.[27]

In fact, a discourse in nineteenth-century political economy emerged that directly advocated the expulsion of the surplus population. For example, British political economist and member of Parliament Robert Torrens argued that Britain could solve poverty not by granting the poor access to the land but by emigration. This position was quite popular, and many policies emerged from it—with Torrens as advocate. Torrens proposed that emigration "be made compulsory and that any person on poor relief who refused to emigrate be denied poor relief."[28] Or, as a Scottish parish journal put it more dramatically, "Emigration is considered a riddance of a diseased population."[29] By 1819, the Select Committee on the Poor Laws recommended emigration to alleviate poverty and made possible the first grant for state-supported emigration/colonization.[30] Thus, the British took national action to mobilize their surplus population—as well as pass laws against immigration. The control over a surplus population required an elastic force to buffer social contractions (unemployment, dissents, criminality) and relocate in preparation for colonial expansions (America, Australia, India).

Emigration, however, was not only for expelling the poor; it was also a military strategy. It expelled unwanted military surplus of old wars and also prepared foreign populations for new wars. For example, after the Napoleonic Wars (1803–15), state-subsidized emigration was used in Britain as a way to expel the military surplus population of over three hundred thousand demobilized soldiers and sailors who were thrown into the labor market at a time when war-related industries were being dismantled.[31] This military surplus could then be redirected as part of a new military strategy to defend Canada from US aggression. Government-subsidized emigration from Scotland and Ulster to Canada (from 1815 to 1819) was also established for this reason.[32] Emigration could also be used against internal enemies of the state. Between 1819 and 1820, the British Parliament subsidized mass emigration to Africa as a way of expelling working-class radicals.

Emigration-expulsion expanded colonial military efforts, but it also expanded colonial commercial efforts. As British magistrate and founder of England's regular police force put it in 1814, emigration to the colonies will provide "beneficial employment of a redundant population."[33] Parliamentary undersecretary in the Colonial Office (1818–28), John Wilmot Horton, more dramatically proposed in the name of colonial development that 12 million pounds be spent to expel 1 million paupers to the British colonies. Later in 1831 (in addition to penal transportation), the British government sponsored large-scale emigration to Australia to bolster the colonies.[34]

The compulsion to emigrate was so intense that throughout the eighteenth and nineteenth centuries, poor Europeans paid for their emigration through indenture. They signed contracts promising to work for an employer for a number of years in exchange for passage, housing, food, clothing, and other necessities. After the period of indenture was complete, the worker was free. "Almost a quarter of the 2.6 million Europeans who moved to the New World before 1820 came under indenture."[35] Social motion thus expanded economically by expelling extensively, through emigration. These are the real conditions behind the so-called age of free migration.

Denationalization

Denationalization solves a social kinetic problem posed by emigration: the migrant might return home, and many early European emigrants did. Return migrants make the elastic management of the surplus population a bit more challenging. Thus, after World War I, a new technology of expulsion was invented that aimed to solve this problem once and for all: denationalization. While emigration leaves migrants with their national status intact, along with their potential right to return home, denationalization strips these rights away permanently.

After WWI, the Austro-Hungarian, Russian, and Ottoman Empires were dissolved and reformed into a new constellation of nation-states. This process resulted in a series of bloody civil wars and mass expulsions. As Hannah Arendt describes them,

> Civil wars which ushered in and spread over the twenty years of uneasy peace were not only bloodier and more cruel than all their predecessors; they were followed by migrations of groups who, unlike their happier predecessors in the religious wars, were welcomed nowhere and could be assimilated nowhere. Once they had left their homeland they remained homeless; once they had left their state they became stateless; once they had been deprived of their human rights they were rightless, the scum of the earth.[36]

The price to pay for eastern nation-states was the division between national majority and minority groups. The victors of national conflicts reserved the right to expel the losers, but as new enemies of the nation-state, the losers were promptly denationalized. "To this group belong, in chronological order, millions of Russians, hundreds of thousands of Armenians, thousands of Hungarians, hundreds of thousands of Germans, and more than half a million Spaniards—to enumerate only the more important categories," Arendt reports.[37]

Between the two wars, almost every country in Europe passed some sort of legislation that allowed for denationalization expulsions. In 1915, France passed a war measure that allowed for the denationalization of naturalized citizens of enemy origin. In 1916, Portugal allowed the denationalization of all persons with a German father. In 1922, Belgium revoked the citizenship of naturalized persons engaged in antinational acts during the war. In Italy in 1926, all persons could be denationalized who were not "worthy of Italian citizenship." In 1926 and 1928, respectively, Egypt and Turkey allowed the denationalization of people who were a threat to the social order. Austria in 1933 could denationalize any citizen who participated abroad in any action hostile to Austria. In 1933, Germany, following Russia's lead since 1921, legalized the denationalization of all persons "residing abroad."[38] After the discovery of denationalization, legislation across Europe made it possible to permanently expel any kind of surplus population: an economic, ethnic, national, or enemy surplus (often there was overlap).

Denationalization made it possible to mobilize unwanted surplus populations that affected the countries' economies. Persecuting governments could act upon this surplus stateless population in whatever way they pleased since the surplus had no rights. By denationalizing them, states made it difficult or impossible for stateless people to legally enter a new state (without proper passports from their "home" country) or to deport them once they had arrived, since there was nowhere they could be legally repatriated. These stateless migrants began to form a single, precarious migrant proletariat: a mobile surplus population. Because they had no rights, anything could be done to them. In this way, they constituted a more flexible and freely movable surplus. In fact, as Hannah Arendt comments, even criminal status would grant them more status. "As a criminal," she says, "even a stateless person will not be treated worse than another criminal, that is, he will be treated like everybody else."[39] Proletarian migrants were disappeared, put in camps, or reexpelled elsewhere in the name of achieving certain forms of social equilibrium corresponding to the new distribution of national identities (racial, ethnic, linguistic, etc.).

Not only had the German persecution/expulsion of its migrant surplus inspired eastern minority countries to do the same; it also laid the foundations for the extermination of this surplus. The first step of German democide was always denationalization. Foreigners, Marxists, gays, disabled people, and social surplus of all kinds had to be first deprived of their territorial, legal, and political status. Afterward, anything was permissible—the mobility of this migrant surplus had been radically "freed up." As the official SS newspaper, the *Schwarze Korps*, put it in 1938: "[I]f the world was not yet convinced that the Jews were the scum of the earth, it soon would be when unidentifiable beggars, without nationality, without money, and without passports crossed their frontiers."[40]

Denationalization is, therefore, an elastic force in the sense in which it is able to identify a broad diversity of human surplus (national, ethnic, linguistic, etc.), and expel them from any and all kinetic restrictions

(territorial, political, legal, etc.) once and for all. In this way, denationalization creates a highly mobile surplus that can be relocated anywhere
according to the needs of social equilibrium. Instead of working within the
normal perimeters of intensive expulsion that often resulted in increased
national heterogeneity, including unemployment, poverty, criminality,
and prison costs, which the state often paid for in welfare, states opted for
an extensive denationalization.

External Expansion by Expulsion: Intensive Surplus

It has been shown how the elastic expulsion of the migrant worker is
internally achieved through intensive and extensive mechanisms. But economic kinopower also expands by expelling an external surplus population residing abroad. This external surplus is intensively expelled as a way
to increase competition and production through the Atlantic slave trade
and extensively expelled from the Americas as a way to redistribute a colonial surplus.

The Atlantic Slave Trade

Just as the internal expulsion of an intensive surplus population in
Europe was used as a way to lower wages and intensify production within
the country, so the external expulsion of an intensive surplus population
transported to the Americas was done to intensify production outside
the country. Only this time, the Americas did not constitute a sufficient
native population to produce a colonial surplus because it had already
been decimated largely by disease (killing almost 90 percent of the indigenous population by 1890). Thus, in order to keep wages low and prices
and production high, a surplus population was redistributed from Africa
to the Americas via the Atlantic slave system.

Between the sixteenth and nineteenth centuries, more than 12 million people were transported across the Atlantic alive; if those who died
are included, this number would be much greater. The vast majority (80
percent) of the slave trade occurred between the eighteenth and nineteenth centuries. Half the total alone took place during the eighteenth
century, mainly by the British, Portuguese, and French, taking nine out

of ten slaves from Africa.[41] By the turn of the eighteenth century, tens of thousands of Africans were being captured per year and transported to the Caribbean, Brazil, and North America to produce cotton, coffee, sugar, tobacco, and indigo and to mine for gold and silver for an emerging world market. Mortality rates for transport averaged around 12 percent.[42]

The Atlantic slave trade is an elastic system. It is predominantly defined not by its movement from an outside to a center (centripetal), nor by its movement from a center to a periphery (centrifugal), nor even by legal links between political centers (tension). Rather, the Atlantic slave trade is a driven oscillatory motion, without a center, that is continually in the process of redistributing (often illegally) a surplus between a series of relay points (elasticity). Each point in the series depends on the others but, more important, depends on the continual mobilization of the surplus between them.

However, the Atlantic slave trade is not simply triadic (like the other forms of elastic surplus); it is triangular. Unfortunately, its "triangular" nature has so far been understood purely geographically: the British traded manufactured goods and money for slaves in Africa; shipped them to the Americas as workers to grow cotton, tobacco, and sugar, which were then shipped back to Britain for manufacture; and so on. The spatial location of the three points form a triangle. But this spatio-geographic definition says nothing about the relations of *social motion,* or three-way social codependency involved in the slave trade, only something about their location. Further, it is perhaps not even accurate to talk in terms of a triangle, when in fact, many ships stopped at multiple places of trade in Europe, Africa, and South, Central, and North America. All sorts of geometrical shapes have been traced in polygons across the Atlantic.[43]

Thus, I propose instead a strictly kinopolitical definition of the "triangulation" of the Atlantic slave trade. Kinopolitical triangulation is a process of multiplying and relaying together two or more elastic series. Since, as we established in Chapter 6, each elastic series already consists of three parts (base, floating, and future surplus), the multiplication of series is always a multiplication by three. This is kinopolitical triangulation. For example, we can identify at least three elastic series contained in the triangulation of the Atlantic slave trade.

A first series is British and European. The first point in this series is the base surplus defined by a socially necessary degree of surplus in agriculture and manufacturing labor; in national population; in affordable criminal population; and so on (even though this "necessary" degree was already a surplus gathered from a vagabond population expelled by enclosure laws and then normalized at a certain level). The second point is the floating surplus, defined by the stockpiling of human beings into the workhouses, factories, prisons, and forests. Here, they wait in anticipation of the future surplus. The third point is the expulsion of the surplus from the workhouse, factory, prison, and forests into the expanding manufacturing and/or colonial sector.

A second series is African. A base surplus is defined by a socially necessary apparatus of tribal warfare and the expulsion of the enemy from their land. A floating surplus is then captured in prison camps and awaits the future. A future surplus arrives in the form of an exchange opportunity to sell prisoners of war to the Europeans as slaves. The income from selling the slaves then becomes an impetus for future war and expansion of the base surplus into a larger and larger future surplus.

A third series is American. A base surplus is defined by a colonial right and necessity of land acquisition and native expulsion in the Americas. A floating surplus is then captured in the form of native slaves, reservations, and land claimed through manifest destiny. The people and the land are then held in waiting until a future military and economic apparatus can mobilize the surplus effectively as the colonial population grows.

The triangulation of the Atlantic slave trade conjoins these series by continually mobilizing a surplus between them. Each series has a deficit fillable by another series, but only indirectly through a third series. Europe has a deficit of certain goods like cotton, tobacco, sugar, gold, and silver; Africa has a deficit of manufactured goods; the Americas have a deficit of labor. Europe also has a surplus of manufactured goods; Africa, a surplus population of captured slaves; and the Americas, a surplus of raw materials (cotton, tobacco, etc.). A surplus migrant proletariat is then moved from one to the other through the third. Thus, the Atlantic slave trade mobilizes a triple expulsion: the expulsion of peasants from the land, prisons, and workhouses to work in manufacturing; the expulsion of prisoners of war from Africa; and the expulsion of Native Americans from their land to be cultivated for export. Each expulsion increases the others, just as each expansion also increases the others.

External Expansion by Expulsion: Extensive Surplus

In addition to *intensifying* production and competition in the colonies by expelling a migrant proletariat from a third country via the Atlantic slave trade, colonialism prepares the colony with an extensive expulsion of the "unproductive" or "lumpen" native population. Once the native surplus population is expelled and their land opened up, an intensive surplus from elsewhere can put the land into productive circulation. To be clear, this is not a feature of all colonialism. For example, sixteenth- and seventeenth-century Spanish colonialism was not driven by the imperatives of productivity and intensification and thus did not define "unproductive" populations as a proletarian "surplus." In fact, the problem was quite the opposite. There were not too many natives but consistently *not enough* to be worked profitably, since they were almost entirely wiped out by disease—hence, the failure of the *ecomienda*. Insofar as Spanish colonialism was largely a juridical extension of feudal customary laws by representatives of the state, and not a largely private financial endeavor by individuals to make a profit, the Spaniards had a very different kinetic relationship to the population.

However, with the rise of elastic kinopower in Britain, colonialism takes on a new driving imperative: the economic mobilization of a proletarian surplus. The first forms of this new elastic colonialism are the creation of an Irish and American surplus, which, like the Atlantic slave trade, are also bound together in a larger triangular circuit. The expulsion of the Scots fills the gap created by the expulsion of the Irish, and the expelled Irish fill the gap created by the expulsion of the Native Americans. This defines the triangulation of a new colonial project.

The Irish Surplus

The Irish model of colonialism was the first break with the previous age of the tensional imperialism based on the Spanish model. A new concept of an elastic proletarian surplus was mobilized against the natives. Ireland became more than a classical colonial military campaign for the British; it became a moral and economic matter of mobilizing (expelling) an unproductive native surplus and liberating their "wasted" land for redistribution by other means. Years later, this will be the same logic used to justify the expulsion of Native Americans.

Even as early as the seventeenth century, there is a hint of the beginning of a legal battle aiming to reconceptualize the basis of colonial motion. In a letter written to the Earl of Salisbury by the English lawyer Sir John Davies concerning the state of Ireland in 1610, he articulates a novel justification for the expulsion of the Irish and their replacement by the Scots and English. His argument is that the king is bound not only by law but by moral conscience to remove the surplus Irish population because the Irish will

never, to the end of the world, build houses, make townships or villages, or manure or improve the land as it ought to be; therefore it stands neither with Christian policy nor conscience to suffer so good and fruitful a country to lie waste like a wilderness, when his Majesty may lawfully dispose it to such persons as will make a civil plantation thereupon. Again, his majesty may take this course in conscience because it tendeth to the good of the inhabitants many ways; for half their land doth now lie waste, by reason whereof that which is habited is not improved to half the value; but when the undertakers [the settlers] are planted among them . . . and that land shall be fully stocked and manured, 500 acres will be of better value than 5000 are now.[44]

Since Ireland's people were unproductive and allowed their land to become "waste," they constituted a redundant proletarian surplus that it was morally right to expel from the land so the land could be settled (redistributed) by a more productive population of Scottish and English plantation directors.

This new strategy of expelling the unproductive surplus population and replacing it elastically with another one, driven by the needs of social contractions and expansions, slowly took hold. Thus, in addition to the purely military attempts by the Tudor governments of the early sixteenth century, Britain began using military force to impose a strictly economic system as well as a new political and legal order in Ireland: capitalism.

In 1585, for instance, the English government announced a plan to re-create the conditions of south-east England in Munster by granting expropriated lands to settlers who would introduce English agriculture to the region. . . . The very conscious intention was to establish an English-style commercial order, a new kind of economy based on new social relations on the land, new relations between landlord and tenant, like the ones that were driving improvement in England.[45]

If Ireland could not be taken militarily, perhaps it could be taken economically. The military expulsion of the Irish from their lands (Cromwell's conquest) could be made permanent by subsidizing the mobilization of another surplus population (the English and Scottish), that was waiting in the wings for an opportunity to relieve their own surplus population.

The English and Scots as landlords thus expanded their range of economic motion by expropriating Irish lands. These landlords would then institute commercial trade within the English market system, thus making rents competitive and land "improvements" necessary, just as they were in the English system. From the sixteenth through seventeenth centuries, Ireland was enclosed, just as England was during the first age of the Tudor enclosure. Only in this way could the Irish be controlled by direct economic means. Accordingly, just as English peasants had been expelled (as vagabonds), so the Irish were expelled from their land and made into tenant farmers on English-owned plantations.

The expulsion of the Irish from the land is only the first expulsion that prepares the way for a second and much larger one: the Irish Famine. Since peasant customary ties to the land had been removed by force and replaced with the English landlord-tenant market system, the peasants had little control over what was being grown and held no ownership of the land to turn to when the potato blight occurred. What land was still held by the Irish was rapidly subdivided as the population grew, just as in Europe. Land plots became small and unproductive and eventually were sold off to English landlords to consolidate as potato fields. The landlord-tenant potato system then produced a further surplus population—for twenty weeks a year the peasants grew and harvested potatoes, but for thirty weeks there was absolutely no other work. Thus, by 1835, 2.3 million people were unemployed thirty weeks a year.[46]

The potato was brought to Ireland from the Americas around 1600 and quickly became the staple food of the country's peasants. The potato was cheap, easy to cultivate, and nutritionally satisfying, and it quickly became the almost exclusive agricultural product of Ireland. As a result in part to the mass cultivation of the potato, the Irish population increased from around 2.5 million in 1700 to 8.1 million in 1841.[47] Ireland became the most densely populated country in Europe and had the highest rate of population increase. When the potato crop failed, due to a blight also originating from the Americas, there were no cheap substitutes available and the country plunged into crisis. The Irish Famine was perhaps one of the largest, per capita, demographic catastrophes of the modern period. Between the years of 1846 and 1848, Ireland lost 2.5 million of its population of 9 million—half due to emigration and half from famine-related deaths.[48]

Just as England expelled its own population from the land, workhouses, and prisons during the eighteenth and nineteenth centuries, when famine became widespread, the landlords were eager to expel the Irish peasants, who they knew would not be able to pay their rent. The Irish peasants had already been expelled once from the land; now they were expelled again, this time from their status as tenants. Due to English market imperatives toward productivity, the tenants were evicted from their lands in favor of farmers or sheep raisers who could produce a cash crop. The Irish expulsions were some of the worst aspects of the famine:

Starving, impoverished peasants were turned out of their holdings and their cabins immediately torn down. The lucky ones found shelter as squatters in nearby ditches. The unlucky ones were driven from the ditches by troops or local police. Instead of declaring a moratorium on debts or offering some kind of disaster relief, the English government employed its troops to drive away famine-stricken families.[49]

In the Kilrush district, for example, seven thousand families were evicted from their homes in a six-month period.[50] Thousands of such evictions occurred all over Ireland in the worst parts of winter. When a landlord decided to secure a legal judgment against a tenant who was delinquent on his rent, the tenant was thrown in jail and his family left to starve (and likely die). In one district alone, County Mayo, there were more than six thousand applications to the courts for such judgments.[51] Rather than help relieve the poor, the government was used to help expel these proletarian migrants.

The expulsion of the Irish was not simply a "natural" phenomenon of the famine. It was part of a kinopolitical strategy of elasticity, insofar as it handled the famine according to the market imperatives of expansion and contraction. The oscillations of the food supply (famine and surplus) were dealt with according to the laws of supply, demand, and the production/redistribution of a surplus population. England's leaders dealt with famine strictly according to these laws and provided insufficient aid to Ireland. While the Irish starved, three thousand tons of Indian corn remained in government warehouses. The English worried that if cheap corn were released and price protections on corn (the Corn Laws) repealed to feed the Irish, the economy would crash. Even during the famine years, the Irish continued to export grain in large quantities to the distilleries of England and Scotland, while their own people starved. In 1846, Relief Commission leader Randolph Routh appealed to colonial administrator Charles Edward Trevelyan to ban the export of grain from Ireland so that food produced within the country would be available to feed the people. Trevelyan refused. But when protests broke out, Trevelyan certainly had the funds to send British troops to put rioters down and in some cases kill them.[52] But instead of providing sufficient aid, Trevelyan advocated for the expulsion of the Irish:

I do not know how farms are to be consolidated if small farmers do not emigrate and by acting for the purpose of keeping them at home, we should be defeating our own object. We must not complain of what we really want to obtain. If small farms go, and then landlords are induced to sell portions of their estates to persons who will invest capital, we shall at last arrive at something like a satisfactory settlement in this country.[53]

The goal of British colonial efforts were clear: do not intervene in the kinetic contractions of Ireland, but instead facilitate the expulsion of their proletariat to expand English land acquisition. But the "contraction of the market" entailed not only emigration to England and America but also the deaths of over 1 million people. Either way, the market would be opened for those "persons who will invest in capital." Trevelyan was supported in his actions by the prime minister, Lord John Russell, who in 1848 refused to grant further public funds to aid Ireland.

After substantial deaths, the Irish began to emigrate. They immigrated to the workhouses of England in search of food, but many were soon expelled again in June 1847 by a law granting local authorities the power to return Irish paupers to Ireland (and to certain death).[54] More than 1 million immigrated to America to fill the social contraction left by the expulsion of the natives. However, safety laws were not regularly enforced on what came to be known as "coffin ships." On one such ship, only 42 out of the 276 emigrations from Ireland to Quebec survived, because they were not given sufficient food and water.

The experience of the ship *Virginius* was typical. It left Liverpool with 476 passengers: 158 died *en route*, 106 arrived with typhus. The quarantine station also became a breeder of disease. One ship, the *Agnes*, arrived with 427 passengers; two weeks later only 150 were alive. Over-crowding became so bad that the authorities were forced to release "healthy" immigrants.[55]

But for all this mass expulsion and death, the economy did not suffer one bit. As a writer for the *London Economist* says,

The departure of the redundant part of Ireland and Scotland is an indispensable preliminary to every kind of improvement. . . . The revenue of Ireland has not suffered in any degree from the famine of 1846–47, or from the emigration that has since taken place. On the contrary, her net revenue amounted to £4,281,999, being about £184,000 greater than in 1843.[56]

In fact, the Irish expulsion resulted in one of the most successful expansion strategies ever, according to Marx:

The Irish famine of 1846 killed more than 1,000,000 people, but it killed poor devils only. It did not do the slightest damage to the wealth of the country. The exodus of the next twenty years, an exodus which still continues to increase, did not, as for instance the Thirty Years War did, decimate the means of production along with the human beings. The Irish genius discovered an altogether new way of spiriting a poor people thousands of miles away from the scene of its misery. The exiles transplanted to the United States send sums of money home every year as traveling expenses for those left behind. Every troop that emigrates one year draws another after it the next. Thus, instead of costing Ireland anything, emigration forms one of the most lucrative branches of its export trade.[57]

The American Surplus

Just as an Irish proletarian surplus was expelled by defining the base population as the ones who improve the land, the same tactic was used to morally justify the expulsion of an American surplus population. Nineteen years after Sir John Davies's letter justifying the expulsion of the Irish, there was a similar argument made by John Winthrop, the first governor of Massachusetts and former Irish settler. Winthrop's moral and social justification for the intended plantation of New England in 1629 was that the Native Americans had failed to make productive use of their land. He writes: "[F]or the Natives in New England they inclose no land, neither have they any settled habitation nor any tame cattle to improve the land by."[58]

But it was the English philosopher John Locke who, sixty years later (1689), formulated the most well-known version of this argument justifying the colonial expulsion of surplus Native Americans. Although Locke claims that God "hath given the world to men in common," and "every man has *property* in his own *person*," as well as "the *labour* of his body and *work* of his hands," an individual can also increase his property by taking something out of the state of nature by mixing it with his labor "and thereby mak[ing] it his *property*." For Locke, the improvements made by this labor are what "puts the difference of value on everything." But the value added to nature through labor (as property) is not defined by the effort of labor or how useful the labor is but rather by the exchange value of the labor. Locke makes this clear in his example of calculating how much an acre of land in America is worth compared to an acre of naturally fertile land in England if we calculate "all the profit an Indian received from it were it valued and sold here."[59] The value of the land is thus not related to how hard the Indian works but to the Indian's failure to realize a profit. Locke thus concludes that all unimproved land is waste, and enclosing (privatizing) the land and displacing natives or peasants are not taking anything away but giving something back to society.

Wasteland is theft from its possible improvement and exchange value in circulation. Those who waste the land by not improving it are at best redundant surplus populations and at worst kinopolitical thieves. In both cases, their redundancy is justification for expulsion. What Locke is describing is precisely one of the major economic factors "driving" oscillation and exchange: the imperative to increase productivity. If movement is consonant with liberal freedom, for Locke then the unmoved "wasteland" of the native and peasant commons must be liberated through increased production and circulation.[60] Of course, Locke was not the only one to think this at the time. But what is unique to Locke is that he redefines the value of labor and property as exchange value, and in doing so he simultaneously defines a vast surplus population whose expulsion and mobilization are justified entirely according to larger elastic demands of the social field of improvement and expansion.

This philosophical point also justified similar expulsions elsewhere. During the seventeenth and eighteenth centuries, English judges used Locke's arguments to resolve property conflicts to decide in favor of exclusive private property (enclosure) over common and customary property rights.[61] Whoever could produce the greatest exchange value from the land had the right to the land. Further, in the eighteenth century, Parliament took an active role in accelerating the enclosure process, citing reasons of "improvement" to evict the tenants and transform wasteland into profit.[62] The goal of liberal government is not to take public control of all the land and improve it but to elastically mobilize an unproductive proletariat through expulsion and expand colonial surplus through redistribution. Liberalism is not a centrifugal totalitarianism but an elastic government that removes all juridical barriers, customary laws, or public property that obstructs the free movement of surplus.

Locke also provides a philosophical and natural legitimation for treating the products of slave labor as the private property of the owner. He says that "the grass my horse has bit; the turfs my servant has cut; and the ore I have digg'd in any place where I have a right to them in common with others, become my property."[63] In effect, the labor of the servant is no different from the owner's own labor. The economic force of improvement that drives oscillation and exchange includes not only the owner's individual labor and its profit, but all the products of the labor of animals and other humans who are employed in the improvement also become the owner's property.

This is the second key concept for the kinetics of elasticity: redistribution. It is moral to expel the surplus proletariat who is not sufficiently working the land and justified to enslave the labor of these migrants under the command of a master who will make them work more productively. The result is not that the servant and slave will gain property by mixing their labor with objects, but since they do so under the command of the "true improver," it is the master/boss who expands his own property. In this way, expansion occurs under the condition of a primary expulsion. According to this rationale, the expulsion of the surplus from the land is not theft or taking anything away; it is giving something back to the community. It gives productive land and productive labor to a previously unproductive population.

This argument for improvement and the redistribution of a migrant surplus population is also seen in the colonial logic of Thomas Jefferson's "Indian Policy." In an 1803 letter to William Henry Harrison, Jefferson writes that if the Native Americans cannot be forced to give up their land by military struggle, then they should be dispossessed by economic means. If they can be convinced through trade to take up cultivation of a small piece of land, they will see how all their forests and fields are truly being wasted. However, if they cannot be educated about their wasteful ways, Jefferson proposes that they be encouraged to incur a large enough debt that they will have to sell their land.

When they withdraw themselves to the culture of a small piece of land, they will perceive how useless to them are their extensive forests, and will be willing to pare them off from time to time in exchange for necessaries for their farms and families. To promote this disposition to exchange lands, which they have to spare and we want, for necessaries, which we have to spare and they want, we shall push our trading uses, and be glad to see the good and influential individuals among them run in debt, because we observe that when these debts get beyond what the individuals can pay, they become willing to lop them off by a cession of lands.[64]

Conclusion

More than at any other time in history, modern social motion dramatically expands and diversifies its modes of expansion by expulsion. However, Part 2 of this book has also limited its inquiry into migration in a significant way. It has defined the migrant exclusively with respect to the forces of expansion and expulsion that produce migration. This is only half the theory and history of the migrant. The figures of the migrant that emerge at different points in human history, in addition to being produced by expulsion, invent their own regimes of social motion that are irreducible to the four kinetic forces that expelled them. To understand this second positive definition of the migrant, it is important to explore the forms of social motion that the migrant invents on its own and that pose an alternative or counterforce to those of expansion by expulsion. The task of Part 3 is to discover the force of social motion created by the migrant.

PART III

FIGURES OF THE MIGRANT

CHAPTER 8

Pedetic Force

The nomad, the barbarian, the vagabond, and the proletariat are four figures of the migrant. Each emerges under different historical and social conditions of expansion and expulsion, but each also invents a form of kinetic power of its own that poses an alternative to social expulsion. Although each figure of the migrant deploys this force in a unique way, each is also the social expression of a more general "pedetic" social force. This chapter briefly outlines the concept of pedetic social force deployed by the four figures of the migrant analyzed in the following chapters of Part 3.

Pedesis (from the PIE root *ped-*, meaning "foot") is the first motion of autonomous self-transport: the motion of the foot. Pedetic motion is the force of the foot—to walk, to run, to leap, to dance. As a social force of motion, it is defined by its autonomy and self-motion. It is different from the social forces of centripetal, centrifugal, tensional, and elastic power because it has neither center nor surplus. Instead, its movement is irregular and unpredictable. It is turbulent.[1] It does not expand by social expulsion but by inclusive social transformation. Pedetic social force coexists in an undivided social distribution alongside other forms of motion in a *confluence*—like a drop of ink diffuses into a glass of water—not a conjunction. The ink does not divide the water as something else expanding or expelling it around kinetic social centers or series but diffuses and becomes ink-water. Henri Bergson similarly describes the "real movement" of qualitative change as the dissolving of sugar in a glass of water—the sugar becomes water, and the water becomes sugared in the same autonomous movement.[2] Diffusion occurs through pedesis.

Pedesis may be irregular and unpredictable, but it is not random. Specific movements appear random only from the perspective of those who do not understand or see the enormous number of complex collisions and vectors that determine a given motion. From the perspective of those who do not hear the music, the dancers (*pedetes*) appear insane. The autonomous motions of migratory movements have been subject to the same charge of historical and social "chaos." But it appears as chaos only from the perspective of the kinopolitical order. It is said that migrants have no social order and no history, but this is not the case. It is precisely the irregularity and unpredictability of certain figures of the migrant that are capable of giving birth to a new form of social motion not defined by expulsion. Or, as Nietzsche, the great migrant-philosopher of dance puts it, "one must still have chaos in oneself to give birth to a dancing star."[3] This section of Part 3 outlines the theory of this pedetic social force as it is expressed historically in the four figures of the migrant discussed earlier.

Continuous Oscillation

Pedetic force has three social kinetic characteristics. First, it is defined by a continuous oscillation "to and fro." This is not to be confused with the driven oscillations that define elastic or economic kinopower. Elastic force *drives* motion "to and fro" according to social imperatives like equilibrium, competition, efficiency, and surplus redistribution. Continuous oscillation, however, is not driven by any of these social imperatives. It moves without center, origin, or ultimate destination. It moves as a point-by-point response to a thousand tiny molecular movements that collide with it. But the movement of a single body is complicated when it becomes the movement of two or more bodies to and fro.

When the number of oscillations, their connections, and places become very large and unfixed from a frame of reference, the social system approaches "continuity." A "continuous system" does not have a single repeatable pattern or "normal mode" of oscillation. Because the degrees of freedom are so large, continuous systems have an infinite number of oscillations, like the rippling surface of the ocean.

Continuous social oscillation is a mass phenomenon of extensive movement, to and fro, outside the "normal" social modes of motion. The transhumance of the nomad, the brigandry of the barbarian, the defection of the vagabond, and the social movements of the proletariat are all relatively unconstricted forms of social motion compared to those of expansion by expulsion. Social oscillation is a change or *mutation* of social motion from being captured by centric, tensional, or elastic forces to simply moving to and fro freely. In short, continuous social oscillation is the free extensive social movement of peoples to determine and change the conditions of their motion.

Waves

The second kinetic characteristic of pedetic force is that of the creation of waves. A social wave is a transportation of a social force. While continuous oscillation is an extensive transport of something to and fro, a wave does not necessarily transport some "thing." A wave transports a qualitative change or *social force* of solidarity or collective disruption. The medium of a social wave (the territorial, political, juridical, and economic order) is temporarily displaced in such a way that a unified force is transported elsewhere through its motion. This unified force is what links a continuous and undivided distribution of force while maintaining the heterogeneity of the distinct social disturbances. There are no static barriers in a wave. It is a fundamentally undivided phenomenon.

Discontent, revolt, and political turmoil are all social waves insofar as they transport a social force of solidarity or disruption. But a wave is not yet a revolution or a complete kinetic overthrow. A social wave simply transports a disturbance through a social collective that unifies the collective without the source of the transport originating from any single point. In this way, a social wave is the unifying force of heterogeneity: a nonunified whole or undivided distribution.

Social revolt travels rapidly in between the formal channels of power, through "word of mouth," print, association, and all manner of viral underground communications and secret meetings. Thus, a social wave is a distinctly mass or *common* phenomenon that requires a multitude of *mutual* pedetic motions in order to transmit a social disturbance among heterogeneous elements.

It is not surprising then that so many popular uprisings and social revolts are described as waves: waves of migrants, waves of riots, waves of discontent, waves of protest. This is partly due to the unified irregularity and unpredictability (pedesis) shared both by fluid waves and social waves, not because one is modeled on the other.

Pressure

The third kinetic characteristic is that of pressure.[4] Social pressure is the ratio of social force distributed across the kinopolitical order. It is based on the pedetic motion of rapidly oscillating elements in constant collision. Pressure occurs when a wave of social disturbance encounters the limits of a wall, container, or closed system. The force of these collisions against the limits of their motion in a given area produces social pressure.

Social and political pressure builds as certain forms of motion are limited or restricted. Single individuals rarely topple these restrictions. Rather, migrants of all kinds who are expelled, or whose social motion is blocked, begin to create waves: temporary or seemingly isolated outbursts that together transport a force. Social discontent, riots, protests, and the like are the waves of force whose pressure crushes armies, topples governments, kills tax collectors, and occupies the streets. Their collision creates a kinetic pressure against the forces of expansion by expulsion.

Social pressure strikes against the limits of mobility imposed by the dominant regimes of motion.[5] But kinetic social pressure should not be understood simply as a conflict between free motion and constraint. Pressure is created anytime there is a blockage of flows (a conjunction). This can create pressure in any social system. But, as indicated earlier, there are different regimes of social pressure, each with its own form of circulation—and of pressure. Each relies on a certain logic of circulatory expulsion in order to expand. So pressure is not free motion versus constraint but pedetic motion versus various forms of social circulation.

The pedetic force of oscillation creates social pressure in two ways. First, it may try to move or flow in a direction that is blocked by a given regime of conjunction. The pedetic force of oscillation then strikes against these barriers (i.e., territorial borders and walls, political conditions or limits of participation, juridical restrictions or limited rights, and economic wage or mobility limits). Pressure aims to *permeate* the limits of social mobility. Second, one of the most effective ways to change the dominant regime of social motion is to create an artificial kinetic blockage in social circulation. The pressure "to strike" may mean physical or social revolt and violence, but it may also mean a kinetic strike: a refusal to move. The refusal to move or work is a way of creating a blockage in the dominant form of social circulation and thus a way of building a social pressure. Protests, demonstrations, occupations, and general strikes are all forms of creating such a social pressure.

But these are only the general characteristics of pedetic force. The next four chapters demonstrate how the four major figures of the migrant have deployed this pedetic force historically. Part 4 concludes with their deployment in the case of contemporary Mexico-US migration.

CHAPTER 9

The Nomad

The nomad is the first figure of pedetic social force. The nomad is not simply the result of a primary territorial, centripetal expulsion. Early hunter-gathers were not simply left out from territorial society; they also actively left it and invented an entirely different form of social motion. Hunter-gatherers moved to the mountains and cultivated the newly discovered art of animal raising. In cultivating this art so exclusively, they had to invent a form of social motion most conducive to it.

The nomads never died out; they were only ignored by the histories of states. They continue to exist today, although in new forms and with a profoundly neglected history that archeologists are only now discovering.[1] Thus, contrary to Hegel, Toynbee, and others, the nomad has its own history. But it is not in the written history of states but in the history of social pedesis: a counter-history. The nomads were not only chased out; they deserted. Social conflict produces both oppression and counterpower. The exodus and raids of the nomad are the first in a long history of counter-power to kinopolitical domination.[2]

Continuous Oscillation

As opposed to the centripetal force of territorial kinopower, which aims to harness the earth's flows into a series of junctions and curved vessels, nomadism oscillates continually by following the earth's flows wherever they may go, without centripetal capture or accumulation. The aim of nomadism is to allow the grasses, herds, and waters to move, while the aim of agriculturalism is to slow them down and accumulate the surplus of their mobility by conjoining it. While hunter-gatherers and agriculturalists move toward resources based on direct human consumption, pastoral nomads move toward resources based on flock or herd consumption (independently of direct human resources).[3] Nomads follow the flows of the flock, while agriculturalists conjoin a flock from the flows.

The nomads migrate between different seasonal pastures according to unpredictable weather patterns.[4] Generally, however, in the winter their flocks graze on the valley grasses and drink from streams fed by snowmelt. In the summer, they move to the mountains where it is cooler and various grasses, shrubs, and wild herbs grow. There is no essential center or periphery, inside or outside, since the two are only relative to each other—and are equally important. Once one arrives "outside" (in summer pasture), this becomes the new "inside," and vice versa for winter pasture, when the seasons change. From the perspective of the motion itself, neither side is ontologically distinguishable as inside or outside. The concepts of inside and outside make sense only from a fixed referent or perspective (inward or outward curves, inside or outside a centripetal center). However, from the perspective of the movement of oscillation itself, every place is an inside/outside. Kino-geometrically speaking, instead of the centripetal ring of accumulation with its inner side and outer side, oscillating movement is like the movement "across" a Möbius strip, where the movement between inside/outside is absolutely continuous.

Early nomads were not timid fugitives seeking to escape the brutal life of the mountain and steppe, but they wanted to make themselves at home there.[5] Instead of conjoining the flows of the earth, they oscillated alongside them as just one more flow. Even Toynbee praises nomadism as the "more audacious" and "superior" mode of life insofar as it successfully confronts its conditions without becoming master or slave.[6] Thus, the question of the "perpetual movement" of the nomad cannot be simply contrasted with the supposed "immobility" of sedentary societies. The nomads stayed in the same place (the mountains) in order to continually oscillate and change with the highly variable climate and migration patterns. Sedentary peoples, however, moved away (into Europe) in order not to change—to keep the same climate and agriculture, as the earth changed climatologically.[7] Centripetal grain farming, as James C. Scott states, is "inherently expansionary, generating, when not checked by disease or famine, a surplus population, which is obliged to move and colonize new lands."[8] On the other hand, Scott writes, following the work of Pierre Clastres, "[The] movement and subsistence techniques [of nomadism] were designed to ward off incorporation into the state."[9] The difference between these two ways of life is not movement versus non-movement but the type of movement that distinguishes them: centripetal versus pedetic oscillation.

Waves

The second pedetic strategy the nomads deploy is a transportation of social kinetic disturbances: waves. The nomads' kinetic wave is a mass or common phenomenon that links them by a force without producing a division in their motion. Nomads continually oscillate across the mountains and steppe, but they do not divide the steppe into territories. They move locally and temporarily from pasture to pasture based on the seasons and rainfall. Their temporary displacements also give birth to a mutual social force that binds them to one another despite their aterritoriality.

French historian Emmanuel Laroche portrays this nomadic social wave phenomenon in *Histoire de la racine NEM- en grec ancien* (1949). He argues that the Greek origins of the word "nomad," from the root νεμ (*nem*), signified a "mode of distribution" (*moyen de distribution*), not an allocation of parceled-out or delimited land (*partage*). "The idea [that *nomos* meant] law is a product of fifth and sixth-century Greek thought," Laroche argues, that breaks from the "original Homeric root νεμω meaning, 'I distribute' or 'I arrange.'"[10] Even "the [retroactively] proposed translations 'cut-up earth, plot of land, piece' are not suitable in all cases to the Homeric poems and assume an ancient νεμω 'I divide' that we should reject. The pasture in archaic times is generally an unlimited space (*espace illimité*); this can be a forest, meadow, river, or mountain side."[11]

Before the ancient Greek appropriation of the word *nomos* (as law), the social organization of nomadic peoples was defined primarily by an occupied, but undivided, space without segmentation, or fencing: as a continual process of oscillating allotment and reallotment. The nomads were distributed to variably assigned and sized grazing areas, which are mobile depending on the weather.

The unlimited distribution of the steppe does not mean that there is no form of social organization or assembly: there is a wave phenomenon of solidarity. Solidarity is, as its root *sol-* indicates, a fluid and undivided, pedetic phenomenon. The social bond of solidarity unites the undivided wave of nomads in a collective and continuous motion without dividing them into territories. For example, Ibn Khaldūn, in *The Muqaddimah: An Introduction to History* (1377), argues that the Bedouin nomads do not define themselves primarily by their ethnic, geographic, state, or familial genealogy or any static criteria for inclusion/exclusion. Rather, the nomads deploy a wave solidarity "between persons who . . . share a feeling of solidarity without any outside prodding." "By taking their special place within the group solidarity, they participate to some extent in the common descent to which that particular group solidarity belongs."[12]

The only condition for nomadic group solidarity, according to Khaldūn, is "a commitment" to a particular group solidarity, but this mutual solidarity then creates a new common line of descent (similarly open to solidarity with other groups). Thus, Khaldūn can claim that "genealogy is something that is of no use to know and that it does no harm not to know . . . [because] when common descent is no longer clear and has become a matter of scientific knowledge, it can no longer move the imagination and is denied the affection caused by solidarity. It has become useless."[13] The most primary form of social belonging is, for the Bedouin, according to Khaldūn, neither sedentary (state) nor genealogical (family), but mobile (nomadic).

Pressure

The third pedetic strategy that the nomads create is social pressure. Nomadism is the continuous oscillation across the steppe in wavelike solidarity. In this sense, nomadism is a relatively low-pressure social system. Once the ruminants exhaust one pasture, a flow opens up a new pasture elsewhere. Since there are no sedentary or territorial divisions, social motion simply flows to and fro without encountering much resistance or pressure. The only pressures are the flows of water and grass. This does not mean, however, as Toynbee says, that their movement is an "identic orbit," between pastures. In fact, earlier Toynbee describes the nomad's meticulous adaptation to a constantly changing environment. "They must combine the pastoral with the military virtues. . . . They must know, by sure intuition, when to be benevolent and when to be severe; when to be prudent and when to be prompt in action."[14] Far from an identical "orbit," the nomads strive for a dynamic transformation of themselves according to the relative *pressures of the environment.* Without the possibility of sedentarism or the surplus of stored food, the nomads must continually launch and relaunch themselves back into movement. There is no stable ground to rely on, so the nomad must become its own ground in a continual oscillation of rigorous self-transformation and self-cultivation of pressure and counterpressure.

The Raid

Nomadism also produces a social kinetic pressure against the expanding agricultural forces of territorial kinopower in the form of "the raid." Since the figure of the nomad is the one who has been abandoned by the centripetal force of territorialization, its point of counterpower or pressure is precisely its attempt to break into the territory via the raid. The nomadic raid thus defines the mountain peoples who come out of nowhere, riding their mounts to take what they need from the territorial agricultural peoples of the lowlands.

The primary aim of the nomads is not war or violence.[15] When territorial societies begin cultivating the valleys closer to the mountains or steppe, they destroy the pasturelands that the nomads rely on for the winter. When the nomads reach the limits of their motion, a pressure builds up and they raid. They do not raid from revenge or negation but simply because the cultivators have refused to move from the conjoined pastures. The social division or territory creates a limit, and the possibility of a pressure raid against the boundary releases the pressure. The nomads are thus those who oscillate across the steppe, form an undivided wave of social solidarity, and produce a pressure or raid against territorial societies when their movement is blocked. In this way, nomadic pedesis forms an alternative to, and counterpower against, centripetal territorialization.

CHAPTER 10

The Barbarian

Refuge and Revolt

The second figure of pedetic social force is the barbarian. The barbarian, like the nomad, is not merely the result of a kinetic expulsion. The barbarians also invent their own form of social motion that functions in a pedetic manner. Just as the name "barbarian" in the ancient world was often etymologically or literally the word for the "slave by nature," it is not surprising that the ancient art of pedesis appears most predominantly in refugees and slave revolts.

The Refuge

Only when there is barbarism and slavery can there be the escaped slave who seeks asylum. It is therefore no surprise that we find for the first time in ancient history, among the nested figures of the barbarian (*nitakur, shasu, arad*), the emergence of the figure of the refugee and the practice of asylum. Centri*fugal* force comes from the center and forces people from their homes (*corvée,* kidnapping, etc.). The *re*fugee (also from the Latin word *fugere*) is the one who reflees: first being forced to flee one's homeland as a captured slave and then having to flee one's captor in favor of the *refugium,* or ἄσυλον (*asulon,* asylum).

The asylum is the politically sanctioned place where one has the right not to be seized or captured. In the ancient empires of Mesopotamia, Egypt, Greece, and Rome, large-scale slavery emerges, but also the right of asylum. In Mesopotamia, the *amargi* granted amnesty for debt slaves and refugees who had run away to the mountains (and very occasionally immigrant refugees from other cities).[1] In Greece, the famous laws of *asylia* protected slaves, debtors, and criminals. In Athens especially, there was a vast network of temples dedicated to asylum: the temple of Theseus; the Altar of Pity in the agora; the altar of Zeus Ayopcuos; the Altar of the Twelve Gods; and the altar of the Eumenides on the Areopagus. Elsewhere, in Laconia the temple of Poseidon and in Tegea the temple of Athena Alea offered asylum. In Rome, the *jus asyli* (right of asylum) was offered in temples (and later extended to churches) but applied only to slaves (not debtors or criminals). In the port town of Canopus, Egypt, Herodotus (ca. 450–420 BC) describes an ancient temple built to the Egyptian god Amun (later known to the Hellenic world as the temple of Hercules) "in which if any man's slave take refuge and have the sacred marks set upon him, giving himself over to the god, it is not lawful to lay hands upon him; but this custom has continued still unchanged from the beginning down to my own time."[2]

In conjunction with the right of asylum, each of these societies had extensive laws regarding the punishment of runaway slaves. As politically expelled barbarians, slaves were subject to blinding, beating, and death. Anyone who harbored slaves could be punished similarly.[3] While the right to asylum did grant some relief to harshly treated slaves, it is important to note that the refuge (asylum), at its core, is a kinetic strategy for diffusing the pressure of revolt in favor of the refuge and is thus ultimately in the service of political power. The slave flees one master in favor of another in the refuge (the temple master, or god). The revolt, however, is a more radical returning that moves beyond the refuge and returns home.

The Revolt

The slave revolt, unlike the refuge, posed a real threat to political kinopower in the ancient world. While not the only form of counterpower, it was by far the most frequent and statistically significant, since most of the lower classes were slaves or noncitizens. While the nomad could simply retreat to the mountains and deserts, the barbarians were relentlessly pursued and captured by a farther-reaching centrifugal force. The fact that the barbarian migrant is captured and enslaved by a centrally directed political force thus changes the coordinates of kinopolitical domination from one of aterritorial abandonment to apolitical disenfranchisement. Accordingly, the coordinates of counterpower are also different. The aterritorial nomad is abandoned by a centripetal force, so forces its way back *in* through the raid. However, the apolitical barbarian is disenfranchised by a centrifugal force that captures it, so the barbarian tries to reflee (as a refugee) or return home (revolt). The slave revolt is more than a flight to a refuge; it is the effort to return home, even if this means finding new homes elsewhere. Accordingly, the origins of revolt are in barbarian counterpower.

Continuous Oscillation

The first pedetic strategy of the barbarian slave revolt is continuous oscillation. Opposed to the centripetal force of territorial kinopower and the centrifugal force of political kinopower, oscillation is a noncentric movement to and fro *between* at least two points: a vibration. From the perspective of the polis, barbarian oscillations appear as random and pedetic. According to Aristotle, "[S]laves and animals do little for the common good, and for the most part live at random [ἔτυχεν]."[4] Barbarians and escaped slaves live among the flows that are too hard to capture: the mountains that are too rocky to cultivate, the deserts that are too hot and dry to irrigate, the steppe pastures that are too windy and distant from trading ports, the swamps that cannot be built on, and the uninhabitable dense forests.

In Mesopotamia and Syria, this continuous oscillation is expressed in the revolt of brigandry: the return of slaves to their nomadic homes. During the Middle Babylonian period, many peasants gave up city life and returned to the mountains and roadways to become brigands, oscillating to and fro against the kings and merchants of the region. According to Daniel Snell, from 1500 to 1200 BCE, these brigands (termed SA.GAZ, "murderer" in Sumerian, *hāpiru* in Akkadian) constituted a "mass phenomenon."[5] Urban runaways disenfranchised by political life also combined forces with mountain nomads leading raids on traveling merchant caravans and on expanding agriculturalists who occupied year-round the fertile pastures that nomadic pastoralists in Mesopotamia used in the winter. These brigand revolts constituted a new form of nomad barbarism. Rather than follow the flows of grass and milk with the occasional raid, brigands engage in one continuous raid following only the flows of blood and treasure—always searching for a home denied to them by political disenfranchisement.

In ancient Greece, this continuous oscillation occurred in the slave revolt at Chios (ca. 290 BCE). The need for slaves was so great after the Second Great Peloponnesian War that the Greeks began to buy slaves in great quantity from barbarian slave traders. The historian Theopompus of Chios, writing in the third century BCE, noted that the island of Chios had become the first great slave market of the Hellenic world. Chios was capable of sending and receiving ten thousand slaves per day. Around 290 BCE, however, hundreds of slaves escaped from the centrifugal political forces directing them across the Mediterranean to die in battle for the Greeks. The revolt is attributed to Drimacus (Drimakos), who organized a group of rebelling slaves and a group of fugitives already living autonomously in the mountains of Chios. The group acquired arms and fought their way to the mountains. The successful rebellion was short-lived because Drimacus was able to negotiate a deal with local elites that allowed the slave community to remain in place and periodically come down from the mountains and pilfer provisions from local estates "as long as they were not deemed too excessive."[6] The slave community was thereby sustained by oscillating between the mountains and the valley estates on the condition that they were not destructive: their revolt had found a new home in the mountains of Chios.

Outside Rome, the Huns, nomads forced out of China along with others by the Great Wall, which blocked their access to fresh pastures,[7] oscillated across the steppe, trying to "return to their new homes" until they found the green pastures of the Volga River (in modern-day Georgia). Finding these pastures and others in eastern Europe occupied by other barbarian migrants like the Goths, the Huns followed the flows of blood and treasure instead and became a *permanent* raiding party. Without a home to return to, the raid has nowhere to retreat, so it just moves on in a continual revolt. When the Huns' search/revolt continued west, the Romans were just another group of people in the way of their search. Despite the Romans' superior armor and military strategies, they were frequently pushed back by the military pedesis of the Huns. As the Roman historian Strabo recounts, the Huns "carried on a guerrilla warfare in swamps, in pathless forests, and in deserts."[8] In between towns and cities are the geographic sites of the migrant. The Hunnic battles with Romans were more than raids; they were sustained revolts against the Roman Empire in an attempt to carve out a new home and/or destroy the homes of others. As Genghis Khan was heard to say, according to the only remaining Mongol document of Khan's life, "[K]ill them all and destroy their homes."[9] Once the barbarians' homes have been entirely destroyed, their return home or revolt looks a lot like "invasion," or a "raid." But the difference is that nomadic raids are periodic and seasonal, after which nomads return to their seasonal home. For the barbarian migrant revolt is a permanent way of life.

Waves

The second pedetic strategy of the slave revolt is the wave. The slave revolt is a transportation of social disturbance that spreads throughout society. The great Roman historian Ammianus Marcellinus describes the wave structure of barbarian battle: they "shouted their battle cry, and the uproar, through the heat of the conflict, rising up from a gentle murmur, and becoming gradually louder and louder, grew fierce as that of waves dashing against the rocks." The barbarians, he continues, are as numerous as the "waves in the African sea." In battle the Roman soldiers are like swimmers floating or being swallowed up in the violence of waves, streams, and eddies discolored with barbarian blood. Elsewhere, Ammianus describes the barbarians in similar fluid dynamic terms: "The Goths," he says, "that a race of men, hitherto unknown, had suddenly descended like a whirlwind from the lofty mountains." "The armies of barbarians spread over [the Romans] like the lava [flows] of Mount Etna."[10] The movement, action, and distribution of the barbarians are, for the Romans, most closely akin to uncontrollable waves of water, air, and lava rapidly running out of the mountains. Even Hegel adopts this hydrodynamic language in his description of barbarian migration: "Nordic and eastern barbarians of the mass migrations who, like a river, gushed forth over the Roman Empire, something no dam can any longer withstand."[11]

In Mesopotamia, former peasants displaced by debt, slavery, or war joined highly heterogeneous brigand groups who did not distinguish between slaves and nonslaves, inside and outside. Former peasants-turned-brigands robbed their own farms (now occupied by others). Former nomads (now agriculturalists) were attacked by their "own people" (now brigands). The barbarian brigands saw themselves as trying to survive on the only available disjoined flows. Without a home, one has to make a home on the road. Barbarian brigand groups are not organized according to kings, ethnicity, fences, or walls. They are heterogeneous yet unified through a common transportation. They move down from the mountains like an undulating wave: a social turbulence.

In Greece, the Chios slave revolt was also not organized according to family, state, fences, or walls but according to a unified wave formation (solidarity) of highly heterogeneous fugitives from all over the Mediterranean. Fugitives marooned on Chios would have spoken many different languages, making formal organization difficult. Slave owners in ancient Greece were often advised to "avoid the practice of purchasing many slaves of the same nationality" to keep slaves from organizing.[12] In the Maroon at Chios, family or traditions from their respective regions would not have been socially relevant. The heterogeneous group carried out a collective action but was unified like a wave of force coming down from the mountains to gather necessities from the surplus of the estates on Chios.

In the Roman world, barbarian social groups were for the most part not divided according to territorial fences, political walls, money economies,[13] and formal kingships. They were often multiethnic,[14] multilingual hodgepodges of various tribes throughout Europe organized according to a "fluid state of affairs"[15] and an "improvised leadership."[16] One tribe would conquer an area and absorb some of its people, who would then become part of the new tribe. Some from the group would settle for a bit, and others would move on like the ebb and flow of waves crossing Europe. Solidarity is something that passed through and unified these heterogeneous groups. It transported their social disturbance of Roman kinopower.

Since power in these barbarian tribes was sometimes based on success in battle and sometimes on charismatic leaders who could arbitrate disputes, leadership among the tribes changed constantly.[17] Due to this pedetic and wavelike transport of power, the Romans were not able to control barbarian leadership effectively—even though treachery, murder, and kidnapping were all employed. Lesser barbarian leaders were bribed by the Romans to topple mightier rulers, and rival tribes were paid to attack powerful informal kings.[18] Instead of riding the barbarian waves, the Romans tried to control them—and failed.

Eventually, however, the barbarians tired of Roman manipulation and imperialism and occasionally created their own alliances against the Romans. The barbarian alliances were horizontal like the wave transport of social force, quite different from the vertical, centralized hierarchies characteristic of the Roman Empire. For example, the barbarian conspiracy (*barbarica conspiratio*) of 367 brought together the Scots, Picts, and Saxons and transcended linguistic barriers.[19] No single group was superior to any other. Other short-term alliances occurred between the Goths, Huns, and Alans during the Gothic Crisis of 376–82. But the Goths, like the Saxons, Franks, and Alamanni, themselves already "comprised a number of other ethnic identities: former Roman provincials, Dacians, Carpi, Sarmatians, Taifali, and so on."[20] The barbarians were hydra-headed but also capable of collective conspiratorial waves. Thus, the ethnic identity of the barbarians cannot be fully understood simply according to the verticality of genealogical descent, language, or even political rulership. In contrast to ethnocentric and nationalistic arguments for the traceable identity of these ancient peoples (Franks, Goths, Huns, etc.) to modern European nation-states (France, Germany, Italy, etc.), Patrick Geary proposes instead a wave theory of ethnogenesis that argues for the undivided distribution of fluid alliances and identities, which the Romans only haphazardly called "the Huns" or "the Goths."[21]

Barbarian wave distributions are also not centric or accumulative; they move to and fro as pedetic collectives, alternately accumulating and then dissipating. For example, instead of accumulating surplus, barbarians often destroyed or buried their wealth during funerals.

By disposing of large quantities of potential booty, presumably in a gift to the gods, the leader at once demonstrated his authority, removed from circulation valuable items that might have been used by others as gifts, and enhanced the value of those items that he did bestow upon his followers.[22]

Revolts across the ancient world thus attest to the socially, ethnically, and linguistically diverse organization of barbarian groups in contrast to the bordered, divided, and centralized societies of empire.

Pressure

The third pedetic strategy of the slave revolt is pressure. Opposed to the centripetal force of territorial power (attraction) and the centrifugal force of political power (repulsion), kinetic social pressure is the result of a multiplicity of noncentric micro-movements and collisions at varying velocities within certain constraints. At the macro-level, the motion of slave revolts (when and where they will strike) appears to be relatively unpredictable.[23] The ancient empires struggled to determine how to predict and deter slave revolts since the barbarians often seemed to "suddenly descen[d] like a whirlwind from the lofty mountains, as if they had risen from some secret recess of the earth."[24]

Slave revolts, however, are not predictable based on the centric forces of attraction and repulsion. The transport of their force is the result of a multiplicity of relatively freely moving micro-movements (pedesis). Accordingly, slave societies are also characterized by a high degree of adaptation and mutation. As highly mobile societies without a central organization, they have to more frequently adapt to a changing environment than those in kinetically centric societies. The force of slave motion is thus not the static pressure of attraction or repulsion but rather the dynamic mobile force of a multiplicity of moving bodies striking against the walls and roadways of the empire.[25]

The kinetic social pressure of slave revolts is also attested to on the Greek island of Chios. As the capital of the Hellenic slave trade, Chios moved a high number of diverse slaves across a relatively small space (the island's ports). As the surface area of movement shrinks, so the pressure and frequency of collision between barbarian bodies in motion increase. The slave revolt in Chios was not necessary or inevitable; it was only more likely given the increased kinetic pressure and force of collisions against confinement. More discontented slaves and worse treatment entail a higher risk of revolt. Under this kinetic pressure the slaves revolted against their containment, and the transport of social disturbance was released in a wave of destruction. Eventually, the pressure of the revolt was regulated by allowing the periodic release of the barbarians to pilfer the estates.

The force of kinetic pressure is also attested to both inside and outside Rome. Inside Rome, it is not surprising that the slave revolt led by

Spartacus around 70 BCE appears at the height of Roman slavery. Slavery began as an expression of the Roman capacity to hold great masses in motion under its centralized governance. By the first century BCE, small farms throughout Italy were replaced by enormous slave plantations owned by an aristocratic elite. Inexpensive slave labor increased unemployment among average citizens to overwhelming proportions and had a destabilizing and pressure-increasing effect on the transport of social disturbance in the republic. During the Late Republic, the slave population rose from 12 percent in 225 BCE (600,000) to between 33 and 40 percent or higher under Augustus (a range of 1.9 to 3 million total slaves).[26] As in Chios, the higher quantity of restricted mobility (slavery) produced a higher pressure and frequency of revolt in Rome.

Around 70 BCE, Spartacus, "a Thracian from the nomadic tribes" kidnapped from the mountains and forced into gladiatorial combat,[27] led a slave revolt beginning with seventy men and culminating with seventy thousand. As they won battles against the better-equipped Roman military, they gained new equipment and more recruits from the other slave groups—including "many of the herdsmen and shepherds of the region," according to Plutarch.[28] The continuous oscillations of tens of thousands of displaced people moving together across the empire, like a great wave, exerted a force of kinetic pressure against all the borders that the Romans had placed on their mobility.

The slave revolt looted towns and freed slaves. The Spartacus slave revolt was a great explosion of kinetic pressure built up by mass confinement. Just as the mountain nomads attack, not from the desire for expansion but only when their movement to pasture happens to be blocked by agriculturalists and creates a kinetic pressure (relative to the current surface of pasture area), so the slaves revolt once their return home has been blocked by the empire. The Spartacus slave revolt mutated and adapted rapidly as it gathered increasingly diverse barbarians, nomads, refugees, and ex-slaves to their cause. Perhaps this is the reason that Marx identifies the nomad-barbarian Spartacus and his slave revolt as an heir to the modern proletariat: "the most splendid fellow in the whole of ancient history . . . a real representative of the ancient proletariat."[29]

Outside Rome, walls restricted the movement of the barbarians across the border. At Rome's port walls taxes and tributes were collected and immigration restricted. The Goths lived, quite literally, pressed up against Rome's walls until the violent pressure of the Huns was too great. The Goths had nowhere else to go but across the river as refugees under the protection of Rome's walls. However, once the Goths were across, the Romans forced them into an even smaller area of the refugee camps, where starvation and disease killed hundreds of people (disproportionally the young and old). This increase in confinement only raised pressure, which resulted in an explosion of social kinetic force.

The Goths, under confined mobility, attacked the Roman guards and fought their way to Rome. Along the way, deals were made to give the Goths relative autonomy in exchange for military service. But the Romans broke the deals: Goth soldiers were killed or put deliberately in the front lines of battle against other barbarians. The Goths then organized under Alaric, and from the battle of Adrianople in 378 to the sack of Rome in 410, the Goths were the largest and most successful refugee revolt in ancient history. They were also one of the most thoroughly widespread and adaptable barbarian forces in Europe. The kinetic social pressure of their situation—they were trapped between the Romans and the Huns—contributed significantly to their force. As they conquered, they absorbed many smaller barbarian groups and even took on Roman and Christian customs and laws as they saw fit—becoming a great mutational hodge-podge flowing over Europe.

The Vagabond

The third figure of pedetic force, the vagabond, is not only the criminalized migrant expelled by the tensional force of law as the tramp, the debtor, the beggar, the pauper, the vagrant, the heretic, the witch, the Jew, the minstrel, the foreigner, or the homeless. The vagabond, from the Latin *vagus*, meaning "to wander," and the Latin *proprius*, meaning "one's own way," is also the name of the migrant whose free wandering has its own techniques of pedetic force.

Heresy and Rebellion

The vagabond is both the figure that allows juridical kinopower to expand and legitimate its apparatus of enforcement and also serves as a counterpower to it. As a migratory counterpower, vagabondage can be conceptually unified under a vast array of rebellions: social, economic, and religious ideologies, often persecuted under the name of "heresy." Many vagabonds held heretical beliefs, but even if they did not, the church still used the charge of heresy to attack all forms of social and political rebellion, which became heresy. For example, when textile workers in Flanders took up arms against their bosses, they were hanged as rebels, but the Inquisition also burned them as heretics.[1]

In 1234, the Bishop of Bremen referred to a crusade against the peasant tenants who refused to pay tithes "as though they were heretics."[2] Even secular authorities recognized the subversive power of heretical beliefs and responded accordingly. The subversive action of the criminal migrant was called heresy. According to Silvia Federici,

Heresy was the equivalent of "liberation theology" for the medieval proletariat. It gave a frame to people's demands for spiritual renewal and social justice, challenging both the Church and secular authority by appeal to a higher truth. It denounced social hierarchies, private property and the accumulation of wealth, and it disseminated among the people a new, revolutionary conception of society that, for the first time in the Middle Ages, redefined every aspect of daily life (work, property, sexual reproduction, and the position of women), posing the question of emancipation in truly universal terms.[3]

Thus, the history of heretical struggle (from serf refusals to work, to wandering subversive Cathar preachers, to the anti-enclosure struggles of the Diggers)[4] is the most important opposition movement of the Middle Ages.[5] Kinetically, to rebel is to turn "back" or "backward" (*re*) in direct battle (*bellare*) against one's own society: to "fight back."

Just as the nomad carries out raids and the slave revolts, so the vagabond carries out rebellions. All forms of migrant counterpower are defined by the dominant type of social motion they confront. The nomad is centripetally left out, so the raid bursts in. The barbarian is centrifugally captured and disenfranchised, so the revolt is an escape or return. The rebel vagabond adds a new type of kinetic counterpower. While barbarian slaves could potentially escape the limits of their empires, by the Middle Ages there were fewer and fewer places left to flee "outside" the jurisdiction of some lord or another. Thus, vagabonds increasingly began to directly confront authority from *within*: rebelling. This is not to say that there were not also raids or revolts of some kind, or that direct violence was missing from raids and revolts in previous ages, but simply that during the Middle Ages the *primary* goal of most counterpower was less about supplies (raiding) or radical escape (revolt) than about direct assassination, political murder, burning, revenge, and desecration from *within* society without the goal of leaving it. Counterpower before the eighteenth century, as Charles Tilly points out, was predominantly defined by direct, often spontaneous and violent, attacks on local targets: killing tax collectors, burning effigies, attacking grain seizers, burning or looting the homes of the rich, desecrating churches and clergy.[6] Yves-Marie Bercé identifies over 450 separate such rebellions in southwestern France alone between 1590 and 1715—organizing them according to four distinct types: (1) rebellions over the price of bread, (2) rebellions against soldiers, (3) rebellions against taxmen, and (4) rebellions against taxes on farming.[7]

Rebellion and heresy are about seizing power directly without fleeing, returning, or making new homes.[8] On the more radical end, this includes directly inflicting violence against authorities as retribution and seizing power, land, food, and money through violence. When there is nowhere left to go, the migrant is forced to engage in a direct battle for seizure of goods and power. Thus, the vagabond, the rebel, and the heretic all turn back on their societies with the primary aim of battle.

We can more precisely locate in the medieval rebellion of the vagabond the construction of three pedetic strategies that pose an alternative to those of juridical kinopower. Instead of conjoining flows into a system of linked rotational motion of tension, vagabonds create continuous oscillations of disjoined flows. Instead of creating a grid of divided but linked cells, vagabonds create an undivided wave distribution. Instead of expanding through the tensional force of expulsion, vagabonds are defined by their force of pressure.

Continuous Oscillation

Vagabondage is a continuous oscillation insofar as it is a wandering movement without origin or final destination. It is not the curvilinear movement toward a center of power, nor a radial movement outward toward a subordinate periphery, nor even spatial movement of multiple linked centers in the tension of land contracts and waged labor. Rather, vagabondage is continually disjoined from land, labor, and law. It emerges from all the wretched of feudal society: serfs, peasants, beggars, the sick, prostitutes, defrocked priests, witches, urban and rural day laborers, and migrants and refugees of all kinds. "Vagabond" is the legal name for this oscillatory or wandering group of disjoined migrants under juridical kinopower.

The vagabond's oscillation is first attested to in the peasant defections, evictions, and roaming bands of fighters in the fifth through twelfth centuries. Feudal society is often incorrectly depicted as static (contracts tie everyone to the land), but during this period the mobility and rebellion of vagabond peasants were constant. Peasants were always running away from work or military service:

[S]ometimes they joined the bands of pious pilgrims traveling to sacred shrines. . . . [S]ometimes they went to swell the troops of vagabonds who thronged the roads, men without home or fealty, outlaws, who sought in the shelter of forests and mountain gorges a refuge for their freedom and their rapine.[9]

These rebels also armed themselves in roaming bands. For example, in the fifth century, peasants fed up with the constant battles between Romans and barbarians stole farm tools (as weapons) and horses from the estates, forming an armed, wandering group. Townspeople joined them, and they created a self-governing Maroon society in Gaul called Bacaude, or "band of fighters."[10] Bacaude was the largest of the increasing number of rebel Maroon societies that proliferated at the time. Yet the group was continually on the move and under attack. In response to the defeat of their battalions, they adopted "guerrilla warfare" (the warfare of pedesis) tactics against the Romans and barbarians until the end of the century, when they were finally defeated and partially absorbed by the Visigoths and Alans. The Bacaude is thus an oscillatory organization in the sense in which it continually moves to and fro without center, origin, territory, state, or feudal contract: neither Roman nor barbarian.

After commutation in the thirteenth century, a new population of vagabonds was forced into continual oscillation across Europe and England. Many peasants could not afford their new money rent and were evicted. If they were not evicted, they accumulated debt and then ran away to the towns to try to survive on poorly paid waged labor. The population of early towns grew by mass migration from the countryside, often from considerable distances. These populations were disproportionately male and youthful, rootless, without ties of family, and desperately dependent on casual employment of the most demeaning kinds. They were subject to the discrimination often directed at impoverished immigrants.[11]

[T]hese itinerant workers movements are precisely the cause of the problems States have always had with journeymen's associations, or *compagnonnages*, the nomadic or itinerant bodies of the type formed by masons, carpenters, smiths, etc. Settling, sedentarizing labor power, regulating the movement of the flow of labor . . . and, for the rest, relying on forced manpower recruited on the spot (*corvée*) or among indigents (poor/workhouses)—this has always been one of the principal affairs of the State, which undertook to conquer both a *band vagabondage* and a *body nomadism.*[12]

Given their poverty and criminalization, it is no surprise that vagabonds were particularly receptive to movements for social, economic, and religious reform. For example, in 1224–25, underpaid textile workers in Flanders were the main supporters of a man claiming to be (the presumed dead) Baldwin IX and initiated a civil war for social and economic reform against the rule of Baldwin's daughter Jeanne.[13] In 1251, a movement of peasants and urban workers called Pastoreaux (Shepherds) roamed through northern France, attacking monasteries, expelling archbishops, and burning the homes of the rich.[14] By the fourteenth century, up to four thousand day laborers (weavers, fullers, dyers) could be found in each of the main textile cities of Europe (Flanders, Florence, and Siena). Urban wageworkers were controlled by despotic cloth merchants and forbidden to form workers' associations or meet outside work. Strikes were punishable by death, and merchants frequently arrested, tortured, and expelled workers who caused trouble.[15]

All across Europe, oscillating migrants from the countryside moved to the cities and rebelled at every possible chance against the rich, the nobility, and the clerics. These movements met in secret and often spread ideas of rebellion through the words of the "wandering preacher movement," the Cathar (the largest heretical sect).[16]

[M]obility was a keynote of the lives of many of those involved in Catharism. . . . The workers traveled from house to house and town to town making and selling their wares and at the same time making heretical contacts. Inns, workshops and mills were casual meeting places for supporters.[17]

At various times from the thirteenth to the fifteenth century, rebels even succeeded in establishing temporary workers' governments in the cities of Bruges, Ghent, Florence, Liege, and others.[18] In these vagabond struggles, tens of thousands of men and women lost their lives or were forced into further migration.

The brigands and anti-enclosure struggles in England provide another example of the oscillatory movement of vagabonds. The fourteenth-century system of English commutation and enclosure displaced a large number of peasants who had no other means to live than by direct theft. Thomas More describes this in *Utopia*:

By hook or crook, they must needs depart away, poor, silly, wretched souls, men, women, husbands, wives, fatherless children, widows, woeful mothers, with their young babes, and their whole household small in substance and much in number, as husbandry requireth many hands. Away they trudge, I say, out of their known and accustomed houses, finding no place to rest in. All their household stuff, which is very little worth though it might well abide the sale, yet being suddenly thrust out they be constrained to sell it for a thing of nought. And when they have wandered abroad till that be spent, what can they then else do but steal, and then justly pardy be hanged, or else go about a-begging? And yet then also they be cast in prison as vagabonds, because they go about and work not, whom no man will set a-work, though they never so willingly proffer themselves thereto.[19]

English vagabonds oscillated across the countryside, in and out of towns, in and out of jails, punished and expelled—always one step away from the gallows. Of these vagabonds, Marx cites that "72,000 great and petty thieves were put to death" during the reign of Henry VIII.[20] These roaming bands of beggars and thieves camped in the forests, hills, wastes, and heathlands and survived on hunted game and materials gathered (seized) from the woods.

These vagabonds were the inspiration for several popular myths of the time, including the "rhymes of Robin Hood," first mentioned in the fourteenth-century poem *Piers Plowman.*[21] In the story, Robin Hood is an outlaw who lives in the forest with a band of outlaws. He supports peasant struggles, disguises himself as a beggar, hates the clergy, and fights the sheriff and his men. In the ballad of *Adam Bell, Clym of the Cloughe, and Wyllyam of Cloudeslee,* the three men are made outlaws for hunting deer and gathering wood on the lord's land (a popular vagabond crime). They live in the forest and fight against the sheriff. In the seventeenth century, the name "highwayman" emerges to describe the vagabond figure who continued to oscillate along the country roads stealing for a living.[22]

Vagabond oscillation is also expressed in the anti-enclosure movement in England, which began in the fifteenth century and continued into the seventeenth as the "most common species of social protest."[23] During the night, peasants and vagabonds would dig up fence posts that marked the enclosed sheep walks and kept the peasants from their land. The largest and most famous anti-enclosure rebellion was Kett's Rebellion in Norfolk in 1549. The sixteen thousand rebels captured artillery and defeated the government army of twelve thousand in the second-largest city in England (Norwich). The rebels demanded an end to all enclosures and the liberation of all bondmen.[24]

In 1649, a group called the True Levellers demanded radical social and land reform based on the common use of the land. Their egalitarian beliefs were supported by "heretical" readings of Acts 4:32 in the Bible: "The group of believers was one in mind and heart. No one said that any of his belongings was his own, but they all shared with one another everything they had." The group was popularly known as the Diggers because they believed in the right of anyone to dig up and cultivate unused soil. "England is not a Free People," according to their manifesto, "till the Poor that have no Land, have a free allowance to dig and labour the Commons, and so live as Comfortably as the Landlords that live in their Inclosures."[25] The kinetic position of the True Levellers was against the blockage of the earth by enclosure law and for the free oscillation of people and cultivation.

In all of these struggles against criminalization, oppression, poverty, and enclosure, the vagabond is defined by the pedetic force of continuous and rebellious oscillation.

Waves

The second pedetic strategy that vagabond heresy creates is wave distributions. Opposed to the cellular tensions created by juridical kinopower (the enclosure, the prison, and the workhouse), the wave is an undivided distribution of mobility found in the common property, egalitarianism, and internationalism of vagabond and heretical rebellions.

The first expression of wave motion in vagabond heresy is the practice of common property, the undivided distribution of collectively managed land. It is the land practices relating to lands that are not owned that pass across each individual in turn, according to shared agreements. No one owns the lands, but everyone alternates in their usage. The commons are the meadows, forests, mountains, wild pastures, and other "undivided land belonging to the members of the local community as a whole,"[26] which provided peasants and vagabonds with many shared resources, such as fuel wood, building timber, fish ponds, hunting grounds, and grazing grounds.

After commutation, nongrazing lands were not desirable for cultivation or sheep walks and thus laid fallow or frequently harbored vagabonds of some sort. But, as Gary Snyder emphasizes, "the commons" was not only a system of shared land; it was also a system of land management. In England and in Swiss villages, peasants agreed that they would turn out to common pasture only as many head of cattle as they could feed over the winter from their own corrals, in order to stop overgrazing.[27] Other common laws regulated how much fishing, hunting, and wood gathering were permitted to prevent depletion of forests. These sorts of customary laws were determined by the peasants themselves, occasionally in antagonism to the lords' determination. Thus, common property is a wave distribution insofar as it is an undivided (nonprivate) realm that is collectively transmitted and shared in solidarity with others.

The second expression of wave motion in vagabond heresy is the practice of egalitarianism: an undivided distribution of people. Although vagabond egalitarianism is not without its flaws, it does express a distinctly different ethos from that of social expulsion. Instead of regulating the movement of bodies from one cell to another based on the linked tensions of hierarchical laws, vagabonds created, through popular assemblies, rebellions, and heretical ideology, a significantly more egalitarian form of movement. The popular assembly is, in part, a practice brought by the barbarians into Europe, according to Pierre Dockes. For many barbarian groups, the "assembly of free men" is the undivided distribution of decision-making people who had the right to bear arms and hence share in the distribution of booty in accordance with customary rules.[28]

Popular assemblies were used across Europe by peasants struggling against the taxation of the lords. For example, in the fifteenth century, Spanish peasants formed assemblies for the purpose of coordinating their refusal to pay the *remensas* tax. The assemblies allowed them to leave the land without being criminalized. Peasants also used assemblies to organize themselves, form an army of recruited peasants, and fight for peasant property rights.[29] Popular assemblies were used in the management of common property, such as when to plant or harvest, when to drain the fens, or how many animals to allow on the commons.[30]

Vagabonds also expressed an undivided wave motion of equality in their rebellions. Peasants, urban workers, and all manner of vagabonds formed alliances demanding social and economic equality. In Bruges, a large-scale peasant revolt was sustained from 1323 to 1328 due, in large part, to the peasants' alliance with city workers and craftsmen. "Bruges, by now under the control of a weaver and fuller party, took direction of the revolt from the peasants. . . . A war of propaganda began, as monks and preachers told the masses that a new era had come and that they were the equals of the aristocrats."[31]

In Tuchins in central France, a group of mountain bandit vagabonds joined with city artisans against the power of the lords for the equality of all.[32] The largest revolt in the Middle Ages, the Peasants' Revolt or Great Rising of 1381, was a massive alliance of rural peasants and city workers that spread across England in a wave, demanding social equality. One of its leaders, John Ball, writes that "nothing will be well in England until we are of the same condition":[33] in other words, until the force of this social wave has passed through everyone and united them against the powerful.

Vagabond egalitarianism is also expressed in the beliefs of many heretical sects in voluntary poverty and shared goods. The Diggers, for example, argue from Christian scripture that

every single man, Male and Female, is a perfect Creature of himself; and the same Spirit that made the Globe, dwells in man to govern the Globe . . . all looking upon each other, as equals in the Creation; so that our Maker may be glorified in the work of his own hands, and that every one may see, he is no respecter of Persons, but equally loves his whole Creation, and hates nothing but the Serpent.[34]

Other heretical sects, like the Taborites in Bohemia, adopted a form of primitive communism based on equality and communal ownership.[35] The Waldenses in France even avoided all forms of commerce, fraud, and oaths and engaged in voluntary poverty, living only on vagabond begging and preaching.[36]

The third expression of wave motion in vagabond rebellion and heresy is its internationalism: the undivided distribution of the people at the widest level. This was accomplished, in particular, by the contacts made by the roaming bands of wandering heretical priests, pilgrims, and border-crossing refugees fleeing persecution—all of whom received the criminal designation "vagabond heretics." The wandering Cathars and Waldenses preached from town to town, establishing a network of safe houses, schools, and contacts open to anyone interested in their teachings and political organizing. As peasants, workers, and others were expelled from their land and jobs, they joined these roaming bands as they passed through and spread across Europe as a wave of migrant vagabondage.

Pressure

In addition to the continual oscillation of vagabond heretics and their undivided wave distribution of property and people, they created a third pedetic tactic: the force of social pressure. Vagabond pressure has both an internal and external aspect. Vagabond heresy exerted an internal pressure on the believer through the adoption of new social, economic, personal, and religious beliefs. The vagabond heretic wanted a personal transformation, a release of his or her spirit from confinement.

Heretical ideology thus expresses these transformations. Many heretical sects taught that since Christ had no property, the church and the people should relinquish theirs. They taught that external forms of worship (buildings, images, symbols, etc.) should be discarded because they only bound one's inner belief. They exhorted people not to pay the tithes, denied the existence of Purgatory, and rejected the sale of indulgences (a very profitable activity for the church).[37] The refusal to work, voluntary poverty, celibacy, and inner belief all required an inner rebellion and pressure of the individual, but without the monastery and institutions of tensional expulsion. Heretical pressure is not bound by contract to the abbey, the lord, or the boss but rather creates a kinetic pressure from an inner transformation: a heretical pedesis.

Another inner transformation of the vagabond heretic was the sexual practice against reproduction. The Bogomils, for example, believed that the visible world was the work of the devil and thus refused to bring children into this world to become slaves to it.[38] Many other vagabonds tried not to have children because they could not support them or did not want to bring them into the world of expulsion, begging, and starvation. During and after the Black Death, population growth became a major social concern and thus contraception, infanticide, abortion, and nonreproductive sex (sodomy) were criminalized as acts of heresy. Again, the actions of the vagabonds were made heretical.

The external pressure of vagabond heresy is expressed in its social rebellion against the clergy and lords of juridical kinopower. Even when vagabond peasant revolts failed, and tens of thousands died (in the Great Uprising of 1381 and German Peasants' War of 1524), the physical and social pressure at the gates of the city had an impact on the clergy and lords. Constant peasant pressure and rebellion (such as refusing to pay taxes, killing tax collectors, slowing down work, conducting food riots, and burning down homes) explain why between 1177 and 1350 the lords of Loraine alone granted 280 charters recognizing the land and social rights of the peasants. Peasant rebellions against expulsion, poverty, and the persecution of the Catholic Church also advanced Protestant reforms.[39]

Commutation, too, for good or ill, was motivated by hundreds of years of social pressure by peasants. In 1381, the English peasant vagabonds' refusal to pay the poll tax (levied by King Richard II) initiated a servile war against the government. The peasants destroyed the Savoy Palace, stormed the Tower of London, and executed government officials associated with the tax—including the Lord Chancellor, Simon of Sudbury, and the Archbishop of Canterbury. The revolt was led by renegade Lollard priest John Ball, who preached before battle the famous heretical line, "When Adam delved and Eve span, who was then the gentleman?" In other words, if there was no hierarchy of lords and clergy in the Garden of Eden, why then is it good and holy to have one now? It is no coincidence that the Lollards and Diggers resurrected and transformed the Syriac myth of the Garden of Eden in order to valorize it as a symbol of undivided distribution before the first kinetic expulsion of Adam and Eve from their land, and before Cain's territorial expulsion of Abel the nomad. In Eden, there was no division, no territorial, political, or juridical expulsion, only the free movement of all across undivided commons in continual transformation: there was only pure pedesis.

CHAPTER 12

The Proletariat

The final figure of the migrant covered in this book is the proletariat, which is both a migratory surplus expelled by the elastic force of the economy and a figure that breaks free from the driving forces of oscillation (profit, equilibrium, competition, etc.). In other words, the proletariat responds to elastic force with a pedetic force of its own.

Continuous Oscillation

Of all the forms of kinetic antagonism, the pedesis of the proletariat and the elasticity of economic power are the most similar. Both are forms of social motion defined by a movement to and fro without a center or an ultimate binding junction (territory, law, state, etc.). However, the aim of elasticity is the "free circulation" of social bodies, with the qualification that these supposedly free circulations be driven in such a way that they produce a surplus population whose mobility will act as protection against the uncertainties that come with large-scale social oscillations (contraction and expansion).

The proletariat's propertyless productivity is the source of this motion, and the proletariat is also capable of directing its own oscillations elsewhere and otherwise without the imperatives of generating social surplus. Thus, the proletariat's mobility is freed from the driven oscillations to produce according to the demands of profit, competition, and efficiency, and the proletariat can move continuously and freely with others.

From the eighteenth to twentieth centuries, this continuous oscillation takes the form of what Lorenz Von Stein was the first to theorize as "the social movement." In two of his earliest works, *Socialist and Communist Movements since the Third French Revolution* (1848) and *History of the French Social Movements from 1789 to the Present* (1850), Stein laid the theoretical foundations that anticipated and influenced Marx's theory of class struggle and social movements.[1] Many scholars cite Stein as the theoretical father of the concept of the social movement, but few, if any, take his concept of social motion to be more than metaphorical (social change is "like" a movement).

For Stein, the social movement is a real movement. In this sense, Stein was the first to have discovered in the theory of the social movement a pedetic motion proper to the continuous oscillation of the proletariat figure. In the very first section of the *History of the French Social Movements,* Stein develops a theory of social motion, what he calls a "theory of the movement of society and the state." "Life," Stein states, "is motion which in any given unit is brought about through the movement and countermovement of the personal [the state] and the non-personal [society]. The former tries to subdue the latter, which in turn constantly tries to detach itself. . . . Life is a movement between [these] opposing poles." Life, for Stein, is nothing other than the continuous oscillation of social movement and state countermovement. The social movement is always trying to move freely in a continuous oscillation, detaching from the state, while the state is always trying to subdue this motion into its own regime. The science of society, for Stein, is the study of social motion "regulated by definite and intelligible laws": the "matrix according to which mankind has to move."[2]

Stein names three principal laws of social motion:

1. "The movement towards independence has to begin and has to run its course not in the area of public life but in the area of the social order." This is the case because the social order (class) is more powerful than the state. The social order is more powerful because it is the order that contains the larger social struggle between two conflicting motions: the movement to subordinate others (dependence), and the movement toward the liberation from subordination (independence).

2. The ruling class and the ruled class battle against one another for control of the state, and for their independence over the other. "This can happen in two ways: either through reform or through revolution."

3. Finally, the victors of the battle (the most liberal elements of society) produce a new state constitution based on this liberty and freedom. The state is the administrative apparatus of this freedom. "The class which rules society also comes to control the state."[3]

In short, "the social movement aiming to change the state originates within the class which is subjugated to the rule of the powerful. It aims at the elimination of this rule as well as of the corresponding privileges."[4] The social movement is thus an emancipatory movement originating from the lower classes against their subjugation. Every time power is conjoined in the state, a new subordinated class emerges to change it. In this way, the social movement is a continuous oscillatory movement of society against the state. Stein's theory of the social movement is also a deeply materialist theory of social motion:

It can be explained by the fact that the original moving force in the revolution is not the idea of equality, but the unevenly distributed social wealth; and that not philosophical theories but social classes make the revolution. The principle of a social movement necessarily implies that property which has made one part of the dependent class powerful shall become the dominant factor in the society by determining the difference between the ruling and the dependent class.[5]

Thus, for Stein, material social movements are the "main determinants of political life . . . and the very essence of social life and social changes." Social movements are not *like* movements because they are related to philosophical ideas of change. The laws of social motion literally and materially order social wealth, property, and human movement. The historical period in which the social movement is the most predominant, according to Stein, is precisely "the most recent historical period [eighteenth and nineteenth centuries]." This is where we find, maybe not for the first time but in the most striking way, the broadly *social* "law of the movement toward freedom."[6]

This is the case for several important historical reasons. The increasingly unified "social" force of continuous oscillation moving between society and the state (social movements) emerged alongside several historical phenomena that dramatically increased social oscillation and migration in the eighteenth and nineteenth centuries. Economic expansion in cities meant that markets connected people together in proximity and quantity more than ever before. The rise of a propertyless proletariat was thus increasingly and collectively dependent on fluctuations in the national economy and its displacements. The transportation revolution of railways, motorized vehicles, and steamships made geographic movement faster, easier, and cheaper than ever before. The communication revolution of the printing press and the telegraph and the massive proliferation of newspapers, pamphlets, and printed materials of all kinds increased the degree to which people became aware of larger "social" phenomena. New forms of association (public meetings, demonstrations, reading rooms, etc.) also emerged around these phenomena and connected ordinary people to social issues across territorial and social strata. Finally and most important, following the forms of elastic expulsion described in Chapters 6 and 7, the eighteenth and nineteenth centuries produced the largest number of migrants in history up until that point.

These proletarian migrants and their struggles gave birth to the first social movements. As Charles Tilly remarks elsewhere at more length, "[U]rbanization, migration, and rapid population growth transformed the organizational bases of local contention, adding weight to those actors who could create, adapt, or infiltrate flexible, efficient associations and assemblies."[7] In other words, it is precisely the holy trinity of proletarianization (expulsion from property, urban labor, and biological fecundity) that gave birth to the social movement. Once a threshold of proletarianization was achieved, local struggles merged into social and national struggles. As a direct result of their biological production (population growth), the proletariat became the propertyless majority and their motion became a larger *social* movement.

In this way, social movements are not formally or kinopolitically different from many nomadic, barbarian, or vagabond struggles against the state. All are defined by a continuous or free oscillation outside the limits of the dominant regime of social motion. All of them are interpreted historically as chaotic and disorganized (just as pedesis is), but they also express their own form of irregular social order.

Authorities and thoughtless historians commonly describe popular contention as disorderly. . . . But the more closely we look at that same contention, the more we discover order. We discover order created by the rooting of collective action in the routines and organization of everyday social life, and by its involvement in a continuous process of signaling, negotiation, and struggle with other parties whose interests the collective action touches.[8]

The social movement, for Tilly, appeared chaotic only because early theorists did not look closely enough at the pedetic and continuous oscillation that defined their daily struggles. However, the important difference between social movements and the raids, revolts, and rebellions of previous migratory struggles is that the social movement dramatically expanded the possible range of issues and size of the associations of contention. Because of changes in commerce, transportation, communication, association, migration, population, and the emergence of national identities, migrants and their points of contention became increasingly interconnected, that is, social. Migratory phenomena affected more and more people until the vast majority of society was proletarianized and became subject to the elastic forces of economic kinopower and surplus redistribution.

In contrast, before the eighteenth century, migrant resistance was largely parochial, segmented, and particular. It was *parochial* in the sense that the points of contention were concentrated around a single community (the feudal lord, the local tax collector). It was *segmented* in the sense that vagabonds and peasants trying to avoid expulsion mostly took direct action against the local patron or authority (the murder of tax collectors, the raiding of local grain merchants during food shortages, the burning of the homes of the rich, assassinations). It was *particular* in the sense that the tactics used varied greatly depending on the group, issue, and locality. For example, the same food shortage might be dealt with by the burning of an effigy, a food raid, the burning of the home of the local grain merchant, or attacks on a local lord, depending on location and group.[9] As Sidney Tarrow puts it,

With the former, grain seizures, religious conflicts, land wars, and funeral processions were segmented from one another and from elite politics. But with the latter [the social movement], it was possible for workers, peasants, artisans, clerks, writers, lawyers, and aristocrats to march under the same banner and confront the same opponents. These changes facilitated coalition formation and made possible the coming of the national social movement.[10]

Early proletarian migrants who were expelled from England in the form of a surplus population developed one of the first social movements in response to British domination in North America. Beginning in 1764, when the British attempted to levy a new tax in the form of the Sugar Act, colonial merchants responded with "nonimportation" agreements or boycotts. "These fledgling efforts," writes Pauline Maier, "were system-atized in September 1765 (with the Stamp Act controversy), and there-after nonimportation associations were organized in other commercial centers." For Americans, "nonimportation could constitute an effective substitute for domestic violence; opposition could retreat from the streets to the spinning wheel."[11] The boycott required large-scale social cohesion, education, and continuous free association, not simply direct or local vio-lence. It required people to freely gather, identify, and formulate a collec-tive and continuous program of resistance in a way quite different from the vagabond struggles of the Middle Ages.

In England, the British developed similar social movement strate-gies, inspired by the colonial proletariat. In 1791, the English Antislavery Association developed a social movement around the boycott of sugar imported from the West Indies to put pressure on Parliament to abolish the forced migration of slaves.[12] The boycott combined the use of the press and the petition to assemble a vast mobile social force. Instead of allowing their oscillations to be driven by profit, they chose to advocate for the free movement of migrants and the free movement of society against the state. In 1788, the first large petition against slavery was circulated in Britain by taking advantage of the dense network of provincial newspapers. "By the 1790s, petitions were being launched regularly at public meetings and were accompanied by boycotts, newspaper advertisements, and lobbying in extended movement campaigns."[13] Petition signers and diverse associa-tion members were then coordinated into a large national social move-ment. What appeared to be the chaotic oscillation of diverse individuals was actually a quite ordered (but irregular) social movement against state and economic policies of forced migration.

The French Revolution was a massive social movement against the ruling class and the state. Unfortunately, the urban bourgeois revolution-aries, philosophes, novelists, and statesmen of the revolution have become an overly privileged part of this social movement.[14] The vast majority of the revolutionary Third Estate was made up of proletarian peasants engaged in a social struggle against the seigneurial regime of expulsion and for the right to common land. The Third Estate composed roughly 97 percent of the French population. Within this group, the smallest population was the property-owning bourgeoisie, both urban and rural.

The remaining majority was composed of urban and rural propertyless workers and day laborers and those who owned some small bit of rural land but survived only by their customary rights to the resources of common lands.[15] These landless or practically landless proletarian peasants participated in large-scale social action against their forced migration at the hands of an arbitrary ancien régime that was buying up peasant landholdings, disproportionately depleting the commons lands, increasing taxation, expelling them from their land, and offering no economic security for the working class.

In 1789, the year the French Revolution began, the proletariat produced a document chronicling their grievances and demands, the *Cahiers de doleances* (Register of grievances). The proletariat (peasants, small shopkeepers, journeymen, and others) demanded equality, freedom of speech, assembly, trade, education, and freedom of arbitrary arrest and taxation. Most important, however, more than 70 percent of all the Third Estate grievances directly address the community's collective land rights.[16] Of these, 39 percent mentioned their rights to the woods and wild lands, while 26 percent directly address the right to the common land itself.

The single most frequent grievance was the lords' monopolization of the woods and common lands. The "right of triage" (1669), as it was called, allowed seigneurs to take up to a third of a village's common land. As seigneurs secured ownership of the commons, fewer peasants could survive on their land, and more had to sell their plots of land, take up tenure on the lord's land, become day laborers for others, or migrate to the city. Throughout the eighteenth and nineteenth centuries, hundreds of thousands of peasants were forced into migration in this way.[17] As one might guess, the bourgeois reception of these migrants was not positive.

Bourgeois reception reveals the clear political connection between all the pedetic migratory forces of history that converged on Paris at the time. In 1848, Lecouturier writes that "[t]here is no such thing as Parisian society. . . . Paris is nothing but a nomads' camp." In 1871, M. Haussmann writes that "Paris belongs to France . . . not to the mobile population in its lodging houses, which distorts the meaning of the polls by the pressure of unintelligent votes; this 'mob of nomads,' . . . whom move to the great city in search of fairly regular work, . . . [and have] the intention of returning in due course to their place of origin."[18] The use of the word "nomad" in these texts designates the specifically *aterritorial* status of the migrant who lives in temporary "camps" and who comes to the city territory only to *raid* it and leave again. Even when the nomads live in the city, they cannot be city dwellers; instead, they deterritorialize the city itself into a camp.

These migrants are described elsewhere by Balzac and Jules Breynat as a specifically racialized and *apolitical* people: barbarians. An article from the Paris newspaper *Journal des débats* (July 10, 1832) describes an "invasion of the new barbarians." And "the victim of these barbarians," Jules Breynat writes, "was to be the bourgeoisie . . . intoxicated with disorder and carnage, this populace disowned by the people laid siege to power."[19] The counterpower of the barbarian, disowned by the people, is not the raid but the revolt. Barbarians love to foment chaos and lay siege to power. But their apolitical and bellicose nature is also part of their biology. These barbarian "ragpickers" of Paris are described by Le Play as "races" who live "tolerably close to the savage state, who subsist mainly by hunting, fishing, and fruit gathering. Obeying the instincts of savage life, they have a pronounced repugnance to the effort required to raise themselves to the wellbeing concomitant with a settled life. They do not willingly obey any master."[20] Balzac's physiological descriptions of the laboring classes also attest to the racial and biological inferiority of the migrants. It is precisely the "exorbitant mobility of the proletarians,"[21] he says, that "explain[s] the normal ugliness of the Parisian physiognomy." Their mobility makes them "a people of ghastly mien, gaunt, sallow, weather-beaten . . . cadaverous physiognomy . . . exhumed people . . . [with] hellish complexion."[22]

These migrants are also described by their specifically juridical name: the vagabond. Thiers writes in a speech given on May 24, 1850:

It is the mob, not the people, that we wish to exclude; it is this heterogenous mob, this mob of vagabonds with no avowed family and no known domicile, a mob of persons so mobile that they can nowhere be pinned down and have not succeeded in establishing any regular home for their family. This is the mob which the law proposes to expel.[23]

For Thiers, the migrants are essentially criminal beings. Their crime is that they have likely earned money by "unlawful means" and that they have no "regular home." They are not "the people"; they are "the mob." The mob is the mob(ile) people who cannot be "pinned down." The problem, according to Thiers, is thus primarily a juridical one caused by the vaga-bond character of the mob's excessive and criminal mobility.

In all of these various descriptions, the name "migrant" is intermin-gled with the name "proletariat."[24] Each, however, expresses a different characteristic of the migrant's mob(ility): aterritorial, apolitical, criminal, or working class. "Perhaps," as Jacques Rancière writes, "the truly danger-ous classes are not so much the uncivilized ones thought to undermine society from below, but rather the migrants who move at the borders between classes."[25] Or perhaps there is continuity between these classes in the form of the migrant itself.

While the rural proletarian peasants banded together as villages and formed their own militias to attack the homes of the seigneurs, the urban proletariat (the *sans-culottes*) joined and formed the bulk of the early revo-lutionary army in the cities.[26] The rural proletariat wanted to protect what little land it had left to avoid expulsion, and the urban proletariat (already expelled from the land) wanted its land back. In the forested commons of the east alone, for example, more than 150 villages were engaged in struggles against their seigneurs over common land when revolution broke out.[27] Together, rural and urban migrants constituted the two sides of the proletarian struggle in France. Unfortunately, bourgeois land reform after the revolution failed to reconcile the two.[28] Even after church and émigré lands were seized by the revolutionaries, they were largely auctioned off to the rich.[29] Landless peasants were not even allowed to bid.

Thus, the great historian of the French Revolution George Lefebvre argues that it is precisely the proletarian peasants' anticapitalist attach-ment to collective land rights that separated them from the revolutionary bourgeoisie's interest in land privatization.[30] In other words, the "history from below" of the French Revolution,[31] as Lefebvre called it, is precisely a history of the proletarian struggle of migrant oscillation against the state.

Waves

The pedetic force of the proletariat is also defined by its undivided wave distribution. A social wave is a product of a continuous oscillation. It is not a "cycle," as Sidney Tarrow has argued;[32] or a general process of "expansion, transformation, and contraction," as Koopmans argued;[33] or a simple "spreading" of tactics, as Tilly has argued.[34] The problem with these definitions is that they all reduce the social wave to the individual expansions and contractions of its crests and troughs. But, most important, the wave is the undivided *continuity*, resonance, and intensive force that travels *between* the crests and troughs. A migratory social wave is the unifying force that weaves *through* the mass of heterogeneous individuals and struggles and moves them together without dividing them.

The undivided wave of proletarian force is exemplified in the invention of social associations, print communication, and communes. Beginning in the eighteenth century, we start to see the widespread usage of boycotts and petitions and a dramatic increase in the creation of social associations of all kinds. Social associations are waves insofar as they bring people together around causes or issues that travel through their individual circumstances. These associations were largely voluntary and based on the mutual interests of the people, regardless of class. Where there was division, the wave of associations that swept across America, Britain, and France created undivided or unified groups.

The increase in social associations was followed by a massive expansion of social claims, a widening of their geographic reach, and a more sustainable and continuous ability to move large amounts of people around issues—from tax resistance in America in the 1760s, to antislavery social movements in England, to the French Revolution. Associations created a place for face-to-face contact and solidarity among diverse people who shared common interests and struggles.

But the new unity of social associations could not have been formed without the advent of print communication, which helped generate a common and undivided distribution of an increasingly unified "social" field. As Tarrow puts it,

[I]t took the experience of reading the same journals, associating in the same groups, and forming coalitions across class and geographic lines to build the formal connective structures that allowed movements to be diffused to new publics, and the scale of contention to mount from the neighborhood and the locality to the region and the nation.[35]

These "waves of contention," as Tarrow calls them, grew larger and faster because of print and association. The newspaper, widely distributed across the social and political spectrum, had a decentralizing effect on its readership. The newspaper brought together a variety of heterogeneous peoples and things into the same print language. Thus, the status of the rulers and readers was leveled to some degree. The newspaper was not handed down from the rulers above to the readers below but circulated horizontally and, as Benedict Anderson puts it, "spoke polyphonically,"[36] according to the many voices and topics expressed therein. Print communication created an intensive or "invisible discourse" that traversed and unified massive groups of people. "Only a newspaper can put the same thought at the same time before a thousand readers," wrote Alexis de Tocqueville.[37]

If a person could read in a newspaper or pamphlet about how the proletariat in other countries was capable of overthrowing its ruler, then it seemed that the same thing could be possible at home. Print communication in the form of pamphlets, circulars (for "free" circulation), newspapers, and written texts facilitated a common discourse among increasingly migratory groups in the form of protest waves. But the cause of strike or protest waves is not simply that a tactic was modeled and then replicated elsewhere. The strike wave is possible only because there is a *common condition of social expulsion* and *solidarity* between each individual crest and trough. The communicational wave is the horizontal movement that passes through each crest—establishing an undivided social surface. It is a fluid phenomenon.

For example, the proletarian peasants of the French Revolution were able to unify and disseminate their demands and grievances through the *Cahiers de doléances*.[38] The peasants formed local associations, produced written documents of the grievances, and disseminated these documents. Elsewhere, others under shared threats of expulsion did the same. Because of increasing literacy, other peasants and urban proletariat were able to read these and identify a common condition of oppression (the ancien régime) and common liberation (land reform, equality, education, etc.). In this way, the *Cahiers* created a literary and associational wave of proletarian movement.

Tax resistance in the British colonies, the antislavery campaigns in England, the revolution of 1848, and many other social movements relied heavily on the mass distribution of printed texts to create and unify an oppositional wave of protest and free association. One can even, as Tarrow argues, correlate the activity of many major social movements with the numbers of periodicals printed at the same time.[39] The more periodicals, the larger and stronger the oppositional wave of the time.

Nationalism and nationalist movements also emerged through print communication but did not have the same form of wave motion as social movements and free associations for two reasons. First, the social movement is fundamentally a movement against the state through reform or revolution. Nationalism is not necessarily against the state. Second, the social movement is based on the free association, and the undivided oscillation, of all persons. For example, one did not have to be a citizen to boycott, petition, refuse taxes, or demonstrate against slavery. Nationalism and nationalist movements, however, are exclusionary or divided insofar as inclusion is predicated on a specific ethnic background, language, class, or political status. Nationalist movements have a strong history of social expulsion (such as anti-immigrant protests, anti-Semitic protests, or fascism). In short, the nationalist movement is not the same as the social movement. The two should not be kinetically confused.

Finally, the undivided wave of proletarian force is also exemplified in the creation of the social commune, a form of organization defined by its attempt to create an undivided or relatively equalitarian social distribution outside or against the state. The form of motion of the commune is a wave in the sense that it aims to create a solidarity, or esprit de corps, that moves through and across the individuals in the social body. The commune occurs when the proletariat breaks free from the driven oscillations of profit, competition, and surplus and attempts to create an alternative society defined according to a relatively inclusive and egalitarian undivided distribution. The commune is a social movement that also proposes an alternative to the state.

The commune is, thus, a wave invention of the proletariat. The nomad invented a wave of solidarity, the barbarian invented a wave of maroonage, and the vagabond invented a wave of international rebellion. All of these previous undivided wave distributions continued into the modern period. But the proletariat adds to them the commune wave. The nineteenth century saw the emergence of alternative societies on a scale never seen before in history. The vast majority of these communes were created by proletarian migrants.

In particular, the United States provided the fertile ground for the realization of European theories of utopian community. "Immigrant groups," Rosabeth Moss Kanter writes, "found that by organizing utopian communities, they could maintain their distinctive culture even in the New World. . . . In one way or another, utopian communities of the 1800s participated in all major social movements of their time: revivalism, temperance, women's rights, free love, nonresistance, anarchism, socialism of the Owenist, Fourierist, Icarian, and even Marxist varieties."[40]

While the utopian theory of Robert Owen, Charles Fourier, Étienne Cabet, and others began in Europe, utopian practice flourished in America, largely by migrants. The surplus population of Europe immigrated to America because of expulsion, but they also desired to create a better world. Robert Owen was a successful owner of one of Britain's largest cotton-spinning enterprises, who inspired many American communes. Owen left Britain because he was disappointed by the slow rate of social improvement in his factory community (New Lanark), and in Britain generally. In 1824, he immigrated to America to start a utopian community in New Harmony, Indiana. Although this community lasted only a few short years, Owen's disciples founded other Owenite communities in Britain and the United States.[41] The communities aimed to create social and labor diversity, internationalism, equality, and agricultural communities.

The utopian writings of French political theorist Charles Fourier were also based on similar principles but emphasized the expression of passion by individuals. Several colonies based on Fourier's ideas were founded in the United States in the 1840s by Albert Brisbane and Horace Greeley. One of the most important goals of these communities was the elimination of the idea of a surplus population that was so characteristic of elastic force. "There should be no paupers and no surplus labor," Greeley writes; "unemployment indicates sheer lack of brains, and inefficiency in production and waste. . . . [O]nly in unity [of the laboring classes] can a solution be found for the problems of labor."[42] Surplus is based on division; thus, the solution to this problem is the undivided unity of the commune.

Another French utopian theorist, Étienne Cabet, inspired by Owen, wrote *Travel and Adventures of Lord William Carisdall in Icaria* (1840) in which he described an ideal communalist society. Cabet then led his followers to America, where they established a group of egalitarian communes (Icarias) during 1848 through 1898, based on a propertyless egalitarianism he called "communism." "Historically," as Kanter writes, "the greatest wave of community-building in America occurred in the late 1840's. . . . Between 1780 and 1860 almost a hundred known utopian communities were founded, with the peak of activity and membership from 1840–1860."[43]

It is, thus, no coincidence that after a century of migrant commune experiments that the proletarians of Paris joined together in 1871 to create an autonomous workers government against the state: the Paris Commune. "The proletarians of Paris," write the revolutionaries on March 19, "amidst the failures and treasons of the ruling classes, have understood that the hour has struck for them to save the situation by taking into their own hands the direction of public affairs."[44] The commune was created not to reform the ruling state but to create an alternative to it. It was meant to abolish inequality and social division and to establish the unity and rule of the propertyless proletarian majority. As Marx writes, "Working men's Paris, with its Commune, will be forever celebrated as the glorious harbinger of a new society."[45] Thus, the commune is not a mere social movement aimed at the capture of the state but a wave of unification that aimed to create an entirely new society that, as Alain Badiou writes, "broke with the parliamentary destiny of popular and workers' political movements."[46]

All over the world, communes have proliferated under the inclusive desire of migrants for a society without expulsion. After the abolition of serfdom in Russia (1861), the peasants formed self-governing villages called *Obshchina* (communes) to protect themselves against the expulsion of the tenant-debt structure and the privatization of common lands that often followed "setting free" the peasants (as occurred in England beginning in the seventeenth century and then France in the eighteenth). Thus, one of the central principles of the *Obshchina* was that no family could ever be deprived of land, house, or agricultural implements. The commune is the opposite of dispossession and expulsion. Not surprisingly, Russian philosophers like Mikhail Bakunin, Leo Tolstoy, and Alexander Herzen were inspired by peasant communes as the germ of a future free society.[47] As Marx writes,

Russia is the sole European country where the "agricultural commune" has kept going on a nationwide scale up to the present day. It is not the prey of a foreign conqueror [capital] and neither does it lead a life cut off from the modern world. On the one hand, the common ownership of land allows it to transform individualist farming in parcels directly and gradually into collective farming, and the Russian peasants are already practicing it in the undivided grasslands. . . . On the other hand . . . [the commune is able to incorporate] all the positive acquisitions devised by the capitalist system without passing through its Caudine Forks [i.e., undergo humiliation in defeat].[48]

The strength of the Russian commune, for Marx, is that it is able to incorporate certain technological advances without adopting capitalist relations of production.

In Palestine, migrant Jews created self-governing autonomous communes called *kibbutzim* (gathering). Between 1870 and 1920, more than 2 million Jews emigrated from eastern Europe because of anti-Jewish pogroms in the Russian Empire. As a migrant proletariat from Russia, approximately forty thousand Jews immigrated to Palestine in hopes of escaping persecution and of creating a better society. The czarist government even encouraged this emigration. In 1890, the czar approved the creation of the Society for the Support of Jewish Farmers and Artisans in Syria and Palestine, dedicated to creating Jewish agricultural settlements in Palestine. In 1910, the creation of the *kibbutzim* was inspired by communism and the Russian Revolution (which was partly inspired by the communism of the pre-Soviet *Obshchina*).[49] The aim of the *kibbutzim* communes was to provide access to land and egalitarian social relations for Europe's migrant Jews. They provided an undivided wave distribution without expulsion or surplus population.

During the Spanish Revolution of 1936, the Confederación Nacional del Trabajo (CNT; National Confederation of Labor) enacted a wide-scale collectivization of social life. After hundreds of years of enclosure and privatization, most land in Spain by the end of the nineteenth century was consolidated in large private estates (*latifundia*). Many peasants and farmers became rural or urban proletarian landless migrants working for private landowner enterprises as day laborers (*jornaleros*). During the Spanish Revolution, however, CNT militias made up of landless peasants, communists, anarchists, and international proletariat forces collectivized these lands with great success. Émigré lands were turned into rural communes based on equality, common property, and a labor-based credit system of exchange. Property owners were allowed to keep the amount of property they could work themselves, and the rest was turned into communes like those of Alcañiz, Calanda, Alcorisa, Valderrobres, Fraga, and Alcampel.[50] In addition to land collectivization, the CNT took over collective management of city halls, hospitals (such as in Barbastro or Binéfar), barber shops, grocery stores, and many other sorts of institutions.

These are only some of the more significant communes created by proletarian migrants in the nineteenth and early twentieth centuries. Although all these communes are quite different from one another, the kinetic form of their social motion remains similar. The social motion of the commune is an undivided wave distribution to protect against the elastic force of social expulsion and the creation of a surplus population.

Pressure

The pedetic force of the proletariat is finally defined by its creation of social pressure. If the form of kinetic counterpower of the nomad is predominantly defined by the raid, the barbarian's power by the revolt, and the vagabond's by rebellion, the form of power proper to the proletariat is resistance. Kinetically, to resist is to stand one's ground, stay back, or stop (*sistere*). Elastic social force compels the proletarian migrant to continually move according to the contractions and expansions of society. Thus, the proletariat's counterpower to this motion is to stop moving, to stay where it is.

Resistance is a form of social pressure, a ratio of continuous oscillation against a surface or barrier. Just as the English word "strike" has two meanings ("to move against or hit" and "to refuse to move"), so proletarian resistance similarly creates an artificial barrier or *blockage in social motion* and, in doing so, *moves against* the dominant form of social motion (territorial, political, juridical, or economic). Unlike centripetal, centrifugal, and tensional force, elastic force does not act directly on social subjects as passive objects or bind them to one or many centers of power. Rather, it simply drives and redistributes their "free" motions. Thus, proletarian resistance takes a different form from previous migratory forms of counterpower. Against the economic silent compulsion to move, the proletariat *refuses to move.*

This does not mean, however, that the proletariat refuses to move at all. Rather, the kinetic antagonism is between a driven oscillation and a free or continuous oscillation that moves according to its own diverse values. In this way, proletarian resistance can be expressed in many concrete tactics, but none more important than the "strike."[51] The first, and most obvious, form of the strike is the labor strike: the refusal to work. But the labor strike is not just a negative refusal to reproduce the dominant mode of elastic social motion (the production of surplus value). The labor strike has its own pedetic motion of free and continuous oscillation in the form of the labor association or the factory occupation. The proletariat does not just stop moving; it moves together in the picket line, the public demonstration, the occupation, and even the sit-in.

Accordingly, the social pressure of resistance is not just a metaphor. The refusal to move elastically (driven by the demands for surplus) literally stops the movement of products and people. The blockage of elastic circulation in one sector produces an increased demand for it in another sector. Pressure is the threat of a breakdown or explosion (in the factory, the field, the workshop) if movement is not resumed. The refusal to produce surplus poses a crisis for economic kinopower. In most cases, the goal of the labor strike is to literally increase the intensity of a demand for one thing (wages, working conditions, benefits) by increasing the demand for something else (the resumption of "normal" social motion in the form of their labor, products, services, profit).

A second form of resistance is the barricade, a transport strike that blocks the movement of people and things through the normal junctions of social motion. It creates a pressure or backup in the dominant social flows. The barricade is the "people's border" against power. The aim of the barricade is to make the streets, buildings, or bridges no longer yield to the elasticity of power but instead create a space of free proletarian movement: a pedetic pressure that forces power to move otherwise. Thus, the role of the barricade is not simply negative (to stop the movement of power); it is also positive in its construction of a temporary autonomous zone of motion. Strangers band together behind the barricades and create their own kind of social order, what Mark Traugott calls the "revolutionary culture of the barricade."[52] Hence, the barricade is a strategic blockage that allows for the possibility of another kind of social motion. Similar to the labor strike, the transport strike (barricade) has historical precursors elsewhere:

The year 1848 marked a turning point in two important respects: first, the barricade became a recognized component of a pan-European repertoire of collective action; and second, the barricade acquired a *symbolic* significance that increasingly superseded and displaced the pragmatic quality that had earlier defined its essence.[53]

In fact, Traugott argues, revolutionary migrants were "primarily responsible for the proliferation of this technique."[54] The international spread of "barricade consciousness" and revolutionary movements during the nineteenth century was largely due to the work of three types of migrants: students, exiles, and itinerant workers:

Students' ease of mobilization combined with their propensity to move across national boundaries and even to organize themselves on an international basis made them an effective vector of diffusion. . . . Political exiles . . . took full advantage of the diminished capacity of governments . . . to restrict their movements . . . [and] itinerant workers . . . joined political receptivity and geographical mobility with the strength of large numbers.[55]

Furthermore, the mobility of the proletarian migrant is reproduced in the material structure of the barricade itself. The barricade is a "mobile barrier." The French word *barricade* comes from the French word for barrel (*barrique*), because most of the early French barricades were made largely from barrels filled with bricks, mud, or dirt. A barricade is thus literally "an assemblage of barrels." The advantage of the barrel as a barricade material was (similar to the migrant) its ubiquity and its mobility. When empty, the barrel could be easily rolled into place and filled with heavy materials, becoming an instant solid barrier. The second most common barricade material was wheeled vehicles: for example, carts, wagons, coaches, carriages, cabs, brewers' drays, and omnibuses. These vehicles could be easily driven to a location, tipped over, and filled with heavy materials to barricade an intersection. "But when it was subsequently needed elsewhere, insurgents righted the vehicle and rolled it to a new location, where it could again serve as the foundation for a barricade."[56] A crowd in the rue Saint-Denis was even reported to have used a locomotive to make a barricade in June 1848.[57]

Other types of resistance include the hunger strike and the dirty strike (refusing to bathe or use toilets in prison), both of which follow the general kinetic motion of pressure previously discussed. Other tactics of social pressure, or what Tilly calls "pressure groups,"[58] include the international popularization of public demonstrations, boycotts, and petitions. Although not usually described as a strike per se, the predominant tactic of the public demonstration in the nineteenth century achieved something kinetically quite similar. The public demonstration is most often composed of a mass of people blocking a street, park, or public area. The mobility of the barrier is entirely that of the mob itself. Human bodies form the barrier of a demonstration or the potential strength of collective action. Sometimes they form a line (the picket line or the march); other times they form an asymmetrical gathering around a quasi-central point (the mass). The demonstration is a temporary strike from everyday activity to create social pressure.

The protest, the rally, the vigil, the occupation, and forms of public demonstration formed the basis of a new "repertoire of contention" that rose to dominance in the eighteenth and nineteenth centuries, according to Tarrow.[59] Instead of a directly violent action or social pressure intended to produce immediate breakdown, like burning down the lord's house or assassinating a tax collector, the public demonstration simply aims to "show" that a rupture may occur if the pressure is not relieved. This "showing" or "demonstration" creates a pressure without necessarily creating a rupture.

The petition follows a similar kinetic logic of social pressure but in a purely political capacity. The petition is a political strike: a blockage strictly in the reelection of a political figure. If the figure does not do as demanded by the petitioners, he or she will lose the petitioners' political support and favor. Although many types of strikes may occur as a result of an ignored petition, the petition is a strictly political barricade.

The boycott, like the petition and public demonstration, also gained international popularity in the eighteenth century. The boycott, however, is a consumption strike. As a type of resistance, it also follows the same kinetic pressure model as the demonstration and the petition. The boycott is not the immediate attempt to destroy or rupture an adversary but an attempt to show that if the undesired policies continue, a pressure may build to the point of rupture.

The pedetic pressure of the proletariat migrant, thus, takes the form of resistance. Resistance introduces a blockage into the normal flow of social motion to generate a pressure on the blocked flow. Pressure has kinetic social power because at a threshold of intensity, it threatens to rupture the dominant system of social circulation. In this sense, the labor strike, barricade, public demonstration, petition, and boycott are all forms of resistance and were also the predominant forms of proletarian counter-power from the eighteenth to twentieth centuries.

Conclusion

Part 3 has theorized the kinetic social force proper to the figures of the migrant: *pedesis*. Not only is the figure of the migrant defined as the expelled figure of social history, but the migrant also invents its own history of alternative forms of social motion. With the understanding of all five social forces that define the social and historical role of the migrant (centripetal, centrifugal, tensional, elastic, and pedetic), we can now use these concepts to understand the phenomena of contemporary migration. Since each historical age of the migrant does not replace but adds to the others, contemporary migration is by far the most complex.

PART IV

CONTEMPORARY MIGRATION:
MEXICO–UNITED STATES

CHAPTER 13

Centripetal Force and Land Grabbing

The Age of Globalization

Migration has become increasingly complex since the early twentieth century. There are presently more than a billion migrants worldwide, making the contemporary age of migration the largest and most global in history. Today, the conditions, directions, and figures of migration are not easily predictable or stable.[1] Economic deregulation and neoliberal development define much of contemporary migration since the 1970s.[2] Other factors include increased technological development in transportation (air travel, car culture, etc.) and communication (telecommunications and Internet), widening social and family networks, political transformation, and increasing environmental change. These recent changes have all been written about at length elsewhere.[3] But one of the key consequences is that all these social changes have given rise to an age of "hybridity" for global migration.[4] Today's migrants move more often, farther, and for more reasons than ever before. Thus, diagnosing contemporary migration requires a similarly hybrid theory of migration that can analyze the coexistence of multiple competing conditions and political subjectivities at once—no single framework will be sufficient in itself.

In the age of globalization, the traditional political categories that define the power of the nation-state are also being transformed by the increasing force of nonstate, transnational, and other organizations.[5] These organizations now provide many of the affinities, protections, services, and goods traditionally provided by state citizenship. Such organizations include *transnational entities* (the European Union and the Bolivarian Alliance in South America); *international entities* (the United Nations); *global entities* (nongovernmental organizations and the growing network of doctors, teachers, journalists, farmers, lawyers, and groups "without borders"); *economic entities* (private corporations and the World Trade Organization); and *activist entities* (the Alter-Globalization Movement and the world and regional social forums). Again, these hybrid forms of social organization have been written about at length elsewhere and pose complex challenges for the contemporary study of migration that this chapter will help sort out.[6]

Thus, the aim of the final part of this book is to deploy a hybrid theory of political analysis to the increasingly complex phenomenon of contemporary migration. The history of the migrant traced so far is not simply a history of the past; it is also a history of the present in which all of the historical conditions and figures of the migrant return and mix together. Not only do all of the kinetic conditions of expansion by expulsion (territorial, political, juridical, and economic) return and coexist in the present, but so do the figures of the migrant (the nomad, the barbarian, the vagabond, and the proletariat) and their pedetic forms of counterpower. In Part 4, I demonstrate the strength of the preceding kinetic social theory for understanding one of the most significant migratory phenomena in the contemporary world: Mexico-US migration.

Mexico-US Migration

Part 4 focuses on the Mexico-US migration for three reasons. First, Mexico-US migration is the single largest flow of migrants in the contemporary world.[7] Mexico has one of the largest migratory populations in the world, which includes internal migrants within Mexico and those who have left the country. Almost half of Mexico's population (50 million) has been displaced by poverty,[8] and more of the population from Mexico is living abroad than from any other country in the world (11 percent of Mexican citizens live in the United States).[9] Not coincidently, the United States has the largest population of immigrants in the world, 58 percent of whom come from Mexico. Mexican-US migration, thus,

articulates a wide and dramatic range of migratory conditions and figures for analysis.

Second, Mexico-US migration has produced the single largest
number of undocumented migrants in the world (more than 12 million).
Undocumented migrants, in addition to being subject to racism and
other forms of social discrimination, are subject to multiple and complex
forms of social expulsion (territorial, political, legal, and economic) to a
greater degree than legal migrants. The increasingly large population of
undocumented migrants in the United States thus illuminates better than
many other cases the harshest and most diverse set of social expulsions and
migratory resistances at work in contemporary migration.

Third, recent increases in Mexico-US migration are widely considered to be the direct result of the first big experiment in neoliberal economic policies like the North American Free Trade Agreement (NAFTA)
that have now been deployed around the world with similar results.[10] In
many ways, Mexico was the birthplace or laboratory of neoliberalism. In
the history of Mexico-US relations, we find a microcosm of the forms of
social expulsion that are now used around the world to ensure the expansion of powerful entities like the US government, the World Bank, and
transnational corporations. The process widely called "globalization"
or "trade liberalization" is a redeployment of many of the same types
of expansion by expulsion used to force migration throughout history.
Similarly, however, we are also witnessing today in the struggles against
neoliberalism the redeployment of historically familiar types of migratory
resistance. All of these can be found in this first great laboratory: Mexico.

Given the strategic significance of Mexico-US migration as a microcosm of contemporary kinopower, Part 4 is organized as a microcosm of
the whole book. The next four chapters analyze the contemporary redeployment of the historical types of social expansion by expulsion developed
in Part 2 (centripetal, centrifugal, tensional, and elastic forces). While the
empirical processes of contemporary kinetic social force are in some ways
different from those of their historical antecedents, they nonetheless express
the same kinetic *types* of forces. As Octavio Paz writes, "[I]n Mexico, the
past reappears because it is a hidden present."[11]

The final chapter of Part 4 diagnoses the contemporary redeployment of the historical types of social alternatives or counterpowers to

expansion by expulsion in the pedetic force of the migrant found in Part 3. While the historical figures of the nomad, the barbarian, the vagabond, and the proletariat are all unique to their times, they also express a certain kinopolitical type of counterpower that continues to reemerge and coexist in the present. The pedetic motions of continuous oscillation, waves, and pressure persist in the contemporary world under new names and social anatomies of counterpower. A global account of these motions is beyond the scope of this book, but the case of Mexico-US migration can provide us with a microcosmic guide for further diagnosis.

Centripetal Force

Centripetal force is an inward-directed motion that takes from the periphery and accumulates *toward* a center (without necessarily creating a single center). As a social force, centripetal motion emerged as the predominant type of social force alongside the first human territorial settlements of the Neolithic period. This process was defined by the general process of gathering the wild flows of the earth's waters, plants, animals, and minerals and accumulating them into relatively more central forms. Once this kinetic force emerges in the Neolithic period, it then reemerges throughout history—even if it is transformed or mixed with centrifugal, tensional, or elastic social forces.

The reemergence of centripetal social force can also be seen in contemporary Mexico-US migration. While unquestionably mixed with several other types of social motion, centripetal force in its most basic form remains a crucial condition for the expulsion of the Mexican people and the expansion of US and private power. Today, we call this "land grabbing."[12] But the grabbing (accumulating, consolidating, stockpiling) of large plots of land and raw materials has been around for a very long time (even if its agents, motives, and extractive technologies have changed dramatically). The social kinetics of grabbing are defined by the first dominant form of social expansion by expulsion: centripetal force. Grabbing is precisely the seizing of the outside and bringing it inward toward an increasingly central stockpile. But "land grabbing" is not an entirely accurate term for this process since territorial grabbing often includes a much wider accumulation of the earth's flows than just land into a territorial stock—like water, minerals, plants, animals, and genetic material.

Internal Expansion by Expulsion

Internal expansion by expulsion in Mexico has a long history. However, there are two major periods of centripetal force in Mexican history that have accumulated the flows of the earth into increasingly centralized territories while expelling a population of nomadic migrants.

The First Period of Accumulation: The Porfiriato

The first period is the Porfiriato, from 1880 to the revolution in 1911. Throughout the nineteenth century, much of Mexico's land was owned by the Roman Catholic Church and the indigenous population that lived and worked on communally owned lands called *ejidos*. When Porfirio Díaz became president in 1880, however, he began a massive centripetal land reform that confiscated the so-called unproductive lands of the church and *ejidos*. Díaz's liberal view was that communal landownership was an absolute obstacle to the efficiency and profitability that only private enterprise could bring (following Locke). Thus, his primary agenda as president of Mexico was to aggressively enforce the Lerdo Law, passed in 1856, which prohibited the ownership of real estate by "corporations" like the church and *ejidos*. The church was thus obliged to auction off all of its land except that used in day-to-day operations, and Indian villages were forced to convert their *ejidos* into individually owned plots.[13]

Once church and communal lands were deposed, they were aggressively acquired by new landowners: the *latifundistas*. Like all previous centripetal forces of territorial accumulation, the *latifundistas* accumulated the largest tracts of the most fertile land. This left the remaining indigenous owners of small plots unable to sustain themselves or compete against larger producers (like the situation of the first nomads). Subsequently, the rural and indigenous population was forced to become poorly paid seasonal workers, or debt peons, working and living on the newly centralized hacienda-style *latifundias*. During the Porfiriato, 96 percent of the rural population became landless.[14] In this way, the *latifundia* increasingly centralized the territorial accumulation of the earth's flows of water, cattle, minerals, sugar, coffee, cotton, and India rubber, which had previously been dispersed among indigenous farmers. Further, the government made tax-free agreements with foreign investors in mines. Between the French and the United States, almost all of Mexico's mines (including the El Boleo copper mine in Baja and the silver mines of Guanajuato) were owned by foreign investors.

The death of the *ejido* system, and the centripetal accumulation of land and labor, was compounded by a population explosion between 1875 and 1910 that increased the Mexican population by 50 percent. This population boom flooded the labor market, depressed wages, and inflated the cost of foodstuffs. As a result, hundreds of thousands of people were forced off their land and into the *latifundia* plantations, into the mines, or out of Mexico entirely on the newly (US) created railways.[15]

The international rail system was crucial to both the centripetal expansion of territory (water, land, minerals, plants, etc.) and the expulsion of an abandoned nomadic population sent wandering north into the United States. The international rail system between Mexico and the United States made it easier and cheaper for the United States to purchase, consolidate, and extract the resource wealth of Mexico. During the Porfiriato, US corporations came to own nearly all of Mexico's mineral and oil deposits, vast quantities of choice Mexican farm and pastoral lands, and some key industries. By the early 1890s, the United States was buying 70 percent of Mexico's exports, while Mexico bought 56 percent of its imports from the United States.[16] Mexico's 15,360 miles of railway, 70 percent of it US built, were essential to extracting and stockpiling Mexico's territorial flows. Handfuls of private owners made millions, while the majority of the population paid the price of Mexico's "golden age of economics": territorial expulsion and poverty.[17]

Migrants forced out of Mexico worked largely as nomads, continually following railroad contractual labor. After using Chinese workers for many years to work on the railroads, the United States decided that it did not want these workers to permanently immigrate. Mexican workers offered a cheaper and more deportable solution to the temporary US labor needs. Thus, the US government passed the Chinese Exclusion Act (1882), and displaced Mexicans became the nomad labor of choice. By

1900, between 70 and 90 percent of the track crews on the railroads of the southwestern United States were Mexican migrants.[18]

The figure of the nomad looks different throughout history. But what the Neolithic nomad has in common with the Mexican nomad of the early twentieth century is that the migration of both is the effect of being "left out" of the centripetal process of accumulation. The most fertile territory is consolidated around them, and the nomads are the ones left without enough to survive. They are not so much hunted down and directly expelled as largely abandoned by the centripetal force of land, water, and mineral consolidation. Accordingly, the nomads take up the most recent skills at their disposal and make new lives as seasonal workers: transhumants. During the Neolithic period, the nomad specialized in animal grazing, but during the contemporary period, the nomad specializes in seasonally paid agricultural and railroad work that Marx describes in *Capital* as the labor of the "nomadic population":

Nomadic labour is used for various building and draining works, for brick-making, lime-burning, railway-making, etc. . . . When they are not on the march they "camp." . . . The contractor himself generally provides his army with wooden huts and so on, thus improvising villages which lack all sanitary arrangements, are outside the control of the local authorities, and are very profitable to the gentleman who is doing the contracting, for he exploits his workers in two directions at once as soldiers of industry, and as tenants.[19]

The *traqueros* (Mexican railway workers) lived in shantytowns of old box-cars and mobile tent camps.[20] In the Neolithic period, the nomad is left out of the primitive territory to wander the mountains. In the ancient period, the nomad is again left out of the Roman *latifundia* to live in the mountains. In the modern period, the nomad is left out of the sheep enclosures. These historical points of centripetal expulsion are not kinopolitically different from the way in which the Mexican *latifundias* accumulated fertile land at the expense of nomadizing indigenous peoples.[21] Throughout history, the condition for the consolidation of large territorial accumulations is the centripetal expulsion of an aterritorial nomadic population. This continues today as the mountains continue to shelter migrants in the off season.[22]

This first period of centripetal consolidation of the earth's flows of water, minerals, plants, and animals via the dissolution of church and *ejido* land is responsible for the first major wave of Mexican immigration to the United States. This first wave of transhumant and railway nomadism lays the groundwork not only for the Mexican Revolution and the demand for the redistribution of *ejido* land but also for a reactionary period of centripetal force to again undo any gains in communal land-ownership won by the revolution. This first period of centripetal force remains crucial to understanding Mexico-US migration because, despite the revolution, most *ejido* land was never returned to the peasants.[23] What land was returned to them has been under renewed centripetal expropriation since the 1990s—initiating a second major wave of Mexican migration to the United States.

The Second Period of Accumulation: Neoliberalism

The second major period of centripetal force in Mexico is the neoliberal period from the 1990s to the present. Fourteen years after the revolution, Mexican president Lázaro Cárdenas (1934–40) began the process of land reform and nationalization demanded by the revolution, and many (but not even most) *ejidos* were reinstated. Immigration to the United States dropped significantly. However, after 1940, government policies began again to increasingly favor large-scale irrigated agriculture, disregard legal limits to individual land size, and offer subsidies for electricity, pesticides, water, and fertilizer that favored larger modern intensive farming methods. Again, millions of peasants were abandoned by the centripetal land accumulation and competition of large estates and fled to the mountains, railways, and transhumant seasonal jobs in the United States.[24] Their expulsion from the land is the condition of its centripetal accumulation in the hands of the few. The so-called Mexican miracle of economic expansion and industrialization expelled millions from their land and into poverty and migration.[25]

The most dramatic centripetal accumulation began after Carlos Salinas was elected president in 1989. Salinas launched the "Reform of the Countryside" in 1992 with three major changes to the constitution. First, the Agrarian Law allowed, for the first time ever, commercial associations, private investors, and stock companies to purchase *ejido* land and allowed *ejidatarios* the right to sell it to foreign investors.[26]

Constitutionally inalienable land became alienable in manifold ways explicitly to make way for foreign investment and large-scale land accumulation.[27]

The second major change was the 1992 Water Law, which cut almost all government water subsidies to farmers. Without water subsidies for irrigation, many migrant farmers cited high water prices as a primary reason for renting out their *ejido*. As Jessa Lewis demonstrates, withdrawal of government support and increased economic privatization resulted in *ejidatarios* renting out their land and migrating due to a lack of "capital to compete in a highly mechanized agricultural environment that favours land consolidation and large farm sizes."[28] Alongside these two laws were increased government subsidies for large-scale export agriculture and decreased ones for small farmers. Thus, while Mexico's spending on farming doubled between 2001 and 2008, employment in agriculture plummeted by 20 percent, from 10.7 million to 8.6 million workers.[29]

The third major change was that Salinas and his successors changed Mexico's mining laws to allow unlimited foreign investment in mining operations and eliminated all taxes on these operations. Between the two National Action Party (PAN) administrations (2000–2012), about 26 percent of the national territory was given to mining consortiums for their sole benefit.[30] Much of this land was *ejido* land or directly affected by the water consumption of the mines. For example, the Canadian mining corporation Goldcorp Resources was virtually *given* seventy-seven square miles by the federal government on which they opened two pit mines, filtered the gold using cyanide, and used 400 million cubic feet of water per year, completely depleting the aquifer that farmers depend on and then emptying the poisoned water into toxic ponds nearby.[31] The Grupo Mexico mining operation is destroying the city of Cananea.

The mine pumps water from about seventy wells. Cananea, with a population of thirty thousand, only has two or three. The mine is buying up land throughout this area, and now has more land than the town itself. They use it to dump the mine tailings, which have already buried part of the old town.[32]

Since 2006, "multinational companies have received over 80 federal mining concessions in just Oaxaca, covering 1.5 million acres of land. Mining is only the tip of the iceberg. Other mega-projects include hydroelectric dam construction, tourism and infrastructure, energy generation projects, water privatization, and oil exploration."[33]

These land reforms and the centripetal accumulations or grabbings (of agriculture, water, oil, gold, etc.) that followed have turned millions of Mexicans into nomadic migrants. It is no coincidence that after the passage of these reforms, and others required by NAFTA, that Mexican emigration reached a scale never before witnessed in its history. Mexican immigration to the United States tripled from 600,000 per year in 1990 to 1.8 million per year in 1995.[34] And these numbers do not even include internal migrants who moved to the cities or ran away to the mountains in Mexico. Today's Mexican nomads carry their homes on their backs and sleep in temporary tent cities in places like Sonoma and northern San Diego Counties. They sleep in trailers and cars in the fields and in the mountains outside towns all over the United States during harvest season.[35] The nomad marches and camps, as Marx says.

Within Mexico, Grupo Mexico builds barracks, called *colectivos*, for its nomadic strikebreakers on mine property in Cananea. The company picks up workers, transports them to work, and brings them back at night, completely controlling their mobility. In the United States,

most farmworkers in North Carolina live in labor camps, which are like small company towns where workers depend on the employer for housing, transportation, and food. Almost all those surveyed complained of problems like dilapidated barracks, inadequate showers and toilets, lack of heat or ventilation, and insect infestations, no breaks.[36]

On the west coast, Sierra-Cascade Nursery picks up Mexicans in Nogales, Mexico, and transports them on buses for 24 hours without food, lodges them in county fairgrounds and warehouses, works them according to a high-quota labor system, underfeeds them, pays them minimum wages, and ships them back home.[37]

In all of these cases, migrants expelled by the centripetal forces of territorial accumulation in Mexico make up a nomadic population of temporary, landless, seasonal, aterritorial, and highly mobile labor.

CHAPTER 14

Centrifugal Force and Federal Enforcement

Centrifugal force is an outward-directed motion that uses the power of an accumulated center in order to expel from, or to, its periphery. As a social force, centrifugal motion emerged as the dominant form of social motion alongside the first political societies of the ancient world. The creation of the first cities organized by a central political leadership (kings, emperors, priests, despots) is kinetically defined by the concentric resonance of a central and superior point over its subordinate territories. The state deploys various mechanisms for enforcing obedience, taxation, slavery, transportation, public works, and military conquest. Just as centripetal force does, once centrifugal force emerges in the ancient period, it continues to reemerge throughout history, including the present.

While centripetal force largely "leaves out" the nomad from territorial accumulation, centrifugal force brings the inside and the outside into a hierarchical resonance around a center. Thus, "the barbarian" is the name that designates a specifically *depoliticized* inferiority in relation to a central state.

Internal Expansion by Expulsion

Inside Mexico, the centrifugal force of the central government expands its range of power over social motion in several ways.

Liquidation and Eviction

The centrifugal force of the Mexican state expands its central-ized force (the polis, the politicians, police, policies, and plebeian citi-zens) by the direct expulsion of indigenous farmers from public lands and the reappropriation of their labor by other means. The centralized liquidation of land and people is accomplished through direct state interventions. The Mexican government has practically given away millions of acres of public lands to private companies for the devel-opment of mega-projects like mines, hydroelectric dam construction, tourism and infrastructure, energy generation projects, water privati-zation, and oil exploration.[1] The effect of these mega-projects is the destruction of the land, the depletion of water resources used by farm-ers, wide-scale poverty, and the mass dispossession of people from the land.[2] It is no coincidence that Oaxaca, one of the poorest states in Mexico (75 percent live in extreme poverty), also has one of the larg-est concentrations of mega-projects (eighty federal mining concessions covering 1.5 million acres of land), has some of the highest rates of dis-placement/migration in Mexico (662,000 per year in 2000), and con-tains 20 percent of all indigenous people in Mexico.[3] Displacement is concentrated in the Sierra Norte and Valles Centrales regions, site of the Capulalpam and San José del Progreso mining projects, as well as the Mixteca mining project.[4]

Contemporary liquidation and eviction share two kinopolitical characteristics with ancient expulsion. First, both engage in the direct removal of peasants from their homes by centralized political force. In both cases, the state claims the right to use violence because it is the central power to which the peasants are subjected. The justifica-tion and legitimation reside in the central administration. Second, the expulsion of the peasants from their land is done so with the aim of creating a larger public work, or state-subsidized mega-project, that supersedes the lives of the individual peasants. In both cases, the grounds for violence as a means come from the political center, and the mega-project (roads, mines, waterways, etc.) appears as a superior end to which its violence is directed.

Police and Military Violence

Political kinopower also uses direct police and military violence to expel migrants. When peasants will not migrate or sell their land "voluntarily" to these state-sponsored mega-projects, a centrally directed police and military force is sent out from the city to directly expel people from the territory. For example, when the Canadian company Fortuna Silver Mines began mining in San José del Progreso, the residents complained that the mines were using "more water in one hour than an entire family uses in one year," destroying their agricultural livelihoods; that dynamite blasts were damaging their homes; and that their cattle were dying after drinking contaminated water. When the federal government ignored the complaints, the town residents occupied the mine. After a forty-day blockade of the Trinidad mine in the Oaxacan community of San José del Progreso, "mine representatives and municipal authorities called in a 700-strong police force that stormed into the community in anti-riot gear, along with an arsenal of tear gas, dogs, assault rifles, and a helicopter."[5] Residents were beaten, arrested, and their homes illegally searched.

In addition, the Mexican military is guilty of numerous expulsion-motivated indigenous massacres over the last twenty years. In 1995, seventeen peasant activists were shot and killed by state police in Aguas Blancas, Guerrero.[6] In December 1997, a massacre led by a paramilitary group composed of members of "the local PRI, armed and trained by state policy and an ex-soldier from the Mexican army" killed forty-five Tzotzil people who refused to leave their home village in Acteal, Chiapas.[7] The Tzotzil were sympathizers of the Zapatistas—an indigenous revolutionary movement in resistance against neoliberal expulsions. In August 1999, approximately thirty-seven thousand troops "surrounded three [indigenous pro-Zapatista] communities which have a combined population of no more than 500," in order to expel the indigenous people from their communities.[8]

Military forces have now taken up permanent residence in rural indigenous communities.[9] In the poorest migrant states in Mexico (Chiapas, Oaxaca, and Guerrero), local, state, and federal police forces are now under military control. The Public Security Police use "army vehicles, weapons, and tactics but have blue [police] uniforms instead of green

[army]."[10] Just like the centrifugal force of ancient militaries, the Mexican military is launched from the center capital over the territory through a vast network of road projects created for the purpose of controlling transportation and subordinating the territories from the center. Once the periphery is expelled, the state can appropriate their property and migrant labor—expanding its social force. The kinetic goal, then and now, is the same: the centralized control over the transportation and social motion of the people across the territory.

This police-military process receives hundreds of millions of dollars in US aid under the premise of fighting drug cartels and continues (with President Obama) to ignore Mexico's human rights violations. In fact, in an unguarded moment, Thomas Shannon, the Bush administration's top diplomat for the Western Hemisphere, admitted that Washington was in the process of "armoring NAFTA."[11] And the Obama administration has not made any changes to this policy (the Merida Initiative). Thus, the centrifugal power of the government is expanded the more it expels the part of its population at the periphery.

Depoliticization

The third mechanism of centrifugal expansion by expulsion in Mexico is the creation of a depoliticized and barbarian migrant population. Historically, the barbarian is defined according to three political incapacities: (1) the inability to speak the *language* of the political center (Greek); (2) the inability to use the *reason* of the political center (*logos*); and (3) an excessive geographic *mobility* in relation to the political center (polis). All three are realized in Mexico's "barbarians."

First, Mexico's migrants are disproportionally indigenous farmers who frequently do not speak the language of the political center (Spanish). Mexico's indigenous languages are not sufficiently represented in political speech, government documents, and legal records. In Mexican politics, this linguistic difference is largely treated as a natural political inferiority that justifies not having to respect indigenous negotiations. For example, the Mexican government continues to ignore the 1996 San Andrés Accords that President Ernesto Zedillo signed in negotiations with the Zapatista Army of National Liberation. The agreement granted autonomy, recognition, and rights to the indigenous population of Mexico. These agreements were translated into ten indigenous languages and were all ignored by the Mexican government.[12]

Second, indigenous communities are not allowed full participation in state affairs. This is the case, in part, because there is an implicit understanding that indigenous peoples have a more primitive "apolitical" system of decision making that cannot work within Mexican politics. Indigenous people, it seems, have their traditions, but Mexico has the political rationality of the state and does not need to respect the decisions and community leaders of its native peoples who lack the proper *logos*.[13]

Third, Mexico's indigenous and migrant population is perceived to be an inferior and apolitical population insofar as it expresses an excessive mobility and geographic distance from the political center (Mexico City). In the same way that the Greeks viewed their neighbors as barbarian because of how mobile they were and how far away they were, Mexican politics today similarly depoliticizes its most remote indigenous populations who live in the mountains and jungles of the southern states by defunding government provisions for their water, food, housing, education, electricity, and health care. Further, those who have been expelled from their state or country as migrants have an inferior or secondary political status in Mexican politics as well.

These three aspects of historical barbarism continue today to justify the depoliticization of indigenous people in Mexico, and the centrifugal power of the state continues to expand by expelling the migrants of its periphery.

External Expansion by Expulsion

Just as the central authority of the Mexican state has actively expanded its executive, police, and military power through the expulsion of its rural and indigenous population, so has the US government expanded the central power of its federal immigration enforcement agency with the executive aim of "prevent[ing] all un-lawful entries, by any means necessary."[14] Given that there are currently more than 12 million undocumented migrants in the United States, this is a very ambitious project. This centrifugal force thus deploys three major kinds of quasi-military "operations."

Anti-Migrant Operations

The first centrifugal strategy of federal expansion by expulsion is Operation Secure Communities, which fosters cooperation between local law enforcement and federal immigration officials. Kinopolitically, it uses central (federal) authority to bring its peripheral (local) authorities into a shared resonance around a center point of enforcement. In particular, this operation requires local law enforcement to turn over to federal agents the fingerprints of anyone with whom they come into contact.[15] Centralizing these fingerprint databases and searching them for immigrants, Operation Secure Communities led to the detention of hundreds of thousands of migrants with no criminal record who were apprehended simply because they were undocumented. In this unique operation of directing central immigration enforcement over its radial localities, the Obama administration deported over a million people in the first two years.[16]

The second strategy is Operation Wagon Train, which used federal immigration enforcement agents to raid local workplaces looking for undocumented immigrants. Kinetically, it directly deploys centralized (federal) force to control the subordinate movements of peripheral workplaces through raids. Operation Wagon Train culminated in the largest workplace raid in US history in December 2006 when the Immigration and Customs Enforcement (ICE) officers raided six Swift & Company packing houses.

Some 1,282 workers were detained by hundreds of heavily armed I.C.E. agents in military garb. Afterward, Homeland Security secretary Michael Chertoff openly linked the raid to the administration's reform proposals. At a Washington, DC press conference he told reporters that raids would show Congress the need for "stronger border security, effective interior enforcement and a temporary-worker program."[17]

In 1999, Operation Vanguard conducted similar raids using Social Security databases to find discrepancies among the 24,310 workers in forty Nebraska meatpacking plants (17 percent quit, were fired, or arrested). And again, in 2001, raids dubbed Operation Tarmac targeted airports around the country, leading to the firing and deportation of hundreds of mostly food-service workers.[18]

The third major anti-migrant operation is Operation Gatekeeper, which began in 1994 (not by coincidence, the year NAFTA went into effect) as a massive federal project to build walls through border cities and increase the number of Border Patrol agents. Kinetically, this operation was used "as a central component of a national strategy," as Joseph Nevins writes,[19] to direct central (federal) force to control and direct all movement entering and exiting its outermost territory. Operation Gatekeeper marked the beginning of the next twenty years of increased federal border enforcement on the southern border (from 3,747 agents in 1994 to 18,516 in 2012),[20] as well as the creation of the 2006 Secure Fence Act to build a continuous wall across the two thousand–mile US-Mexico border. A 2013 Senate bill was passed proposing to increase patrol numbers to 37,716—which would make it approximately twice the size of the Federal Bureau of Investigation (FBI).[21] In order to build the wall, dozens of laws were suspended by executive (central) power.[22] Interestingly, however, the border fence has had little or no demonstrable effect on deterring unauthorized migrants, according to the US government's own reports.[23]

Furthermore, the success rate of unauthorized migration, on the second or third try, remains upward of 95 percent, according to immigration scholar Wayne Cornelius.[24] On the other hand, the wall has had the highly demonstrable effect of increasing the number of deaths of border crossers. Building a wall at popular border-crossing locations has diverted migrants into more treacherous areas such as deserts, rivers, canals, and rugged terrain, resulting in more than 6,000 deaths along the border (continually increasing from 1994 to 2008).[25] The year 2012 alone marked a 27 percent increase in border deaths (477) from the previous year.[26] No doubt these numbers will continue to increase as the US government continues to spend billions of dollars developing the wall's reach. It is thus difficult to interpret this gross violation of human rights as anything short of a centrally directed military violence against Mexican migrants.[27]

Mexican Barbarians

This brings us to a final point: the barbarism of the migrant in the United States. There are three shared kinopolitical characteristics between the ancient and contemporary Mexican barbarian.[28]

First, Mexican immigrants are perceived by many in the United States (including the government) to have a negative impact on the states. It is for this same reason that the entry of barbarians in the Greek polis,

Roman Empire, and even in ancient Sumer was carefully restricted. In the United States, and in the ancient empires, large military-style walls were built and guarded to control the movement of undesirable foreigners into the community. The reasons for the undesirability of their respective foreign populations vary in each society, yet all these centrifugal powers are associated with massive wall projects. Significant portions of US and ancient societies also found these populations of foreigners undesirable because they would have a negative impact on the "culture" of the host country—yet barbarians were also required as manual laborers to support that culture. In part, it is the language of the immigrant's culture that is perceived as inferior or incompatible to the host's language (Hellenic/English). This matches Aristotle's first key characteristic of barbarism: the inability to speak the language of the political center. Anti-immigrant discourse in the United States is filled with rhetoric about Mexican immigrants who cannot or "refuse to" learn English and whose populations are changing the "American way of life."[29] Both contemporary and ancient societies believed that these immigrations were not benign but constituted a political and military "invasion" that required a military response (walls, deportations, military operations).

In the United States this concept was reanimated in popular and political discourse by Samuel Huntington in his 1996 book, *The Clash of Civilizations*, to explicitly describe the "Mexican immigrant invasion" of American civilization.[30] For the last fifteen years or so, right-wing author Patrick Buchanan,[31] along with others,[32] has been popularizing this political concept of "barbarian invasion" for conservative audiences in the United States. It seems to be catching on, given the way that recent Central American child refugees to the United States are being discussed in the media and treated by the government.[33] Buchanan writes:

History repeats itself. After the Roman republic spread out, Rome became a polyglot city of all creeds and cultures of the empire. But these alien people brought with them no reverence for Roman gods, no respect for Roman tradition, no love of Roman culture. And so, as Rome had conquered the barbarians, the barbarians conquered Rome. In the 5th century, beginning with Alaric and the Visigoths in 410, the northern tribes, one after another, invaded and sacked the Eternal City. And the Dark Ages descended. And as Rome passed away, so, the West is passing away, from the same causes and in much the same way. What the Danube and Rhine were to Rome, the Rio Grande and Mediterranean are to America and Europe, the frontiers of a civilization no longer defended.[34]

Buchanan argues that the decline of the United States and the decline of Rome are both due not so much to the strength of the "invaders" (barbarians and "illegal immigrants") but to the so-called Christian generosity of "emperor Valens, who has his modern counterpart in George W. Bush,"[35] which has been taken advantage of as migrants are allowed to cross the border. Buchanan's historical parallel is deeply disturbing on many levels, since Rome has always been the go-to model for Western imperialism from Napoleon to Hitler.[36] But the comparison with the United States is true in many ways—just not in the ways Buchanan thinks.

In 376, an "incalculable multitude" of barbarian refugees arrived at Rome's Danube border,[37] asking for asylum from the Huns. But the reason Valens eventually helped them cross the river was not "generosity" but power and greed: he required them to be enlisted in the Roman army and pay heavy taxes in exchange for land, grain, and protection.[38] As they crossed, many drowned.[39] Corrupt Roman soldiers allowed barbarians to keep their weapons if they sold their wives and children into prostitution and slavery.[40] Once they arrived on the other side of the river, they were put into deplorable refugee camps where Ammianus describes the exchange of Gothic slaves for dogs to be eaten as meat.[41] Food was insufficient, and the barbarians were never given the land, grain, and protection they were promised. Instead, thousands starved to death, watched their younger children die, and their wives raped or sold into slavery or prostitution for food. Finally, the barbarians were so desperate and dispossessed that they revolted.[42] "In this way," as Ammianus writes, "through the turbulent zeal of violent people, the ruin of the Roman empire was brought on."[43]

There is a contemporary parallel to this in Mexico-US migration. Mexican migrants are frequently recruited in Mexico by American corporations with the promise of a good wage, food, and the American dream (land, protection, etc.).[44] If they arrive, they are promised the possibility of a pathway to citizenship through military service in one of the foreign wars in which the United States is engaged.[45] But many of those who try to cross illegally die because of the US-Mexico border wall (more than six thousand have died since 1994).[46] Mexican migrants pay the *coyotajes'* exorbitant fees to smuggle them across the border, and the *coyotajes* in turn bribe US officials and others to get them across. Sometimes, however, the *coyotajes* kidnap their clients, rape them, or sell them to human traffickers. Once on the other side of the river, migrants are caught—taken from their families and put in a detention camp, where more than 107 migrants' deaths have been covered up by ICE since October 2003.[47] Or the migrants get a job and are often cheated by their employers, who charge them excess fees for their transport, pay them less than they promised, physically abuse them, and generally take advantage of their partial or lack of status. Migrants work some of the hardest and most slavish jobs in the United States and still live below poverty. ICE raids on elementary schools take migrants' children away from them. Migrants are also frequently deported away from their children, who then grow up in poverty. Without legal means of work, migrants are more likely to end up in the underground economy of prostitution, drugs, and so forth. This is the real historical parallel between the United States and Rome. The question now is, "When will the empire fall at the hands of a migrant revolution?"

The second shared kinopolitical characteristic between the ancient and contemporary barbarian is that significant portions of the population of the United States believe that immigrants are naturally inferior, as they did in ancient empires. Although the idea of a natural political inferiority was invented and came to dominance in the ancient world, it repeats itself again and again throughout history and mixes with other mobile subjects to varying degrees. Thus, if it is true that many mobile subjects have also been treated as naturally inferior, it is precisely because this political idea was first invented and incarnated in the ancient barbarian and then redeployed historically. Hence, the persistence of the term "barbarian" throughout all of history to designate one's cultural and political enemies as "naturally inferior."[48] Nazi propaganda described migrant Jews as "uncivilized oriental barbarians,"[49] and the nineteenth-century French bourgeoisie described migrant peasants in Paris as "savage barbarians."

Today, this ancient political idea of the natural inferiority of some persons is repeated by the United States against Mexican migrants, using terms such as "invasion," which directly refers to migrant barbarism as a security threat. To the degree that this type of American racism exists against Mexican immigrants today, a "new barbarism" is being constructed by people like Buchanan. Following in the style of Roman greed, if barbarian immigrants today are allowed entry into the United States, it is precisely under the condition of a highly restricted mobility proper to their servitude to citizens. As George W. Bush emphasizes, "Latinos [as a race] have a strong work ethic that will strengthen our country."[50] In the case of the ancient empires, this would have meant slavery or forced labor. In the United States today, Mexican barbarians are instead subject to the "slavelike" conditions of historically slave-labor occupations (agricultural, domestic, and janitorial work) as undocumented or guest workers.

As a 2007 Southern Poverty Law Center report on temporary migrant labor shows,[51] there are several slavelike features of guest-worker programs in the United States: (1) workers are bound by legal contract to a single employer without the ability to work anywhere else; (2) contracts are entirely under the control of the employer and can be terminated at any time, resulting in the deportation of the worker; (3) workers are often cheated out of their low wages and threatened by employers or labor brokers who seize their documents; and (4) workers are often forced to live in squalid conditions and denied medical benefits for on-the-job injuries.

Most Americans do not consider immigrant labor to be "like slavery." However, many immigrant rights groups make a political point to describe their conditions as "slave labor." Charles Rangel, of the House Ways and Means Committee and founding member of the Congressional Black Caucus, describes the US "guest-worker program [as] the closest thing I've ever seen to slavery."[52] And even historically, former Department of Labor official Lee Williams described the old Bracero Program— the guest-worker program that brought thousands of Mexican nationals to work in the United States during and after World War II—as a system of "legalized slavery."[53] Mexico-US immigration is often explained by the volunteerism of desperate migrants, but poverty alone is not a sufficient explanation for large-scale undocumented immigration.[54] One must also consider the recruitment agenda of many US companies that actively facilitate the flow of cheap (and undocumented) labor from Mexico to the United States (another feature shared with ancient centrifugal power).[55]

The third characteristic of the ancient barbarian still active today is political disenfranchisement. According to Aristotle, the barbarian lacks the *logos* or mental capacity for (Greek) political engagement. In the ancient world, barbarians could not become citizens and had no right to vote or engage in politics. Today's migrants are similarly expelled from political life. They do not have the right to vote and are not represented politically. Whatever explanations are offered for this disenfranchisement, the fact remains that governmental, legal, and popular discourse remains committed to the depoliticizing terminology of calling undocumented migrants "illegals."[56] Never before in history has such a large group of people been labeled as "illegal people" in this way.[57] As a technical or legal term, the word is entirely void of content. No being is, in itself, criminal. Only acts can be criminal, according to most Western constitutions.[58] However, as a political tool, "illegality" is used rhetorically to dismiss non-status people and their activism as apolitical in a way similar to that of the Greek rhetoric of "barbarism" (i.e., something about the "type of their being" is apolitical).

CHAPTER 15

Tensional Force and Illegal People

Tensional social force expands social motion by increasing confinement linkages between new objects and expels by breaking links with older objects. Tensional force emerged as the dominant form of social kinetic force alongside the linked rotation of feudal suzerainty and its innumerable layers of subinfeudation. Instead of one big empire or state, feudalism "was never focused in a single centre," as Perry Anderson argues. "The functions of the State were disintegrated in a vertical allocation downwards, at each level of which political and economic relations were, on the other hand, integrated." This new form of social circulation thus produced a new dominant force of motion, "a dynamic tension . . . within the centrifugal State."[1] This dynamic tension was held by a vast system of contracts and customary laws.

The tensional expulsion of the vagabond is created by the dissolution of juridical linkages: a release of social contracts. The "vagabond" is the name of the migrant whose status is specifically *criminalized* in relation to an expanding system of local, state, national, and international law. The strategic reemergence of this historical social force can be seen in contemporary Mexico-US migration in the following ways.

Internal Expansion by Expulsion

Contemporary tensional force is created by the rise of multiple legal powers: international, supranational, humanitarian, and corporate law that now poses entirely new limitations on the executive power of sovereign governments. Today's tensional forces that bind social motions, although no longer feudal, still take the form of a vast network of legal contracts binding at every level of society: between individuals, local law, states, nations, and other nonstate international organizations.

Reform of the Countryside

In the case of Mexican migration, several juridical forces whose tensions used to give people the right to the land have now been broken and replaced with new links that allow for people's expulsion and the centripetal accumulation of the land by private companies. In particular, Mexican law has increasingly diminished the centrifugal intervention of the state and increased the tensional force of private and international contracts over the last twenty years. The first major postrevolutionary tensional transformations occurred after Carlos Salinas was elected president in 1989.

First, the Mexican constitution had previously protected the hereditary right of people living on *ejido* land to retain their land indefinitely and forbade the renting or selling of this land. In 1992, Salinas abolished this tensional right with the Agrarian Law, which made it possible for common and public lands controlled by the state and its people to be sold off to foreign investment and large-scale land developers. And they were.[2]

Second, Mexican law had previously protected the people's right to subsidized water costs. This allowed farmers to subsist and even compete on the market. In 1992, this law was abolished and replaced with the 1992 Water Law that provided subsidies favoring larger farms.[3] Alongside this law were other kinds of government subsidies for large-scale export agriculture and decreased subsidies for small farmers.

Third, Salinas and his successors eliminated all taxes on mining operations. The tensional force protecting public land and its occupants was thus abolished and replaced with a new law that largely reduced the state's centrifugal power (to collect taxes, to limit foreign investment, etc.) and increased contractual rights to private and foreign investors.

NAFTA

The second major tensional transformation binding social motion is the North American Free Trade Agreement (NAFTA). Mexico adopted a host of laws, a binding set of legal links between international actors, that reduced the power of the state to regulate movement and made trade easier for private corporations to profit through international trade. In particular, the implementation of NAFTA on January 1, 1994, brought the immediate elimination of tariffs on more than half of Mexico's exports to the United States. Within ten years of the implementation of the agreement, all Mexico-US tariffs would be eliminated except a few US tariffs. In effect, NAFTA reduced the Mexican state's tax revenue and thus its ability to provide social and civil support for its population. At the same time, it allowed large, powerful corporations to outcompete Mexican companies in their own country and in the world market. As a result, the United States was able to dump large amounts of highly subsidized corn and other agricultural products into Mexico, outcompeting Mexican farmers and driving them to poverty, debt, renting and selling of their *ejidos,* and finally, migration.[4] NAFTA eliminated tensional tariffs that bound the motion of the Mexican people to the land (through social services) and hurled the people into migration. According to the World Bank, the poverty rate in Mexico jumped from 35 percent (1992–94) to 55 percent (1996–98) after NAFTA took effect as a result of "the 1995 economic crisis, the sluggish performance of agriculture, stagnant rural wages, and falling real agricultural prices."[5] As a consequence of poverty, annual emigration tripled.

The new tensional linkage of NAFTA also "allows companies to sue governments for cash compensation if a country implements legislation that 'expropriates' the company's future profits."[6] For example, when the American waste management company Metalclad was ordered to be closed "by local officials on the grounds that it was not environmentally sound,"[7] Metalclad filed suit under NAFTA's Chapter 11, claiming that government actions were "tantamount to expropriation" and discriminated against it as a foreign firm. In the end, the Mexican government was forced by international law to pay around $15 million in damages. In this case and others, international legal contracts like NAFTA undermine local rights, national sovereignty, and government's ability to protect health and the environment, *producing migrant expulsions.*[8]

Free-Trade Zones and the Maquiladoras

The third major tensional transformation of social motion in Mexico is the creation of free-trade zones (FTZs), areas of intensive social kinetic readjustment—where old tensions that held the people and land under the control of the centrifugal state are increasingly broken and replaced with new private legal contracts. These contracts are based on reduced or no land fees, government subsidies, tax breaks, waivers, no export duties, and unrestricted circulation of foreign currency. The Mexican government negotiates these privately made legal frameworks for certain areas in Mexico to provide incentives for private companies to extract profit with little or no fiscal possibility of intervention from Mexico.

The manufacturing operations in these free-trade zones in Mexico, *maquiladoras*, are factories that import material and equipment free of tariffs in order to assemble, process, or manufacture them for export. As David Bacon writes,

In a desperate attempt to generate jobs and revenue for debt payments, the government encouraged the growth of *maquiladoras*, the foreign-owned factories on the northern border. By 2005, more than three thousand border plants employed more than two million workers making products for shoppers from Los Angeles to New York. In 1992, they already accounted for over half of Mexican exports, and in the NAFTA era, became the main sector of the economy producing employment growth.[9]

Any kinetic tensions that may limit mobility, labor, or land use in these areas or might discourage investment are broken and replaced with new tailor-made legal frameworks defining the maquiladoras as "in-bond" plants—kinetically "bound" by law to their US "twin."

Once the power of the centrifugal state has been diminished through the reduction or elimination of taxes, the enforcement and regulation of these zones diminish, resulting in unenforced government protections for workers and the environment. In this way, workers are either immobilized under these new private labor contracts or driven to migrate elsewhere under increasingly criminalized conditions. For example, women make up the majority (60 to 80 percent) of *maquila* labor and are often hired illegally (with forged documents) at ages twelve to fourteen. In violation of Mexican federal labor law, they are regularly tested for pregnancy to screen out women who will need maternity benefits.[10] The right to unionize and collectively bargain are federal rights in Mexico, but in practice this is not enforced in the maquiladoras. For example, in 2002, seafood workers in Santa Rosalía denounced the Maquila Hanjin and Brumar for numerous violations to labor law, child labor law, and basic human rights, but ninety-six of them were subsequently fired for trying to form a union.[11] Workers are paid $3.40 an hour, which barely covers the cost of food in the area. Some maquiladoras lack proper waste management facilities and the ability to clean up disposal sites, which leads to disposing of hazardous waste illegally. Without taxes in these areas, the Mexican government often cannot afford to regulate this dumping. This has led to polluted rivers and contaminated drinking water. Further, since the government cannot pay for proper sewage treatment infrastructure, all of the streams and rivers in the border region have been devastated by the *maquila* industry.[12] All of this leads to further migration North.

Just as commutation in the Middle Ages severed the previous laws binding the serfs to the soil in order to rebind their motion as tenant farmers and criminalized vagabonds, so the social kinetics of FTZs sever old legal bonds with the state and introduce new private ones to regulate the social motion of migrant workers under harsher and increasingly criminalized conditions.

Colonias

The expansion of private legal contracts like FTZs causes expulsion of people from local and federal legal protections and results in their direct criminalization as vagabonds. Since the companies in these FTZs are not required to pay local taxes, the cities have no funds for basic residential infrastructure or social services for the workers. Thus, makeshift residential areas such as *colonias*, or slums of "criminal squatters," have emerged in the canyons surrounding the factories. Hundreds of thousands of *maquila* workers have been forced to build shanty houses from pallets on often undeeded land. In Tijuana, one of the largest maquiladora sites, over 50 percent of all new housing is in *colonias*. Similar to Mexico City, over 60 percent of the city's population lives in irregular settlements. Since taxes are not collected to pay for infrastructure, the *colonias* also have inadequate access to safe drinking water and sanitation. They are overcrowded, poorly built, located near garbage dumps and industrial pollution zones, and the people have no secure title to the land.[13]

The *colonias* are also home to large numbers of poor rural migrants from all over Mexico hoping to find work in Tijuana or Southern

California, without the money to afford adequate housing. Many may try to cross illegally into the United States, and those who fail or are deported will likely end up homeless in Tijuana. When political action is called for, the Mexican state strategically enforces anti-vagabond "cleanup" laws. Vagabond migrants are then subject to all manner of criminalization by local and federal enforcement: they are arrested and expelled from the city for "charges of vagrancy, begging, and trespassing";[14] the *colonias* are routinely raided by local police to demonstrate their "crack down on crime";[15] and even *colonias* built by developers (without proper infrastructure) do not offer a deed of trust to legally protect residents. If a buyer falls behind in his or her payments, the property is repossessed, often within forty-five days, without going through the traditional foreclosure process.[16] Thus, even when migrants pay rent, they remain expelled from their legal rights. They are again thrown into vagabondage. The same *limpieza social* (social cleaning) is happening in Ciudad Juárez, Guadalajara, and other towns with large populations of deported and homeless migrants.[17]

External Expansion by Expulsion

Vagabond migrants legally expelled from Mexico by the dissolution of the old juridical tensions that held them in place are expelled again when they enter the United States. The network of juridical tensions in the United States also expands its legal apparatus through the expulsion of vagabond migrants. In fact, much of contemporary immigration law in the United States and the United Kingdom is directly inspired by the earlier anti-vagabond legislation of the thirteenth to nineteenth centuries.

The History of Vagabond Laws in the United States

Vagabond or vagrant laws are juridically unique. While most crimes are defined by actions, vagrancy laws are defined by states of being. This language is already at work in fifteenth-century English legal documents directly naming *criminal types of persons*, such as "vagabonds," "beggars," "homeless," "jugglers," and "minstrels." Similarly, in France, vagabonds were named by the law but made by the action of the arrest, not by the action of the "criminal." As Tim Cresswell writes on the figure of the tramp, "[T]he threat of the vagabond and the tramp is a virtual threat, for they have not committed any crime above and beyond that which makes them a vagabond or a tramp." The criminalization of vagabonds is thus anticipatory. "The 'crime' of vagrancy," Cresswell continues, "is importantly not a quality of an act a vagrant commits but a consequence of the application of rules and sanctions to an offender. Law and legal definitions created the legal type vagrant."[18] Vagrant laws are based on personal condition, states of being, and social and economic status. The criminal vagrant is the one who "looks like" he or she may commit a crime. Thus, anti-vagabond laws are some of the most flexible tools for criminalizing all types of socially undesirable migrants.

In fact, some of the first immigration laws in the United Kingdom were explicitly anti-vagabond laws. For example, in 1824 the Vagrancy Act forbade the landing of any foreigner who was "deemed a rogue and vagabond within the meaning of the Act." "In view of the similarities between the poor laws and early immigration norms," Ana Aliverti argues, "it is no coincidence that the first comprehensive immigration legislation in 1905 penalized the unauthorized landing of immigrants with the penalties imposed on 'rogues and vagabonds' and vagrancy was one of the grounds for expulsion of foreigners from the British Isles."[19]

Following England's lead, the United States Congressional Select Committee in July 1838 reported that immigration rates were a threat to the "peace and tranquility of our citizens" and classified immigrants as "paupers, vagrants, and malefactors . . . sent hither at the expense of foreign governments to relieve them from the burden of their maintenance."[20] Accordingly, the 1917 Immigration Act explicitly excluded "vagrants."[21]

Vagrant laws were also used to racially criminalize internal "foreigners" and to enforce the California Greaser Act of 1855 that directly discriminated against Mexicans. The law defined a vagrant as "all persons who are commonly known as 'Greasers' or the issue of Spanish and Indian blood . . . and who go armed and are not peaceable and quiet persons."[22] Vagrant laws were also used in the post–Civil War South to require blacks to obtain licenses, "certificates of good character," from whites before doing business; to take children from "unfit" black parents and gave them to white masters; and to prohibit black immigration until 1865.[23]

Given the intentionally (and etymologically) "vague" nature of vagrancy laws in the United States, the US Supreme Court eventually declared a Florida state statute unconstitutional in February 1972 on the grounds that its terms were not sufficiently explicit to inform those subject to it what conduct would render them liable to its penalties. Since 1972, laws under the title of "vagrancy" have slowly disappeared from the books, replaced with a host of related anti-migrant laws against "loitering," "riotous activities," "the obstruction of streets and side walks," "camping," "sitting/lying in public places," "panhandling," and "begging."[24] Although these laws are more clearly directed at criminalizing actions, they are still flexibly enforced and specific to the actions typical of vagabonds.

Vagabond Laws Today

Contemporary US immigration law remains influenced by the historical criminalization of migrant vagabonds. For example, Arizona SB 1070 (Support Our Law Enforcement and Safe Neighborhoods Act) requires all aliens over the age of fourteen who remain in the United States for longer than thirty days to register with the government and to have their registration documents with them at all times—violation of this law is a federal misdemeanor crime. In the United States, the inability to present immigration documents or having an expired visa was previously not considered a criminal offense but a civil infraction, like a speeding ticket. Now, SB 1070, and numerous attempted copycat laws in the United States (in Utah, Indiana, Georgia, Alabama, and South Carolina), have tried to make one's status, not any particular action, a criminal offense. Furthermore, SB 1070 requires state law enforcement officers to determine an individual's immigration status during a "lawful stop, detention or arrest" or during a "lawful contact," *not specific to any activity*, when there is reasonable suspicion that the individual is an illegal immigrant.[25] Without reference to any specific activity, how is an officer supposed to suspect that someone's visa is overdue? In this way, SB 1070 and laws like it are part of the history of "vague" anti-vagrancy laws that use profiling techniques to criminalize a target population of migrants.

The historical legacy of immigration and anti-vagrancy law is also clearly expressed in certain popular and political rhetoric about immigrants in the United States. For example, South Carolina representative and supporter of SB 1070 Jeff Duncan has made the connection quite clear:

It's kind of like having a house . . . taking the door off the hinges and allowing any kind of vagrant, or animal, or just somebody that's hungry, or somebody that wants to do your dishes for you, to come in. And, you can't say, "No, you can't come in." And you can't say, "No, you can't stay all night." Or, "No you can't have this benefit, using my deodorant."[26]

Although critics are quick and right to point out the derogatory animalization of immigrants in this comment, they were not as quick to point out the inherent criminalization of immigrants implied by the term "vagrant." Vagrancy is not just a derogatory term like "animal"; it is a term with a very specific legal and often racist history of (unconstitutional) criminalization of migrants that is now being reanimated in US politics.[27] Today's migrants are the criminalized heirs of medieval vagabondage.

The Criminalization of Work

Not only is migratory status increasingly becoming a criminal offense in the United States, but so is the basic (and largely necessary) activity of work. The criminalization of work in the United States takes anti-vagabondage legislation to a new level. Today, forced labor is illegal and workhouses no longer exist, but the labor conditions of undocumented and guest workers are the contemporary equivalent. The goal of English anti-vagabond legislation was not just to put vagabonds to work (even if there was no work); it was to pressure them into undesirable low-wage work. Today, the goal is the same even if its explicit punishment is no longer whipping and branding. The true effect of criminalizing the migrant's right to work is not "self-deportation" (as US enforcement hopes) but rather that migrants will work illegally for cheaper wages, under more dangerous conditions, without benefits or collective bargaining—in conditions much closer to those in English workhouses than to those of most professional jobs in the United States. Thus, the creation of oppressive and fragile tensional linkages like guest-worker programs leads to their breakage and the expulsion of undocumented workers from the protections of the law altogether.

The criminalization of work for undocumented migrants in the United States is a recent invention. Prior to the Immigration Reform and

Control Act (IRCA) passed in 1986, workers could be detained for being in the United States without a visa, but hiring undocumented workers was not a crime, nor was working itself.[28] However, in the last ten years the United States has launched a dramatic series of immigration enforcement "operations," supported by new legislation that criminalizes not only undocumented labor but also strategically targets the "identity theft" of migrant workers giving false Social Security numbers to their employers. During the Bush administration, worksite enforcement cases jumped from 850 in 2004 to 4,940 in 2008. In Mississippi, under SB 2988, an undocumented worker holding a job now faces felony charges carrying one to five years in prison and fines of up to ten thousand dollars.[29]

The social kinetic insight here is that the criminalization of undocumented migrant labor is actually a way of controlling social motion. Criminalization forces migrants into increasingly confined and oppressive work relations. The criminal status of migrants is used as leverage to control their mobility within low-paid and hyperexploited labor. As David Bacon writes,

The very industries they target for enforcement are so dependent on the labor of migrants they would collapse without it. Instead, immigration policy and enforcement consign migrants in those industries to an "illegal" status, and this undermines the price of their labor. Enforcement becomes a means for managing the flow of migrants, and making their labor available to employers at a price they want to pay.[30]

Another way of criminalizing work and controlling migrant flows is through the highly restricted tensional links of one kind of work: guest-worker programs. From the Bracero Program (1942–64) to Bush's H-2A visa program, the United States has had a long history of using guest workers from Mexico.[31] Interestingly, in both cases, the result has actually been an increase in criminalized motion: undocumented migration and labor.[32] This is the case because guest-worker programs restrict migrant kinetics to employment with only one company and for a limited period (one to two years), after which migrants must return to their country of origin. Thus, workers have no leverage to negotiate wages or conditions and can be deported at the discretion of their employers. Guest-worker visas do not lead to permanent residence and are limited to a certain number of people per year. These restrictions lead to increases of migrants overstaying their visas, breaking these restrictive kinetic links, or finding undocumented work elsewhere. Furthermore, a 2007 report by the Southern Poverty Law Center documents extensive abuses of workers under this visa program. No one gets overtime, the report says, regardless of the law. Companies charge for tools, food, and housing. Guest workers are routinely cheated.[33]

Detention and Expulsion

Not only does tensional force in the United States expand its specifically juridical control over the status and labor of the criminalized migrant, but it also aims to maintain direct control over as much criminalized movement as possible. The aim of tensional expansion is to increase its jurisdiction over social motion through the legalized detention and expulsion of vagabonds. One of the interesting paradoxes of immigration law, however, is that the more laws there are, the more criminal migrants there are; the greater the need for more laws and enforcement, the more criminals there are; and so forth. This is the same kinetic juridical logic operative during the expansion of tensional social force in the Middle Ages during the Inquisition. The more tensional force expands its network of laws, the more people will be found in violation of these laws, and the more need for detention and processing facilities. When legal tensions are dissolved, vagabonds appear, and criminal detention centers emerge. Even "regularization programs," as Peter Nyers writes, "always budget for significant increases in resources for monitoring, apprehending, and deporting failed applicants."[34]

As in the anti-vagabond and Inquisitorial apparatus in the Middle Ages, the purpose of criminalizing migrants is another way of rapidly "cleaning up" the streets and expanding the force of law. But the expansion of law and its linkages also increases incarceration. As US immigration law has expanded, so has the juridical apparatus for detaining and expelling migrants. Once undocumented migration is criminalized, it begins to pose a uniquely legal problem for the United States: 12 million people live without the same legal rights and protections as everyone else in the country. Yet legal equality and political equality are the founding ideas of liberal law in the United States. This tensional antagonism of tolerated illegality can be reconciled in two ways: either the law can be adjusted to include these people, or it can be expanded to detain and expel these people. The United States has chosen the latter.

The force of law has expanded its powers of expulsion in what Arizona calls "Operation Streamline," the creation of special courtrooms where those caught by the Border Patrol are criminally prosecuted en masse. According to the Spanish news agency EFE, this court process convicted 5,187 migrants from January 14 to June 10, 2008.[35] Unfortunately, many of these migrants are indigenous to southern Mexico and do not even speak Spanish. There is no legal support in Mixtec or Zapotec languages.

Accordingly, the force of law has expanded its powers of detention as well. The detention circuit can begin from the crossing of migrants, but it can also pick up from a territorial or political expulsion. Instead of being quickly deported, migrants are harnessed into a detention junction: the prison, detention, or camp junction. Instead of migrants being turned back at the border and deported, the flow of migrants is now harnessed and used to expand the tensional force of the courtroom, prison, and detention center. The detention center, as a junction, is also a vehicle that harnesses or extracts a negative mobility from the migrants in their nonpublic circulation: "the streets are clean."

The truth of this drive toward tensional expansion can be witnessed in the fact that more than half of migrants in detention do not even have a criminal conviction. "Of the detainee population of 32,000, 18,690 immigrants have no criminal conviction. More than 400 of those with no criminal record have been incarcerated for at least a year."[36] Conviction has become secondary to the more primary process of applying criminal charges, arresting, detaining, and expelling migrants. In other words, just like the Inquisition and vagabond laws, the process of criminalization is about much more than conviction. It is also about the expansion of kinetic social power over criminalized movement. The detention system that housed 6,785 immigrants in 1994 holds nearly five times that number in 260 facilities across the country in 2015. The US Congress has even doubled the budget dedicated to incarcerating immigrants since 2003 to now over $1.7 billion.[37]

Furthermore, many female migrants are criminally charged for status or work violations but then monitored with ankle bracelets so that they can care for their children while they await their trial. "They can't work, they have no way to pay rent or buy food, their husbands or brothers are in prison or deported, and they're being held up to ostracism in this tiny town," says Luz Maria Ramirez, who headed the support network for forty-eight braceleted women at Postville's St. Bridget's Catholic Church.[38] Once the maximum degree of mobility has been extracted from this migrant flow (sometimes many years of detention), migrants are deported. Once deported, the circuit can begin again or pick up like a relay into another circuit.

CHAPTER 16

Elastic Force and Neoliberalism

Social elasticity is the force that quickly redistributes itself to fill a deficit or displace an excess to avoid social decline or collapse. As a social motion, elasticity emerged as the dominant form of motion alongside the modern oscillating (expanding and contracting) forces of the population, food supply, technology, transportation, and the capitalist market. But elasticity is more than the mere oscillation of the social field; it is the driving force that redistributes (expands and expels) a surplus of motion to produce an equilibrium. Kinetic social surplus is motion above and beyond the requirements for basic social reproduction. It is a motion that when not needed, can be reserved, and when needed, can be deployed.

Elastic force expands and expels not by creating and breaking juridical tensions between social motions but by creating and redistributing a surplus of motion elsewhere. As long as a society is capable of producing and mobilizing its surplus and deficits, it will be able to achieve an equilibrium and hopefully expand. Thus, elasticity expands and expels, not from the outside to the center (centripetally), nor from the center to the outside (centrifugally), nor by rigid links between centers (tension), but by the redistribution of a surplus wherever it is needed.

Internal Expansion by Expulsion

The most recent sequence of elastic social force in Mexico begins with the expansive force of the Mexican miracle.

Social Expansion in Mexico (1940s–1970s)

From the 1940s to the 1970s, Mexico's population, food supply, technology, transportation, and economic value expanded dramatically. This was all made possible by Mexico's "stabilizing development" (kinetic equilibrium) policies based on stabilizing prices; maintaining a fixed exchange rate between the peso and the dollar; providing energy and government services to industry at low prices; the government investing heavily in roads, irrigation works, and social services; and using foreign credit and foreign investment to complement domestic savings.[1] Mexico thus sustained economic growth of 3 to 4 percent and modest 3 percent inflation annually from the 1940s until the 1970s.[2]

This growth was invested in efficient social programs that reduced the infant mortality rate and increased life expectancy, as well as commitment to primary education for the general population from the late 1920s through the 1940s. The enrollment rates of the country's youth in school increased threefold during this period; consequently, when this generation was employed by the 1940s, their economic output was more productive. Additionally, the government fostered the development of consumer goods industries directed toward domestic markets by imposing high protective tariffs and other barriers to imports. "Thanks to increased agricultural prices, more government credit, and government spending on highways and irrigation, agricultural production increased by 52 percent between 1940 and 1944."[3]

In 1938, Mexico nationalized its oil industry, which fueled the expansion of roads, agriculture, and industry. Even the *ejido*, despite its decreasing subsidies, remained an important aspect of Mexican agriculture. In 1960, 34 percent of agricultural production, as measured by value, came from the *ejido*. "Yield per acre for corn and beans produced on *ejidos* was virtually the same as the yield on large private farms."[4] Even the mining industry in the early 1960s was increasingly nationalized.[5] Between 1940 and 1970, Mexican per capita gross domestic product increased more rapidly than that of the rest of Latin America, the United States, and the world.[6]

This was Mexico's industrial and urban revolution. Industrial expansion through public investment in agricultural, energy, and transportation infrastructure caused cities to grow rapidly during these years as employment shifted from agricultural to industry and service jobs.

The government set guarantee prices for crops, subsidized agricultural credit, food for urban dwellers, and farm inputs such as fertilizer. Between 1970 and 1981, there was a 4.8 percent annual increase in job creation. The combination of rapid job growth, social programs, and government support for labor resulted in wealth becoming more evenly distributed during the 1970s. Those living in poverty declined from 75 percent of the population in 1960 to 48 percent in 1981.[7]

The expansion of roads, services, and industry was even more dramatically fueled after 1974 by the discovery of massive petroleum reserves in Veracruz, Baja California, Chiapas, and Tabasco (8 percent annual economic growth). Mexico further subsidized oil extraction by taking out large international loans between 1977 and 1980.[8] Mexico wagered its internal expansion on its ability to pay back its loans with the value of its oil.

Social Contraction in Mexico (1980s)

Unfortunately, in the early 1980s, the price of oil fell, and Mexico went into debt. The world price of oil, which had reached a peak of more than eighty dollars per barrel in 1979 during the energy crisis, decreased during the early 1980s to thirty-eight dollars per barrel. Falling oil prices, rising interest rates, and inflation caused capital flight. The sudden contraction of the price of oil also caused Mexico to devalue the peso at least three times during 1982 to try to pay back its loans.[9] This had a disequilibrating effect that rippled across the country. The contraction of the peso also contracted the value of real wages and caused inflation. By 1982, Mexico declared that it could no longer pay its debts.

During the 1980s, 400,000 jobs disappeared, while at the same time the labor force increased by 8 million. Few jobs replaced those lost since both public and private investment declined. Those living on wages fared worse than those living on rents and property, thus worsening income distribution. Not only did income become less evenly distributed but there was also less to distribute as the per capita GDP declined by 10 percent between 1982 and 1987. The proportion of the Mexican population living in poverty increased from 68.5 percent in 1984 to 73.4 percent in 1989. By 1990, the average Mexican's calorie intake approached half of that recommended by the World Health Organization.[10]

Redistribution of Surplus in Mexico

Every social kinetic contraction is followed by the creation of a surplus. In contrast to theories of classical economists such as Adam Smith, equilibrium is not necessarily achieved through the expansion and contraction of the price mechanism (supply and demand). Rather, as Joseph Schumpter argues, equilibrium is never attained since everyone is always trying to take advantage of the price system in order to expand the economy.[11] Thus, the surplus is what is left over from the expanded motions that have contracted. In order to achieve equilibrium again, the surplus must be redistributed to accommodate reduced social and economic mobility.

In Mexico, this is achieved in two main ways. First, Mexico privatized major productive sectors of its economy. With the fall of the peso, Mexico's public industries, services, and land had now effectively become unproductive surplus. By selling off the vast social and industrial apparatus it had built (such as railroads, power plants, banks, water supply and treatment facilities, mines, telephone systems, and roads),[12] Mexico hoped to reestablish a kinetic equilibrium of employment, population, agriculture, industry, fuel, and debt payments. After the contraction of oil prices, Mexican president Miguel de la Madrid (1982–88) initiated the drive to privatize some 1,156 government-owned corporations, declaring, "Public enterprises must be profitable and must not constitute a burden for the people of Mexico who have so many needs which we have not been able to attend to because of a lack of resources."[13] Pressures from foreign governments (holding the debt) and companies interested in investing led to some of the first neoliberal "structural adjustments": demands that all public services and industries return a certain profit. But privatization also led to job loss. Foreign companies often lowered wages, hired non-Mexican workers, and fought unions aggressively. Without adequate severance pay, unemployment benefits, retraining, and job-search assistance, Mexican workers were forced to migrate north.[14]

Second, "surplus" agricultural and manufacturing goods were redistributed by export. Between 1991 and 2001, exports increased by more than 300 percent, but formal employment in the export sector increased by less than 50 percent.[15] Agricultural imports soared from $1.8 billion to $19.3 billion between 1982 and 2007, thus exporting agricultural production while importing agricultural products.[16] The effect of exporting agricultural production was that thousands of farmers growing corn and other crops could no longer compete with many US farmers and began raising cattle, which requires fewer workers and thus increased unemployment and migration. Migrants were either redistributed to the northern Mexico border to work at export maquiladoras or into the United States. The annual growth of the maquiladoras increased from 47 percent in 1989 to 86 percent in 1994, as Mexico desperately exported its products at cheap prices to pay back its debt.[17]

Third, the surplus population was redistributed in the form of proletarian migrant workers to the United States. Once Mexico could no longer support its surplus population, it redistributed them elsewhere. A portion of the wages of these proletarians was then sent back to Mexico in the form of remittances, which were then used to support migrant families and ultimately to establish equilibrium in the Mexican economy by offsetting the cost of federal health care, education, housing, and other social costs. Remittances to Mexico from US residents have steadily increased from $10 billion per year in 2000 to $27 billion per year in 2007.[18] Even after the remittances began to decline after 2007 (due to the US recession), remittances still make up 2 to 3 percent of Mexico's GDP: the second-largest source of national income, behind oil.[19] Thus, Mexico continues to have a vested interest in maintaining the surplus redistribution of migrants and their remittances. As Raul Delgado Wise, professor at the University of Zacatecas, argues, "[R]ather than a free-trade agreement, NAFTA can be described as . . . a mechanism for the provision of cheap labor. Since NAFTA came into force, the migrant factory has exported [millions of] Mexicans to the United States."[20] With respect to the elastic force of surplus redistribution, human migrants from Mexico are just another export commodity in Mexico's elastic equilibrium of social motion.

External Expansion by Expulsion

As Mexico socially contracted (low wages, reduced social services, unemployment, devalued currency, and liquidation of its lands), the

United States socially expanded. Now that Mexico's publicly funded projects, export manufacturers, and population had become relatively surplus (in relation to its contracted state), the United States and its companies were able to expand their range of kinopower by purchasing all of these surpluses at very cheap rates—while also raising the interest rates on Mexico's debt.

Privatization

While Mexico redistributed an intensive surplus of public land, export industry, and emigrants, the United States accumulated it as an extensive surplus of private land, import industry, and immigrant labor. Unlike intensive surplus, which emerges through an elastic contraction of social motion, extensive surplus is accumulated through an elastic expansion. In this case, foreign countries bought up Mexico. Extensive surplus appears on the scene as if from nowhere as a devalorized excess to be put to work when and where it is needed. Land, industry, and migrants arrive in the United States as an apparent devalorized surplus to be redeployed according to the needs of social valorization.

This is accomplished in three ways. First, the extensive surplus of devalorized land in Mexico appears as an investment opportunity for US companies when there is a need to redistribute a monetary surplus. Second, the extensive surplus of devalorized industry and agriculture (as exports) arrives in the United States according to the requirements of US valorization (high volume, low prices) regardless of its consequences for Mexico (poverty, internal migration, environmental destruction, etc.). Given their status as relative intensive surplus (worth next to nothing), Mexican land and industry appear as a surplus above and beyond the basic requirements of US homeorhesis. When there is demand for cheap industrial and agricultural products, the United States is free to buy and even direct the output of this surplus from abroad (via US-owned maquiladoras).

Guest-Worker Programs

Third, Mexico's intensive human surplus of migrants is treated in the United States as an extensive surplus of devalorized cheap labor. Historically, the kinetic management of this surplus motion has taken the form of the guest-worker program. When an extensive surplus is needed, it can be brought in to support a social expansion. When expansion is no longer needed, migrant workers can be expelled—following the social motion described by Marx and recounted in Chapter 6. The expansion of US guest-worker programs is directly correlated with the social expansions and contractions of US kinopolitics. For example, from 1870 to 1930, Mexican migrant *traqueros* were recruited and trained in large numbers by the United States to expand its social motion via railways. However, during the Great Depression (1930s), when their labor was no longer needed, five hundred thousand Mexicans were expelled or pressured to leave during the "Mexican Repatriation."[21] During World War II, when a wartime labor surplus was needed again, the Bracero Program (1942–64) was established to provide manual agricultural laborers.[22] Later, when President Kennedy believed that the workers "adversely affect[ed] the wages, working conditions, and employment opportunities of our own agricultural workers,"[23] the program ended and the migrants were again expelled.

More recent history is no exception. Beginning again in the 1980s and 1990s (a time of high demand for construction, agricultural, and low-skilled service jobs), the United States expanded and elaborated the most restrictive guest-worker program to date. In 1986, the Immigration Reform and Control Act (IRCA) divided guest (nonimmigrant) workers by issuing H-2A and H-2B visas. The H-2A program enables farm owners to apply to the Department of Labor to bring in "low-skilled laborers" for agricultural work. The H-2B program is for nonagricultural workers. In both cases, this work must be temporary (one year at a time), seasonal, and restricted to a single employer with no chance of permanent immigration. Current proposed legislation, the Border Security, Economic Opportunity, and Immigration Modernization Act of 2013, calls for the creation of W-visas with more protections for workers but also for a lower cap on visas. The same elastic principle applies. Beginning with the US recession in 2008, over a million migrants were expelled in the first two years of President Obama's administration. Guest-worker and nonimmigrant visa programs take advantage of an extensive surplus population who is willing to be paid low wages for temporary work without the possibility of permanent immigration. The guest-worker program thus functions as a juridical flow regulator to the elastic demands of US valorization.

Undocumented Migrant Workers

The United States also deploys a complementary form of economic expulsion of workers from their labor power: the use of undocumented labor. Although policy makers argue that guest-worker programs are meant to be alternatives to undocumented migrant labor, in reality, they actually facilitate it. Highly restrictive guest-worker programs bring migrant workers in for only a few years. When their contract is complete, rather than return home, workers (still compelled by poverty) choose to remain in the United States without documentation. Many continue working illegally for the same employers but for lower wages and with greater precarity. Thus, the Bracero Program did not, as predicted, reduce undocumented migration. For example, during 1942–64, 4.6 million braceros were admitted, and 4.9 million undocumented migrants were apprehended—many more were not. The "failure" of the Bracero Program as an alternative to undocumented migration thus inspired the launch of Operation Wetback in 1954, which deported 1.1 million Mexicans, including US-born citizen children of braceros,[24] many of whom simply reentered the United States after expulsion.

However, the guest-worker program is a failure only from a tensional perspective—since it encourages de facto breaks in the links of the law. From an elastic perspective, undocumented migrants have always been, and continue to be, the more preferred and flexible form of migrant proletariat. From the perspective of employers and the kinetic redistribution of surplus labor flows, guest-worker programs are flimsy juridical excuses to bring an arbitrarily capped number of migrant workers to the United States and give employers legal recourse to expel undocumented workers at will. The cheaper the wages, the fewer benefits, the fewer labor rights, and the more precarious the term of contract, the more elastic the contraction and expansion of the migrant surplus. Undocumented labor is just more elastic and thus more responsive to the demands of employers, markets, and changing social conditions. Undocumented workers are the migrant proletariat par excellence. They are more purely propertyless since they are denied the right to own property, not de facto but de jure, and they are reduced to nothing more than a kind of bare life since their territorial, political, legal, and economic status has been completely stripped. Thus, as we would expect to find, almost half of all undocumented migrants in the United States entered legally with work visas but stayed to work illegally.[25] In this way, tensional and elastic forces work together to create a criminal population without labor rights (expulsion) in order to redistribute them as surplus labor power according to the needs of US valorization (expansion).

CHAPTER 17

Pedetic Force and Migrant Power

Just as contemporary migration is produced by the forces of social expansion and expulsion, so it is also defined by the pedetic counterforces of oscillation, waves, and pressure. Social pedesis is the irregular movement of a collective body: a social turbulence. It is the force of motion of the social figure who moves outside the dominant forms of social motion: the migrant.

With regard to Mexico-US migration, there is an explicit public and legal acknowledgment of this pedetic force in the popular rhetoric— the "migrant flood."[1] In *Brown Tide Rising*, Otto Santa Ana collects all the words used to describe migrant movements between June 1992 and December 1994 in the *Los Angeles Times* during a debate over California Proposition 187 (a bill to prohibit undocumented migrants from using health care, public education, and other social services in California).[2] Of the total descriptors used to describe Mexican migrants, the dominant type (58 percent) was that of "dangerous waters": floods, tide, sea, influx, flow, waves, drowning, porous, swelling, absorbing, funnel, surging, pouring, streaming, swamp, pool, safety valve.[3] Santa Ana explains the significance of these descriptors:

Moving water is a fluid. Above all other characteristics, fluids are normally understood and measured in terms of volume and mass, not units. . . . The everyday use of such noncount words reflects a mobile energy. Water moves, and when placed under pressure cannot be compressed, but forces its way or is channeled in some direction. This dynamism implies kinetic and hydraulic power, and control

of the movement of water also requires power. . . . Greater volume and movement of water imply greater need for safeguards and controls.[4]

The popular discourse on migrant motion as "dangerous waters" is not
unique to the *Los Angeles Times* but can be found throughout American
newspapers and media over the last twenty years, most recently in the arrival
of Central American child refugees into the United States.[5] In fact, as Part
3 of this book has argued, the concept of "dangerous waters" (associated
with irregular oscillations, waves, and pressure) is a fundamentally pedetic
concept that can be traced throughout the history of migration. The fluid
and turbulent force of migration is not a new discovery. Societies have
always feared the turbulence and irregular movement of migrants and have
described them in the same fluid terms.

    Another study has documented this same dominant description
of migration as "dangerous waters" in the legal discourse of the US
Supreme Court.[6] In this study, the author argues that the legal designation of migrants as a "flood" attributes three distinct characteristics to
them: a direction (oscillation), a form (wavelike), and a force (of pressure).
The US Supreme Court defines the oscillating direction of this flood as
a *"northbound tide* of illegal entrants into the United States." It defines
the wavelike and oceanic form of the *"vast tide* of illegal immigration"
into the United States as creating "law enforcement problems of *titanic
proportions.*" "The immigrant waves described in Supreme Court opin-
ions appear as foreboding bodies that submerge everything in their path,
including American culture." And the Supreme Court defines the force of
these oceanic wave-tides as putting pressure on the border and country.
As the author of the study states: "Just as levees attempt to hold back large
bodies of water, the border is presented as a fragile dike that might burst
at any moment, given the pressure coming from the alien flood." "The
entire system," the Supreme Court says, "has been notably unsuccessful
in deterring or stemming this *heavy flow*; and its costs, including added
burdens on the courts, have been substantial.' '[T]he flow of illegal aliens
cannot be controlled effectively at the border.'"[7]

    The migrant flood is more than a metaphor. The force of migrant
motion is literally a social pedesis akin to the hydrokinetic motion of
irregular oscillations, waves, and pressure.[8] But what the authors of these
studies miss is that pedesis is not a normatively "bad" force. It appears as a

negative one only in popular and legal discourse as a result of thousands of years of certain dominant forms of kinetic social control (centripetal, centrifugal, etc.). The contemporary political task of the migrant is not radically different from what it has been historically: to redeploy its pedetic forces against those of social expulsion. Migrant pedesis today is thus a mixture and redeployment of the four historical figures of the migrant: the nomad, the barbarian, the vagabond, and the proletariat. Let us examine each in its contemporary Mexico-US context.

The Nomad

The nomad is the migrant who is abandoned by centripetal expulsion and who *abandons* the territory to create a life on the road. Nomads are not only chased out; they desert. But their exodus always comes up against a territorial limit. When it does, their pedetic force takes the form of "the raid." The primary motive of the raid is not violence or war but survival.

The contemporary Mexico-US nomad is the seasonal worker: today's transhumance. Instead of moving their cattle from winter to summer pasture, these nomads move their tents, RVs, vans, and trucks back and forth across the border to gather resources that have been centripetally accumulated by expulsion.

Today, the nomad's form of kinetic counterpower is still the raid. Mexican migrants cross the border to gather resources and hopefully return home. If violence or conflict occurs along the way, it is not the primary aim of the raid: violence is only a secondary consequence of the raid. Today, as historically, the raid appears as theft only from the perspective of the true thieves: those who have centripetally accumulated, fenced the earth into territories, and excluded others. It is only because of this initial theft of fertile pastureland that the nomad's own resources appear not be their own (simply because they are not there for part of the year).

The kinetic counterpower of the raid is thus expressed today in groups like the Border Angels, Humane Borders, and the Electronic Disturbance Theater (EDT). These groups are composed of volunteers dedicated to helping migrants survive the seasonal hazards of crossing the Mexico-US border by providing them with food, water, maps of water stations, cell-phone coverage, emergency telephone numbers, clothing, supplies, free legal advice, directions—key items for survival. The Border Angels and Humane Borders have created hundreds of rescue stations along the border to distribute this aid, and EDT has created a Transborder Immigrant Tool (TBIT) using a hacked cell-phone GPS system to provide migrants with a handheld map of all the water stations, highways, places where migrants have died, and so on. With summer desert temperatures as high as 127 degrees and winter temperatures below freezing, the border wall is increasingly pushing migrants into dangerous, classically nomadic areas (deserts and mountains). The Border Angels and the network of safe houses created to help migrants survive their travel facilitate migrant mobility across the desert in search of fertile pastures. The Border Angels and safe houses (*casas de migrantes*) are effectively part of the raiding party. These rescue stations and safe houses, much like nomads themselves, appear and disappear (oscillate) according to the weather, season, the Border Patrol, and shifting zones of construction along the border.[9] Nomadic groups and their allies share a common social bond or wave in their mutual aterritoriality or transterritorial solidarity. The pressure of their movement is created by the existence of the border wall, which blocks their flow and produces a social pressure that rips holes through the border.

The Barbarian

Similarly, the barbarian is not only a historical figure centrifugally excluded from political life and enslaved or recruited by the empire. Today's barbarians also invent their own political agency in the form of a revolt, or "return" to the land and their homes—even if this revolt looks like an invasion or destruction when the barbarians' homes have been destroyed and they search for *new homes*.[10] This search is precisely what Walter Benjamin proposes in his positive concept of barbarism: "We affirm this in order to introduce a new, positive notion of barbarism. What does the poverty of experience oblige the barbarian to do? To begin anew, to begin from the new."[11] This is also what Nietzsche advocates in his call for the "barbarians of the twentieth century,"[12] who will "grant [themselves] the right to exceptional actions; as an experiment in self-overcoming and freedom. To venture into states in which it is not permitted not to be a barbarian."[13] A similar explicitly pedetic form of revolutionary "new barbarism" is also prefigured in the works of French anarchists Ernest Coeurderoy and Octave Vauthier,[14] and ultimately in the great "barbarian manifesto," *L'Humanisphère* (1899) by Joseph Déjacque:

It is at the noise of the social tempest, it is in the current of that regenerating deluge that Civilization will collapse in decadence. It is at the breath of the innovating spirit that the popular ocean will bound up from its gulf. It is the [stormy] turmoil of new ideas that will bring down the heads and thrones of the civilized and pass with its level of iron and fire over the ruins. It is this that will drown in blood and flames all the notarized and certified deeds, and the procurers of those deeds, and will make the parceled and appropriated soil a collective whole. This time it is not darkness that the Barbarians will bring to the world, but light.[15]

In the same way that the Roman Empire was radically transformed by the "old barbarians," so today, Hardt and Negri argue, the contemporary empire of global capital needs to be radically transformed by its "new barbarians."[16] Or, as Italian insurrectionists Crisso and Odoteo write:

May the barbarians break loose. May they sharpen their swords, may they brandish their battleaxes, may they strike their enemies without pity. May hatred take the place of tolerance, may fury take the place of resignation, may outrage take the place of respect. May the barbarian hordes go to the assault, autonomously, in the way that they determine. And may no parliament, no credit institution, no supermarket, no barracks, no factory ever grow again after their passage. In the face of the concrete that rises to strike the sky and the pollution that fouls it.[17]

Today's barbarians, they say, "have other paths to travel, other worlds to discover, other existences to live."[18]

Mexican migrants are part of today's new barbarians insofar as they revolt against their expulsion from their land and their waged guest-work "slavery" and insofar as they try to create a new social force. In the Mexico-US case, this revolt has an internal and an external form. Within Mexico, the mass expulsions and depoliticization of indigenous *campesinos* from their land has resulted in a long history of peasant land seizures and revolts. From the *Palenques* (Maroon societies) of the sixteenth century—composed of runaway slaves living in the mountains—to Emilio Zapata's peasant army and its long legacy of the return of the land to the peasants—the displaced in Mexico have fought for the return of their collective lands. More recently, the contemporary barbarian revolt inside Mexico has been led by the Zapatistas in Chiapas. After the legal and political destruction of the *ejido* system in 1992, then NAFTA beginning in 1994, many indigenous *campesinos* were forced off their land (through debt, poverty, violent cohesion, cattle ranches, and privatization) and into the mountains as internal migrants. On January 1, 1994, the Ejército Zapatista de Liberación (Zapatista Army of National Liberation) revolted against the private ranchers, the local paramilitary leaders, and government so they could return home to their land. Armed men and women from the indigenous communities took by force seven towns and more than five hundred privately owned ranches in the state of Chiapas.[19] Like other barbarian revolts, it was interpreted by the state as an "invasion" against those who had taken the land away in the first place.

Over the past twenty years, the Zapatistas have fought a constant battle against what they call the "nightmare of global migration,"[20] facilitated by the Mexican government, paramilitary forces, and corporate investors. The Zapatistas fight for the right *not* to migrate but to return home (to revolt). Thus, the struggle of the migrant is not only to move freely but also to remain at home in kinopolitical autonomy. The Zapatistas have also been creating a new home: an alternative political power based on the classic pedetic inventions of federated autonomous communes, direct democracy, cooperative economics, and consensus decision making.[21] Today, their struggle remains an internal barbarian force that continues in such a way that it does not become an external one. The Zapatistas proclaim that "if Mexicans could find in their own land what now is denied them, they would not be forced to look for work in other countries."[22]

However, many Mexican migrants are not able to maintain their revolt in Mexico and are forced to become an external barbarian force in the United States instead, where they revolt for the right to return home to Mexico but also to find new homes in the United States. Here, we can identify several types of migrant justice groups (representing hundreds of organizations) aimed at defending the political status and rights of Mexican immigrants: the Binational Front of Indigenous Organizations (to defend their right to return home or stay home), Amnesty International (to defend their political rights in the United States), and Sanctuary Cities (to defend the right to make a new home in the United States).

All of these political efforts to create a migrant counterpower of revolt against social expulsion are again interpreted in legal and popular culture to be a form of "invasion." Writings in the popular media depicting Mexican immigration as an invasion of "barbarians at the gates" (an explicit reference to Roman history) are extensive.[23] Racial, linguistic, and geographic inferiority are often explicit in the analogy (as they have always been). Even the US Supreme Court describes the movement of these migrants as a "silent invasion of illegal aliens from Mexico,"[24] which requires us to "protect" and "defend" our borders and to "combat" their "fertile" (biologically reproductive) and "creative" efforts to stay.[25] Today's barbarian revolts, just like their ancient predecessors (in the Gallic and Gothic Wars) are in defense of the migrant struggle to return home (or stay home) against forced expulsion and servitude under empire (whether Roman or capitalist).

The Vagabond

Vagabondage also has a contemporary manifestation in the pedetic counterpower of the Mexican migrant. Within Mexico, there is a widespread criminalization of begging, homelessness, and vagabondage, particularly in the *colonias*. Just as the criminalized vagabonds of the Middle Ages responded to their tensional expulsion by openly rebelling in the form of mobs against tax collectors and feudal lords and directly seizing the food and tools they needed to survive, so do Mexico's vagabonds of today have their own form of direct rebellion. Mexico's border and urban *colonias* are disproportionately composed of internal migrants forced from their *ejidos*. In response, migrants directly occupy the land and building materials they need as a makeshift community of squatters. Once the land and materials have been collectively taken, residents refuse all forms of tax collection. Just as vagabond feudal peasants occupied and "illegally" hunted in the forests, marshes, and "wastes" of Europe, taking what they needed from the land, so today's vagabond homeless in Mexico squat, refuse taxation, directly take electricity, and dig water wells without governmental approval. Since such communities are poor, a disproportionate portion of their income comes from the informal economy of theft, as it did in many medieval vagabond communities like Bacaude.

In the United States, vagabond counterpower takes the similarly direct form of rebellion in the open rejection of immigration authorities and the illegal seizure of necessary services. First, this is expressed in the direct civil disobedience of nonstatus migrants in groups like No Papers, No Fear; Undocumented and Unafraid; and the DREAMers. These criminalized migrants directly and collectively confront those who have legally expelled them and demand the decriminalization of their status. In the United States, this has had some success: No Papers, No Fear participants have been arrested but not directly deported on their Ride for Justice to Washington, DC,[26] and more than thirty thousand undocumented youth have had their deportations suspended by executive order. Second, many migrants who live and work in the United States find ways to socially participate that are legally denied to them, such as education, political protest, labor, and unionization. On a large scale, in the United States this represents a direct rebellion against the laws that restrict their organization and appropriation of the services they often pay for in taxes.

This brings us to a third form of rebellion against those who would expel vagabonds and then tax them. While the vast majority of Mexican migrants pay US taxes directly through their labor (documented or not) through sales taxes and indirectly pay property taxes in their rent, many migrants rebel against taxation without representation or benefit in public protest because they consider it a kind of political theft. The United States taxes migrants but does not allow them a say in the distribution of these taxes by allowing them to vote. The migrant rejection of unfair taxation is thus similar to the medieval peasants' rejection of arbitrary taxes to the lord that are forced on them without collective benefit. Today's rebellions are perhaps not as physically violent as the medieval rebellions that burned the homes of the rich and murdered tax collectors, but they are similar in the direct confrontation and/or theft of what rightfully belongs to the migrant.

The Proletariat

Migrant proletarianism also has its contemporary manifestation in perhaps the most frequently identified form of migrant pedetic counterpower: the power of the migrant worker. Within Mexico this takes a variety of forms quite similar to those invented by modern social movements.

First, the Mexican proletariat organizes in the form of social movements against displacement. As Mexican migrants become increasingly mobile and dispersed, so do their social networks and associations, which depend on their migratory oscillations. Their collective migrations quite literally form a wave of inspiration, influence, and connection between earlier and current migrants. Across states and across national borders, solidarity movements like the Frente Indigena de Organizaciones Binacionales (Binational Front of Indigenous Organizations, FIOB) connect a variety of different pressure groups in Mexico and the United States around the common issues faced by Mexican migrants (such as law, health, environment, and labor). The FIOB provides resources for the communication (print, Internet, etc.), organization, and direct action of the shared struggle of indigenous migrants in Mexico and the United States. It aims to unite the struggles of migrants into a large-scale international social movement against expulsion.

Another example of the wavelike unity that proletarian migrants have created is the social movement La Via Campesina—an international movement that coordinates peasant organizations of small and middle-scale producers, agricultural workers, rural women, and indigenous communities from Asia, Africa, America, and Europe. La Via Campesina has carried out several international campaigns to protect the food sovereignty of farmers, the recognition of the rights of peasants, and a global campaign for agrarian reform: all protections for the right not to become surplus migrants. As a social movement, it unifies diverse migrants in the common struggle against their shared conditions of expulsion. The social movement provides an undivided continuity, resonance, and force that travels between isolated migrant workers/farmers.

The second way the Mexican proletariat aims to resist expulsion is by pedetic use of the strike. As the Mexican economy contracted (stripped workers of their rights to safe working conditions, benefits, social services, and fair wages) and redistributed its surplus northward, migrant workers (and those not wishing to migrate) organized themselves into national unions and created blockages to this contraction. By moving (pedetically), they refused to move (elastically). The proletariat all over Mexico has used barricades, labor strikes, boycotts, petitions, and other forms of resistance to protect the conditions that allow them to stay home. In particular, some of the largest unions in Mexico are mining unions who went on strike against Grupo Mexico in Cananea over safety conditions (degraded by economic contractions) in June 2007. The strike put pressure on profits and the circulation of profit.

After police attempted to break the strike in January, twenty-five thousand workers went on strike in ten of the largest mines in Mexico. Street battles ensued as police were brought in to beat and jail the workers, and corporate lawyers brought in to change labor laws that protected unions.[27] As Mexico contracted and privatized the productive sectors of its economy (such as automobile manufacturing, oil, mining, and agriculture), unions rose up everywhere to defend their right not to migrate: to resist. But in 2012, Article 123 of the Mexican Constitution, which protected the rights of workers to severance pay, a forty-hour workweek, housing, health care, training, the right to strike, minimum wage, and protection from strikebreaking was "reformed," that is, removed, in order to encourage capital investment and stop strikes.[28] However, Mexican wildcat strikes continue to organize and occupy workplaces in hopes of creating counterpressure against poverty and migration.

The third pedetic tactic within Mexico is kinetically similar to the strike but, given the increasing criminalization of the strike, now takes the form of the *plantón* or the "occupation": the pedetic power of the foot. The word *plantón* in Spanish means to "stand up," "to not be moved," and comes from the Spanish verb *plantar*, "to stand firm, or hold one's ground," from the Latin *plantare*, "to drive in with the sole or heel of the foot." Thus, the pedetic power of the foot is not only the power to move and leap but also the power to stop, stay, and resist, *plantón*. As public and indigenous lands are sold off and their residents forced to move, the Mexican proletarian mobilizes itself in the form of a *plantón*-blockage. It literally aims to "hold its ground" by use of barricades, petitions, boycotts, and labor strikes when that ground is taken from them. When the government gave away public lands to private mining companies in San José de Progreso, residents barricaded themselves at the entrance of the mine.[29] When Smithfield Farms monopolized pig farming and bought up all the land, Perote farmers blocked the highways into and out of factories. When teachers' wages were reduced in Oaxaca in 2006, hundreds of thousands of people organized as the Popular Assembly of the Peoples of Oaxaca

(APPO) occupied the capital of Oaxaca in November for weeks. Proletarian resistance is the pedetic power to stop, to hold ground, to stay home, to not move: to stop the causes of migration (poverty, privatization, and dispossession).

In the United States, there is a long history of cross-border labor solidarity from the time that Mexicans entered the United States to work on the railroads, in mines, and in agriculture.[30] Labor organizers from both countries united in their shared conditions of exploitation in pedetic groups like the Industrial Workers of the World (IWW) and other communist associations in both countries.

[T]he Wobblies had extraordinary success among the vast and mobile immigrant populations because they spoke all the languages of that hybrid labor force. The two accepted stories of the derivation of the name "Wobbly" illustrate these two central characteristics of the movement, its organizational mobility and its ethnic-linguistic hybridity: first, Wobbly is supposed to refer to the lack of a center, the flexible and unpredictable pilgrimage of IWW militancy; and second, the name is said to derive from the mispronunciation of a Chinese cook in Seattle, "I Wobbly Wobbly."[31]

Today, numerous migrant justice social movements exist in the United States to organize and protect migrant workers. Not only are migrant workers being exported from Mexico but so are their experiences of resistance and organizing. For example, the strong history of Mexican labor unions carries over into organizing other kinds of human strikes and boycotts against racial and social discrimination against Mexican migrants in the United States.

On May Day, International Workers Day, 2006, Mexican migrants organized El Gran Paro Estadounidense (The Great American Strike)—during which migrants and their US allies abstained from buying, selling, working, and attending school in order to demonstrate the force of Mexican migrants. In Spanish, the verb *parar* also means "to block a movement" or "stop."

In another example of occupation, the Coalition for the Political Rights of Mexicans Abroad sent a support letter to Occupy Wall Street, outlining their shared conditions of expulsion and calling for public occupations across borders (organized according to the pedetic forces of common property, consensus decision making, and direct democracy). "We greet your movement," it declared, "because your struggle against the suppression of human rights, and against social and economic injustice has been a fundamental part of our struggle, that of the Mexican people who cross borders, and the millions of Mexican migrants who live in the United States."[32] Not long after the Occupy Wall Street camp was set up in Zuccotti Park, a solidarity *plantón* began in Tijuana—home to many displaced migrants from southern Mexico. Despite their differences, the Mexican and American migrant proletariat share something in common: they are both treated as a proletarian surplus to be displaced from their homes for the sake of private profit. Between 2006 and 2010, 13 million homes were foreclosed in the United States.[33] This massive expulsion of migrants was the basis for the largest international occupation movement in history, of which Mexico and the United States were only two countries.

Conclusion

The migrant is the political figure of our time. Most people today increasingly fall somewhere, and at some point, on the spectrum of migration, from global tourist to undocumented labor. As a result, they experience (among other things) a certain degree of deprivation or expulsion from their social status. In this sense, the figure of the migrant is not a "type of person" or fixed identity but a mobile social position or spectrum that people move into and out of under certain social conditions of mobility. The figure of the migrant is a political concept that defines the conditions and agencies by which various figures are socially expelled as a result of, or as the cause of, their mobility.

Rather than view human migration as the exception to the rule of political fixity and citizenship, this book reinterprets the history of political power from the perspective of the movement that defines the migrant. This book begins not from normative or philosophical principles but from the social and historical conditions that define the subjective figures we have become: *migrants*. From this new starting point, it reinterprets political theory as a politics of movement: a kinopolitics.

This new starting point of political philosophy allows us to overcome two important problems set out at the beginning of this book. First, the figure of the migrant has been almost exclusively considered from the perspective of social stasis—and thus as derivative. However, Chapters 1 and 2 provide a new conceptual framework that privileges the primacy of the movement and flow that define the migrant. Stasis is then reinterpreted as a secondary "junction" of motion. The consequence of beginning from this movement-oriented philosophy of flows is that we are able to reinterpret several of the major historical conditions that produced migration according to their different regimes of social motion. We thus discover, in Part 2, that one of the conditions of expanding social motion is the expulsion of the migrant from various territorial, political, juridical, and economic orders.

The second problem we have overcome is that the migrant has been previously considered primarily from the perspective of the history of the state—and thus as ahistorical. But Part 3 develops a kinetic history of several major social formations created and autonomously organized by migrants against the dominant forms of social expulsion. The consequence of this conceptual history is that it gives us a concrete sense of what alternatives have been and can be created to oppose the dominant forms of kinopolitical expulsion.

The final payoff, and consequence, of the conceptual (Part 1), historical (Part 2), and counterpower (Part 3) analyses of migration and social motion is that they provide us with the tools to analyze contemporary migration in a new way: from the perspective of the *primacy* of migration and motion (Part 4). This is possible because the migrant is not only a historical figure but also a contemporary one, produced under certain social conditions that have persisted throughout history in different ways, to varying degrees, and in different combinations. Contemporary migration is a hybrid mix of all of them.

Analyzing contemporary migration according to the primacy of movement thus makes three important contributions. First, it allows us to see that contemporary migration is not a secondary phenomenon that simply occurs between states. Rather, migration is the primary condition by which something like societies and states is established in the first place. Migration is an essential part of how societies move. In particular, the expulsion of the migrant is a condition for social expansion and reproduction: it is constitutive. Second, it allows us to see that contemporary migration is poorly understood according to a single axis of social expulsion. Rather, the social conditions of migration are always a mixture of territorial, political, juridical, and economic types of expulsion. All four are operative at the same time to different degrees. Thus, migrants are always a mixture of different subjective tendencies toward nomadism, barbarism, vagabondage, and proletarian migrancy. Finally, this movement-oriented analysis allows us to see that there are alternatives to the contemporary conditions of migration being developed by migrants today.

However, there is still much work to be done in three major areas. The first area is historical. This book has limited its historical scope for the sake of clarity and brevity to analyzing only four major types of kinopower (centripetal, centrifugal, tensional, and elastic) during their general period of social dominance. Once these types of kinopower emerge historically, they tend to persist and mix with one another, creating various hybrid combinations. For example, the technology of enclosure creates a territorial expulsion from the land, a political expulsion of the peasants from the decision-making process, a juridical expulsion from the customary law, and an economic expulsion from employment. Expulsion is always multiple. It is always a question of type and degree. Thus, what remains to be done in the future is to analyze the kinopolitical technologies presented here (and elsewhere) according to their full historical and kinetic *mixture* or *hybridization*—which this book has presented only in their relative isolation.

The second area is contemporary. This book has used its conceptual and historical framework to analyze only one major area of contemporary migration: Mexico-US migration. Many other major and interesting areas of contemporary migration remain to be analyzed within this framework, such as the landless peasant movement in Brazil, the recent home foreclosure process happening around the world, the recent land grabs and expulsions in Cambodia, and the *sans-papiers* (without papers) struggle in France. So many migrant social expulsions are happening today that much remains to be done to reinterpret them according to the primacy of motion and the figures of the migrant that can pose an alternative to them.

The third area is subjective. In addition to limiting its historical and contemporary scope, this book has limited its subjective scope to focus solely on four major migrant subjects because it is their histories that were in most need of recovery, showed the sharpest visibility of social expulsion, and remain more relevant for most migrants today. But in doing so, it has left out the rich history and contemporary analysis of many other migratory figures much less intensely or dramatically expelled from their social status. Thus, future work also remains to be done to show how such figures as tourists, commuters, diplomats, business travelers, explorers, messengers, and state functionaries are affected by certain degrees of social expulsion with respect to their movement. These figures of the migrant also produce their own dominant and hybrid types (historically and recently) according to the four kinopolitical conditions. Work in this area is already under way in various ways in the journal *Mobilities*—although it is not clear that such work always adopts a movement-oriented philosophy in the way that this book has.

There is much more to be done in the kinopolitical analysis of migration. The aim of this book has been to prepare the way for further analysis by creating a general conceptual and historical framework proper to the migrant (based on social motion) that can be used to perform further historical and contemporary analysis of migration elsewhere. No doubt the coming century of the migrant will require many new hybrid analyses.

Notes

INTRODUCTION

1. In total number (1 billion: one in seven) and as percentage of total population (about 14 percent) according to the International Organization on Migration, "The Future of Migration: Building Capacities for Change," *World Migration Report 2010,* presentation at Migration Policy Institute, Washington, DC, http://www.iom.int/files/live/sites/iom/files/Newsrelease/docs/WM2010_FINAL_23_11_2010.pdf.; and The World Health Organization, "Migrant Health," 2015, http://www.who.int/hac/techguidance/health_of_migrants/en/.

2. As of 2010, there were 215 million international migrants and 740 million internal migrants according to the United Nations Human Development Report, *Overcoming Barriers: Human Mobility and Development,* 2009, http://oppenheimer.mcgill.ca/IMG/pdf/HDR_2009_EN_Complete.pdf, 21.

3. Trends in International Migrant Stock: The 2008 Revision (United Nations database, POP/DB/MIG/Stock/Rev.2008), http://esa.un.org/migration; and The US National Intelligence Council, "Global Trends 2030: Alternative Worlds," December 2012, http://globaltrends2030.files.wordpress.com/2012/11/global-trends-2030-november2012.pdf, 24. On the theoretical implications of this phenomenon for liberalism, see Phillip Cole, *Philosophies of Exclusion: Liberal Political Theory and Immigration* (Edinburgh: Edinburgh University Press, 2000).

4. Future forecasts vary from 25 million to 1 billion environmental migrants by 2050, moving either within their countries or across borders on a permanent or temporary basis, with 200 million the most widely cited estimate. This figure equals the current estimate of international migrants worldwide. See International Organization for Migration, "Migration, Climate Change and the Environment," accessed April 9, 2015, http://www.iom.int/cms/en/sites/iom/home/what-we-do/migration-and-climate-change/a-complex-nexus.html.

5. International Council on Human Rights Policy, "Irregular Migration, Migrant Smuggling and Human Rights: Towards Coherence," 2010, http://www.ichrp.org/files/summaries/41/122_pb_en.pdf, estimates that the approximate number of global irregular migrants has grown to 30–40 million persons.

6. With the rise of home foreclosure and unemployment people today are beginning to have much more in common with migrants than with certain notions of citizenship (grounded in certain social, legal, and political rights). "All people may now be wanderers": Zygmunt Bauman, *Globalization: The Human Consequences* (New York: Columbia University Press, 1998), 87. "Migration must be understood in a broad sense": Nikos Papastergiadis, *The Turbulence of Migration: Globalization, Deterritorialization, and Hybridity* (Cambridge, UK: Polity Press, 2000), 2.

7. World Bank's World Development Indicators 2005: Section 3 Environment, Table 3.11, http://www.worldmapper.org/display.php?selected=141.

8. International annual tourist arrivals exceeded 1 billion globally for the first time in history in 2012. World Tourism Organization (UNWTO), "World Tourism Barometer," vol. 11, 2013, http://dtxtq4w60xqpw.cloudfront.net/sites/all/files/pdf/unwto_barom13_01_jan_excerpt_0.pdf.

9. I use the word "expulsion" here in the same sense in which Saskia Sassen uses it to indicate a general dispossession or deprivation of social status. See *Expulsions: Brutality and Complexity in the Global Economy* (Cambridge, MA: Belknap Press of Harvard University Press, 2014), 1–2. Many scholars have noted a similar trend. For an excellent review of the "mobilities" literature on migration, see Alison Blunt, "Cultural Geographies of Migration: Mobility, Transnationality and Diaspora," *Progress in Human Geography* 31 (2007): 684–94.

10. Michael Hardt and Antonio Negri, *Empire* (Cambridge, MA: Harvard University Press, 2000), 213.

11. Bauman, *Globalization*.

12. Ibid., 96, 85, 78, 83, 84.

13. Ibid., 97.

14. For an excellent introduction to the tradition of thinkers who have granted theoretical primacy to movement and flow, see Peter Merriman, *Mobility, Space, and Culture* (New York: Routledge, 2012). See also Lucretius, *De Rerum Natura* (Cambridge, MA: Harvard University Press, 1975); Henri Bergson, *Matter and Memory,* trans. Nancy Paul and William S. Palmer (New York: Zone Books, 1988); Michel Serres, *The Birth of Physics* (Manchester, UK: Clinamen Press, 2000); Gilles Deleuze and Félix Guattari, *A Thousand Plateaus: Capitalism and Schizophrenia,* trans. Brian Massumi (London: Continuum, 2008); Brian Massumi, *Parables for the Virtual: Movement, Affect, Sensation* (Durham, NC: Duke University Press, 2002); Erin Manning, *Relationscapes: Movement, Art, Philosophy* (Cambridge, MA: MIT Press, 2009); Tim Cresswell, *On the Move: Mobility in the Modern Western World* (Hoboken, NJ: Taylor & Francis, 2012).

15. See Merriman, *Mobility, Space, and Culture,* 1–20, for a review of the criticisms against the philosophy of movement.

16. John Urry, *Sociology beyond Societies: Mobilities for the Twenty-First Century* (London: Routledge, 2000).

17. In this sense, this book can also be placed in the context of what is now being called the "new mobilities paradigm" or "mobility turn" in the social sciences. See Kevin Hannam, Mimi Sheller, and John Urry, "Mobilities, Immobilities and Moorings," *Mobilities* 1, no. 1 (2006): 1–22; Cresswell, *On the Move*; Vincent Kaufmann, *Re-thinking Mobility: Contemporary Sociology* (Aldershot, Hampshire, UK: Ashgate, 2002); John Urry, *Mobilities* (Cambridge, UK: Polity, 2007); Tanu Uteng and Tim Cresswell, *Gendered Mobilities* (Aldershot, UK: Ashgate, 2008); Jørgen Bærenholdt and Kirsten Simonsen, *Space Odysseys: Spatiality and Social Relations in the 21st Century* (Aldershot, Hampshire, UK: Ashgate, 2004); Nigel Thrift, *Spatial Formations* (London: Sage, 1996).

18. This argument, and the idea of a "sedentarist metaphysics," is well supported by Liisa Malkki, "National Geographic: The Rooting of Peoples and the Territorialization of National Identity among Scholars and Refugees," *Cultural Anthropology* 7, no. 1 (February 1992): 24–44; and Cresswell, *On the Move*.

19. Georg Wilhelm Friedrich Hegel, *Introduction to the Philosophy of History*, trans. Leo Rauch (New York: Hackett, 1988), 41–42.

20. This is not a strictly empirical study. For an empirical world history of migration, see Patrick Manning and Tiffany Trimmer, *Migration in World History* (Abingdon, UK: Routledge, 2013).

21. For an example of this sort of historical work on the concept of territory, see Stuart Elden, *The Birth of Territory* (Chicago: University of Chicago Press, 2013).

22. Stephen Castles has also argued that the figure of the migrant needs to be defined in relation to its other overlapping historical figures, such as indentured laborer, refugee, and exile. See *Mistaken Identity: Multiculturalism and the Demise of Nationalism in Australia* (Sydney: Pluto Press, 1992).

23. Here I am using the word "territory" simply to mean "delimited land" (following the *OED*) and not in a strictly historical way since, as Stuart Elden argues in *The Birth of Territory*, 322–30, the usage of the word "territory" varies significantly throughout history and cannot be used in a univocal way.

24. According to Tim Cresswell, "We cannot understand new mobilities, without understanding old mobilities." "Towards a Politics of Mobility," *Environment and Planning D, Society & Space*, 28, no. 1 (2010): 17–31.

25. To be clear, I am not arguing that contemporary migrants are *exactly* the same as the first historical nomads. For a good example of a *philosophical concept* of "nomadism" *derived* from history, see Deleuze and Guattari, *A Thousand Plateaus*, 351–423.

CHAPTER 1

1. See Peter Merriman, *Mobility, Space, and Culture* (New York: Routledge, 2012).

2. "In the living mobility of things the understanding is bent on marking real or virtual stations, it notes departures and arrivals; for this is all that concerns the thought of man in so far as it is simply human. It is more than human to grasp what is happening in the interval. But philosophy can only be an effort to transcend the human condition." Henri Bergson, *An Introduction to Metaphysics*, trans. T. E. Hulme (New York: Putnam's Sons, 1912), 77.

3. "The Internationale," stanza 1, lines 7–8 (author's translation).

4. Henri Bergson, *Matter and Memory*, trans. Nancy Paul and William S. Palmer (New York: Zone Books, 1988), 189.

5. Bergson, *Introduction to Metaphysics*, 53.

6. Henri Bergson, *The Creative Mind*, trans. Mabelle Louise Cunningham Andison (New York: Philosophical Library, 1946), 177, 171.

7. By "whole," Bergson does not mean a "totality," because a totality cannot change or become other than it is. Bergson means something like an open and vibratory whole.

8. "You cannot measure migration in changes of position or location, but only in the increase in its inclusiveness and the amplitude of its intensities. Even if migration starts sometimes as a form of dislocation (forced by poverty, patriarchal exploitation, war, famine), its target is not relocation but the active transformation of social space." Dimitris Papadopoulos and Vassilis Tsianos, "The Autonomy of Migration: The Animals of Undocumented Mobility," in *Deleuzian Encounters: Studies in Contemporary Social Issues*, ed. Anna Hickey-Moody and Peta Malins (Basingstoke, UK: Palgrave Macmillan, 2007), 225.

9. These are all much larger claims that will be argued in more detail later.

10. Bergson, *Matter and Memory*, 193.

11. The proletariat is expelled from the means of production, but this does not always give rise to an extensive motion in the form of migration more often associated with the lumpenproletariat. This point is developed further in Chapter 6.

12. Here this project is quite different from "nomadic" theories of subjectivity found in the work of certain Deleuze scholars such as Rosi Braidotti. See Rosi Braidotti, *Nomadic Subjects: Embodiment and Sexual Difference in Contemporary Feminist Theory* (New York: Columbia University Press, 2011).

13. A paraphrase from Michel Foucault, *Security, Territory, Population: Lectures at the Collège de France, 1977–78* (Basingstoke, UK: Palgrave Macmillan, 2007), 3.

14. See Gilles Deleuze and Félix Guattari, *A Thousand Plateaus: Capitalism and Schizophrenia*, trans. Brian Massumi (London: Continuum, 2008), 367.

15. For a detailed proposal for such a scenario, see Eugene Holland, *Nomad Citizenship: Free-Market Communism and the Slow-Motion General Strike* (Minneapolis: University of Minnesota Press, 2011).

CHAPTER 2

1. Adam Smith, *The Wealth of Nations* (1776; repr., Lawrence: Digireads.com Publishing, 2009), book II, introduction, 162.

2. David Harvey, *The New Imperialism* (Oxford: Oxford University Press, 2003); Silvia Federici, *Caliban and the Witch* (New York: Autonomedia, 2004); Saskia Sassen, *Expulsions: Brutality and Complexity in the Global Economy* (Cambridge, MA: Belknap Press of Harvard University Press, 2014); Saskia Sassen, "A Savage Sorting of Winners and Losers: Contemporary Versions of Primitive Accumulation," *Globalizations* 7, no. 1–2 (2010): 23–50; Fredy Perlman, *The Continuing Appeal of Nationalism* (Detroit: Black & Red, 1985); Massimo De Angelis, "Marx and Primitive Accumulation: The Continuous Character of Capital 'Enclosures,'" *The Commoner*, September 2010, http://www.commoner.org.uk/02deangelis.pdf.

3. Karl Marx, *Capital: A Critique of Political Economy*, trans. Ben Fowkes (London: Penguin Books, 1990), 1:786.

4. Or, as Hardt and Negri frame it: "The mobility and migration of the labor force have disrupted the disciplinary conditions to which workers are constrained. And power has wielded the most extreme violence against this mobility. It would be interesting, in fact, to write a general history of the modes of production from the standpoint of the workers' desire for mobility." Michael Hardt and Antonio Negri, *Empire* (Cambridge, MA: Harvard University Press, 2000), 212.

5. A "politics of mobility" has also been proposed by Tim Cresswell, "Towards a Politics of Mobility," *Environment and Planning D, Society & Space* 28, no. 1 (2010): 17–31. Cresswell advocates for the historical and contemporary study of what he calls "constellations of movement." This is what I am calling "regimes of social motion."

6. This approach has also been proposed by Peter Merriman. In particular, he rejects geography's privileging of space and time and proposes instead a "geography of mobility," which he applies to the case of "driving mobilities." "Mobility and movement," in geography, he argues, "are positioned as important, but they are frequently thought of as functions of space and time. In contrast, [he] seek[s] to suggest a way forward which does not seek to apprehend events—and, in particular, movements—as if they necessarily unfold in or produce ontologies situated in space and time (or space-times), and [he] map[s] out an approach which seeks to reveal how other primitive ontological constituents continually erupt into being and are no less important to situating the unfolding of particular events. . . . Movement,

affect, sensation, rhythm, vibration, energy, force, and much more, then, might be taken to be fundamental to understanding how life unfolds, and we might even go as far as to suggest that space-time is a Western fiction, a series of stories we like to tell ourselves, which in turn structure how we think about the world." Peter Merriman, *Mobility, Space, and Culture* (New York: Routledge, 2012), 2.

7. In my definition of "society" I follow John Urry's definition of the "social as mobility." John Urry, *Sociology beyond Societies: Mobilities for the Twenty-First Century* (London: Routledge, 2000), 2.

8. The concept of "flow" has a long legacy in the history of the philosophy of movement, from Lucretius to Deleuze. Every philosopher who has given philosophical primacy to motion begins with the concept of flow. Lucretius begins his philosophy from the continuous flow of atoms through the void. Bergson begins from the "perpetual flowing" of "pure movement" (*Creative Evolution* [London: Macmillan, 1911], 287; and *Matter and Memory,* trans. Nancy Paul and William S. Palmer [New York: Zone Books, 1988], 149). According to Bergson, "Mobility, or what comes to the same thing, duration" (*An Introduction to Metaphysics,* trans. T. E. Hulme [New York: Putnam, 1912], 47); and "Time is mobility" (*The Creative Mind,* trans. Mabelle L. C. Andison [New York: Philosophical Library, 1946], 11). Michel Serres begins from the fluid dynamic model of physics in which "everything flows" (*The Birth of Physics,* trans. Jack Hawkes [Manchester, UK: Clinamen Press, 2000], 5). Gilles Deleuze and Félix Guattari begin their political philosophy from the "flows of desire." "Every 'object,'" they argue, "presupposes the continuity of a flow" (*Anti-Oedipus: Capitalism and Schizophrenia* [Minneapolis: University of Minnesota Press, 1983], 33, 6).

9. The fluid sciences also have their conceptual origin in the work of Lucretius, as Michel Serres argues in *The Birth of Physics.*

10. The density, pressure, and velocity of fluids are assumed to be well defined at infinitesimally small points, which vary continuously.

11. Otto Santa Ana, *Brown Tide Rising: Metaphors of Latinos in Contemporary American Public Discourse* (Austin: University of Texas Press, 2002).

12. For a detailed philosophical history of statistics, see Ian Hacking, *The Taming of Chance* (Cambridge: Cambridge University Press, 1990).

13. Harvey's discovery of circulation also had an influence on political theories of circulation as "social health" in the work of Thomas Hobbes and others. See Jürgen Overhoff, *Hobbes's Theory of the Will: Ideological Reasons and Historical Circumstances* (Lanham: Rowman & Littlefield, 2000); and Richard Sennett, *Flesh and Stone: The Body and the City in Western Civilization* (New York: W. W. Norton, 1994).

14. "What emerges in the seventeenth century, all at once, is not so much the applied sciences, the practice of exactitude and precision, as the general philosophy of its possibility." Serres, *The Birth of Physics,* 141.

15. Ibid.

16. Nikos Papastergiadis argues that the migrant is defined by an "endless motion, [which] surrounds and pervades almost all aspects of contemporary society." *The Turbulence of Migration: Globalization, Deterritorialization, and Hybridity* (Cambridge, UK: Polity Press, 2000), 1. Similarly, Dimitris Papadopoulos and Vassilis Tsianos argue "that the practices of contemporary transnational migration force us to revise Deleuze & Guattari's split between nomadism and migration. Nomadism's dictum 'you never arrive somewhere' constitutes the matrix of today's migrational movements." "The Autonomy of Migration: The Animals of Undocumented Mobility," in *Deleuzian Encounters: Studies in Contemporary Social Issues,* ed. Anna Hickey-Moody and Peta Malins (Basingstoke, UK: Palgrave Macmillan, 2007), 224.

17. Papastergiadis, Gloria Anzaldúa, Homi Bhabha, and others argue that we should understand the migrant in terms of hybridity. See Papastergiadis, *The Turbulence of Migration,* 168–88; Gloria Anzaldúa, *Borderlands: The New Mestiza = La Frontera* (San Francisco: Spinsters/Aunt Lute, 1987); Homi Bhabha, *The Location of Culture* (London: Routledge, 1994).

18. Michel Serres develops a similar theory of vortices: "The vortex conjoins the atoms, in the same way as the spiral links the points; the turning movement brings together atoms and points alike." *The Birth of Physics,* 16. Deleuze and Guattari then further develop this under the name of "minor science." *A Thousand Plateaus: Capitalism and Schizophrenia,* trans. Brian Massumi (London: Continuum, 2008), 361–62.

19. The kinetic roots of the word junction come from the Proto-Indo-European root *yeug-,* "to join, to yoke."

20. John Lowe and S. Moryadas, *The Geography of Movement* (Boston: Houghton Mifflin, 1975), 54.

21. Lowe and Moryadas have been thoroughly critiqued in Tim Cresswell, *On the Move: Mobility in the Modern Western World* (Hoboken, NJ: Taylor & Francis, 2012), 27–29.

22. Peter Haggett puts movement first, but only arbitrarily: "[I]t is just as logical to begin with the study of settlements as with the study of routes. We choose to make that cut with movement." *Locational Analysis in Human Geography* (New York: St. Martin's Press, 1966), 31.

23. In geography and many social sciences, migration and circulation are often treated as distinctly different phenomena. Migration describes only one trip between two points, whereas circulation describes repeated movements between multiple points. But the two phenomena are the same. Migration is simply an abstracted selection of a more general and primary social circulation. Papastergiadas argues at length against this division. Migration is not about a single pathway but a multiplicity of reversible and unpredictable trajectories or circuits. Papastergiadas, *The Turbulence of Migration,* 7–8.

24. During the first age of mass migration some European migrants moved to New York and never left, but today this is the exception rather than the rule. Today, unemployment, temporary, and "flex-time" labor are turning almost everyone into a migrant to some degree.

25. Many US detention centers will pay one dollar per hour for detained migrant labor even though their legal status forbids them from working. "*Punishment and Profits: Immigration Detention*," Aljazeera.com, 2012, http://www. aljazeera.com/programmes/faultlines/2012/04/201241081117980874.html.

26. Department of Homeland Security, Office of Inspector General, "Immigration and Customs Enforcement's Tracking and Transfers of Detainees," 2009, http://www.oig.dhs.gov/assets/Mgmt/OIG_09-41_Mar09.pdf, 2.

27. Saskia Sassen offers a similar definition of expulsion: "people, enterprises, and places expelled from the core social and economic orders of our time." *Expulsions*, 1.

28. There are even "quite a few things the tourist could complain about." Zygmunt Bauman, *Globalization: The Human Consequences* (New York: Columbia University Press, 1998), 98.

29. See Georges Bataille, *The Accursed Share: An Essay on General Economy*, trans. Robert Hurley (New York: Zone Books, 1988).

30. This is what Marx calls "social metabolism." *Capital*, 1:283.

CHAPTER 3

1. By "compulsion" I do not necessarily mean "forced" movement but rather collectively directed movement in general.

2. The first "great migration" of human movement occurred almost 2 million years ago when *Homo erectus* moved out of Africa into the Middle East. It is strange to call this a migration because for thousands of years *Homo erectus* simply followed the migration of wild game moving north (at about one kilometer per year) to avoid rising temperatures and the desertification of Africa. Whether we call this migration or not, *Homo erectus* and early *Homo sapiens* were initially nonsedentary hunter-gatherers who increasingly settled down in societies. Patrick Manning, *Migration in World History* (New York: Routledge, 2005), 16–39.

3. That is not to say there is no sociality among early hunter-gathers but that there are no clear or large-scale regimes of *socially* compelled movement.

4. Here I follow Manuel De Landa's definition of "territorialization": "The other dimension [processes of territorialization] defines variable processes in which these components become involved and that either stabilize the identity of an assemblage, by increasing its degree of internal homogeneity or the degree of sharpness of its boundaries." *A New Philosophy of Society: Assemblage Theory and Social Complexity* (London: Continuum, 2006), 12.

5. Henri Bergson, *Matter and Memory*, trans. Nancy Paul and William S. Palmer (New York: Zone Books, 1988), 195.

6. "Our aim is not to repeat the common mistake of mapping ideas from natural science on to the social sciences and humanities in order to inherit some of the intellectual cache of 'proper' science." Tim Cresswell and C. Martin, "On Turbulence: Entanglements of Disorder and Order on a Devon Beach," *Tijdschrift Voor Economische En Sociale Geografie* 103, no. 5 (2012): 516–29, at 518.

7. The theory of kinetic social force presented in the remainder of this book is influenced by the theory of social forces developed by Marx, Nietzsche, Foucault, Deleuze, and others. Foucault describes a "moving substrate of force relations" (Michel Foucault, *The History of Sexuality*, trans. Robert Hurley [New York: Pantheon Books, 1978], 1:93). "[P]ower must be understood in the first instance as the multiplicity of force relations immanent in the sphere in which they operate and which constitute their own organization" (92). In his lectures, he describes disciplinary power as "centripetal" and biopower/security as "centrifugal" social forces (Michel Foucault, *Security, Territory, Population: Lectures at the Collège De France, 1977–78*, trans. Alessandro Fontana [Basingstoke, UK: Palgrave Macmillan, 2007], 44–45). Marx writes about "social force" (Karl Marx, *Capital: A Critique of Political Economy*, trans. Ben Fowkes [London: Penguin Books, 1990], 1:308). Nietzsche writes about an "economy of forces" (Friedrich Nietzsche, *The Will to Power*, trans. Walter A. Kaufmann [New York: Random House, 1967], 174). Deleuze and Guattari describe social "relations of force," in which the state acts both "centripetally" and "centrifugally." "In a first phase, information circulates principally from the periphery toward the center, but at a certain critical point, the town begins to emit, in the direction of the rural world, increasingly imperative messages" (Gilles Deleuze and Félix Guattari, *A Thousand Plateaus: Capitalism and Schizophrenia*, trans. Brian Massumi [London: Continuum, 2008], 34, 431n14).

8. Ofer Bar-Yosef, "The Natufian Culture in the Levant, Threshold to the Origins of Agriculture," *Evolutionary Anthropology* 6, no. 5 (1998): 159–77.

9. Lewis Mumford, *The City in History: Its Origins, Its Transformations, and Its Prospects* (New York: Harcourt, 1961), 16.

10. "They found different ways of getting the cattle under control. One Neolithic sculpture depicts a steer with a hole punched through its nasal septum. Removing the testicles was also quickly recognized as a way of improving the animals' temperament. Once the wild cattle had been castrated, they could finally be yoked." Matthias Schulz, "Neolithic Immigration: How Middle Eastern Milk Drinkers Conquered Europe," *Der Spiegel*, October 15, 2010, http://www.spiegel.de/international/zeitgeist/neolithic-immigration-how-middle-eastern-milk-drinkers-conquered-europe-a-723310.html.

11. Mumford, *The City in History*, 7.

12. Stuart Elden shows that the word "territory" emerges with the ancient Greeks and Romans. But the movement of territorialization (as the delimitation of the earth) precedes the Greek and Roman traditions, according to Deleuze and Guattari, *A Thousand Plateaus*, 351–423.

13. Karl Marx, *Grundrisse: Foundations of the Critique of Political Economy*, trans. Martin Nicolaus (London: Penguin Books, 1993), 472.

14. See I. Kuijt and N. Goring-Morris, "Foraging, Farming, and Social Complexity in the Pre-Pottery Neolithic of the Southern Levant: A Review and Synthesis," *Journal of World Prehistory* 16, no. 4 (2002): 361–440.

15. Allison Betts, "Things to Do with Sheep and Goats: Neolithic Hunter-Forager-Herders in North Arabia," in *The Archaeology of Mobility: Old World and New World Nomadism*, ed. Hans Barnard and Willeke Wendrich (Los Angeles: Cotsen Institute of Archaeology, University of California, 2008), 25.

16. Brian Byrd, "The Dispersal of Food Production across the Levant," in *Transitions to Agriculture in Prehistory*, ed. Anne Gebauer and T. Douglas Price (Madison, WI: Prehistory Press, 1992), 49–61.

17. G. O. Rollefson and Köhler-Rollefson, "The Collapse of Early Neolithic Settlements in the Southern Levant," in *People and Culture in Change: Proceedings of the Second Symposium on Upper Paleolithic, Mesolithic, and Neolithic Populations of Europe and the Mediterranean Basin*, ed. I. Hershkovitz (Oxford: Archaeopress, 1989), 73–89; and G. O. Rollefson, A. H. Simmons, and Z. Kafafi, "Neolithic Cultures at 'Ain Ghazal,'" *Journal of Field Archaeology* 19, no. 4 (1992): 443–70.

18. Although material support for this is more difficult to obtain. See Kuijt and Goring-Morris, "Foraging, Farming, and Social Complexity," 361–440.

19. Although social inequality and the concept of the "foreigner" existed during the Neolithic period, they did not constitute the dominant justification for social expulsion.

20. Once nomadism emerges historically, however, not all nomads are defined by expulsion and do not always and in all cases match up with the figure of the migrant as a social position.

21. Deleuze and Guattari, *A Thousand Plateaus*, 380.

22. *The English Standard Version Bible: Containing the Old and New Testaments with Apocrypha* (Oxford: Oxford University Press, 2009), Genesis 4:1–5.

23. Arnold Toynbee, *A Study of History* (London: Oxford University Press, 1972), 3:13–14.

24. Genesis 4:7–8.

25. Desmond Alexander and David W. Baker, *Dictionary of the Old Testament: Pentateuch* (Downers Grove, IL: InterVarsity Press, 2003), 27.

26. Genesis 4:12.

27. The extinction of the Neanderthals has not been conclusively tied to their centripetal expulsion by *Homo sapiens*. However, Jared Diamond has made a

compelling argument for it in *The Third Chimpanzee: The Evolution and Future of the Human Animal* (New York: HarperCollins, 1992).

CHAPTER 4

1. Lewis Mumford calls this a "megamachine." See Lewis Mumford, *The Pentagon of Power: The Myth of the Machine* (New York: Harcourt Brace Jovanovich, 1970), 2:236–360. How central the center of this rotational motion is varies according to the empire. In Egypt and Rome the axis was highly central. In the case of Sumer, and especially Greece, the center was more diffused into the city centers within the empire. The coordinated actions of the city centers in these latter cases still functioned as a socially kinetic central force. As Deleuze and Guattari argue, "Sumer already attests to a town solution, as opposed to the imperial solution of Egypt. But to an even greater extent, it was the Mediterranean world, with the Pelasgians, Phoenicians, Greeks, Carthaginians, that created an urban fabric distinct from the imperial organisms of the Orient." Gilles Deleuze and Félix Guattari, *A Thousand Plateaus: Capitalism and Schizophrenia*, trans. Brian Massumi (London: Continuum, 2008), 432.

2. The English word "politics" comes from the Greek word *polis,* meaning "city," from the Proto-Indo-European (PIE) root **pel -,* meaning "citadel, or fortified high place."

3. "Older societies were organized hierarchically and in function of the distinction between center and periphery." Niklas Luhmann, *Theory of Society: Volume 1*, trans. Rhodes Barrett (Stanford, CA: Stanford University Press, 2012), 91.

4. It is interesting to see how this process compares to those in Eastern empires, especially China. But just because the present book is not able to fully account for this Eastern history does not mean that I share Weber's view that Eastern empires and cities were "clusters of absences." I hope future works will take up this question in greater detail. For an excellent source on this issue, see Engin Isin, *Citizenship after Orientalism: An Unfinished Project* (London: Routledge, 2014).

5. Edith Porada, "The Relative Chronology of Mesopotamia: Part 1, Seals and Trade (6000–1600 B.C.)," and Donald Hansen, "The Relative Chronology of Mesopotamia: Part 2, The Pottery Sequence at Nippur from the Middle Uruk to the End of the Old Babylonian Period (3400–1600 B.C.)," both in *Chronologies in Old World Archaeology*, 3rd ed., ed. Robert Ehrich (Chicago: University of Chicago Press, 1992), 77–121, esp. 87.

6. This can be clearly seen in the creation of Roman *castra* (military encampments), which later would turn into towns and cities. The orientation of the entire grid was first and foremost a central point (*decumanus* and *cardo maximus*) from which the cardinal directions were measured and the *castra* divided. "Meanwhile the survey party was staking out the centre line of the camp (*decumanus maximus*)

crossed by its axis (*Cardo maximus*). These two lines formed the basis of two pathways bisecting the camp, the via principalis about 30 metros wide. All the various *strigae* (or rectangular spaces where the tents were to be erected) were marked off, as were the corners of the square of oblong camp." Martin Brice, *Stronghold: A History of Military Architecture* (London: Batsford, 1984), 48.

7. For an excellent literature review of theories of ancient urban planning, including their cosmological design, see Michael E. Smith, "Form and Meaning in the Earliest Cities: A New Approach to Ancient Urban Planning," *Journal of Planning History* 6, no. 1 (February 2007): 3–47.

8. The square and grid form were also socially significant but were for the most part subordinate to the circle and its centrifugal rotation.

9. See Paul Virilio, *Negative Horizon: An Essay in Dromoscopy*, trans. Michael Degener (London: Continuum, 2006), 48.

10. "An army is always strong enough when it can go and come, extend itself and draw itself back in, as it wishes and when it wishes." Paul Virilio attributes this phrase to the ancient Chinese strategist Se Ma, in ibid., 58.

11. "A human being is by nature," Aristotle says, "a political animal, and anyone who is without a city-state, not by luck but by nature, is either a poor specimen or else superhuman . . . either a beast or a god." Aristotle, *Politics*, trans. C. D. C. Reeve (Indianapolis: Hackett, 1998), book I, chap. 2, 1253a, 1–30.

12. Herodotus, *The Landmark Herodotus: The Histories*, trans. Andrea L. Purvis (New York: Pantheon Books, 2007), book I, chap. 4, sec. 46.

13. Aristotle, *Politics*, book I, chap. 6, 1255a, 25.

14. Ibid., chap. 2, 1252b, 5; chap. 6, 1255a, 30.

15. Anthony Pagden, *The Fall of Natural Man: The American Indian and the Origins of Comparative Ethnology* (Cambridge: Cambridge University Press, 1982).

16. Ibid., 15.

17. Ibid., 17.

18. Isaac Mendelsohn, *Slavery in the Ancient Near East: A Comparative Study of Slavery in Babylonia, Assyria, Syria, and Palestine, from the Middle of the Third Millennium to the End of the First Millennium* (New York: Oxford University Press, 1949), 74.

19. Ibid., 7.

20. Virilio, *Negative Horizon*, 56.

21. This point is argued in more detail in the case of Greece by Moses Finley and in other Near East empires by Isaac Mendelsohn. See Moses Finley, "Was Greek Civilization Based on Slave Labour?," *Historia* 8 (1959): 145–64; Mendelsohn, *Slavery in the Ancient Near East*.

22. Mendelsohn, *Slavery in the Ancient Near East*, 92; Daniel Snell, *Flight and Freedom in the Ancient Near East* (Leiden, Netherlands: Brill, 2001), 3.

23. While this is not exactly the same as chattel slavery, forced relocation and labor are still kinds of expulsion.

24. For a full anthropological account of the emergence of ancient debt and debt slavery, see David Graeber, *Debt: The First 5,000 Years* (Brooklyn, NY: Melville House, 2011).

25. Ibid., 39.

26. Here Graeber claims to be following the interpretation of Michael Hudson's "Reconstructuring the Origins of Interest-Bearing Debt and the Logic of Clean Slates," in *Debt and Economic Renewal in the Ancient Near East*, ed. Michael Hudson and Marc Van de Mieroop (Bethesda, MD: CDL Press), 7–58. Others suggest that interest may have instead originated in rental fees. See Marc Van De Mieroop, "A History of Near Eastern Debt?," in Hudson and Van de Mieroop, *Debt and Economic Renewal*, 59–95.

27. Graeber, *Debt: The First 5,000 Years*, 65.

28. Ibid.

29. Ibid.

30. K. R. Bradley and Paul Cartledge, *The Cambridge World History of Slavery*, Vol. 1, *The Ancient Mediterranean World* (Cambridge: Cambridge University Press, 2011), 16–17.

31. Ibid., 13–14.

32. Moses Finley argues that ancient Greece and Rome were "true slave societies . . . where the economic and political elite depended primarily on slave labor for basic production." Moses Finley, "Slavery," in *International Encyclopedia of the Social Sciences*, ed. David Sills (New York: Macmillan, 1968), 14:310.

33. Although estimations of the slave population in Athens vary greatly, Andrewes places it at eighty thousand to one hundred thousand ca. 500–400 BCE. Antony Andrewes, *The Greeks* (London: Hutchinson, 1967), 135.

34. M. I. Finley, *Ancient Slavery and Modern Ideology*, rev. exp. ed., edited by B. D. Shaw (Princeton, NJ: Markus Weiner Publishers, 1998), 148.

35. Mendelsohn, *Slavery in the Ancient Near East*.

36. Fernand Braudel, *The Mediterranean and the Mediterranean World in the Age of Philip II*, trans. Siân Reynolds (New York: Harper & Row, 1972), 51.

37. "Constructed roads, dug canals, erected fortresses, built temples, tilled crown lands, and worked in the royal factories." Mendelsohn, *Slavery in the Ancient Near East*, 92.

38. For an extended review of the literature and themes of ancient slavery, see Bradley and Cartledge, *Cambridge World History of Slavery*.

CHAPTER 5

1. Feudal land tenure was not completely abolished in England until the seventeenth century and in France until the French Revolution in 1789. See Marc

Bloch, *Slavery and Serfdom in the Middle Ages: Selected Essays* (Berkeley: University of California Press, 1975).

2. March Bloch argues that the word "feudalism" comes from the Frankish term *fehu-ôd*, in which *fehu* means "cattle" and *-ôd* means "goods." Cattle, in contrast to currency, are always tied to the soil, land, and its grasses. Thus, when land replaced currency as the primary store of value during feudalism, the Germanic word *fehu-ôd* replaced the Latin word *beneficium* as the name of stored value. See Marc Bloch, *Feudal Society* (Chicago: University of Chicago Press, 1961), 106.

3. Perry Anderson, *Passages from Antiquity to Feudalism* (London: NLB, 1974), 153.

4. Ibid., 154.

5. Ibid., 141.

6. Daniel McGarry, *Medieval History and Civilization* (New York: Macmillan, 1976), 242.

7. Clifford Backman, *The Worlds of Medieval Europe* (New York: Oxford University Press, 2003), 178–79.

8. Ibid., 178.

9. Anderson, *Passages from Antiquity to Feudalism*, 151.

10. Ibid., 148.

11. Ibid., 152 (my italics).

12. For an in-depth kinetic analysis of human joints, see Vincenzo Parenti-Castelli and Nicola Sancisi, "Synthesis of Spatial Mechanisms to Model Human Joints," in *21st Century Kinematics,* ed. J. M. McCarthy (Springer-Verlag London, 2013), 49–84. Another example of spatial motion is what is called in mechanics "Bennett's linkage," a spatial four-bar linkage with hinged joints that have their axes angled in a particular way that makes the system movable. See K. H. Hunt, *Kinematic Geometry of Mechanisms* (Oxford: Oxford University Press, 1978).

13. Henri Pirenne, *Economic and Social History of Medieval Europe* (New York: Martino Fine Books, 2014), 167–75.

14. Michel Foucault, *The History of Sexuality*, Vol. 1, *An Introduction* (New York: Vintage, 1990), 87.

15. Ibid.

16. Ibid.

17. Silvia Federici, *Caliban and the Witch* (New York: Autonomedia, 2004), 23.

18. Anderson, *Passages from Antiquity to Feudalism*, 122.

19. Ibid., 123.

20. Ibid.

21. Ibid., 139.

22. Ibid.

23. Guy Geltner, *The Medieval Prison: A Social History* (Princeton, NJ: Princeton University Press, 2008), 55.

24. Federici, *Caliban and the Witch*, 27.

25. Ibid., 26–27.

26. H. S. Bennett, *Life on the English Manor: A Study of Peasant Conditions, 1150–1400* (1937; repr., Cambridge: Cambridge University Press, 1967), 295–96.

27. Bronislaw Geremek, *Poverty: A History* (Oxford, UK: Blackwell, 1994), 56.

28. A. L. Beier, *Masterless Men: The Vagrancy Problem in England 1560–1640* (London: Methuen, 1985), 19.

29. Eric Kerridge, *The Agricultural Revolution* (New York: A. M. Kelley, 1968), 39–40, 181.

30. Beier, *Masterless Men*, 20.

31. Ibid.

32. This history is explored at length by Marx on primitive accumulation. Karl Marx, *Capital: A Critique of Political Economy: A Critique of Political Economy*, trans. Ben Fowkes (London: Penguin Books, 1990), vol. 1, chaps. 26–28.

33. M. W. Beresford, *The Lost Villages of England* (Stroud, UK: Sutton Publishing, 1998), 102.

34. "'Forsooth, my lord,' quoth I, 'your sheep that were wont to be so meek and tame and so small eaters, now, as I hear say, be become so great devourers and so wild, that they eat up and swallow down the very men themselves. They consume, destroy, and devour whole fields, houses, and cities.'" Thomas More, *Three Early Modern Utopias* (Oxford: Oxford University Press, 1999), 21–22.

35. Cited in William E. Tate, *The Enclosure Movement* (New York: Walker, 1967), 63.

36. Guy Geltner, "Medieval Prisons: Between Myth and Reality, Hell and Purgatory," *History Compass* 4 (2006): 2.

37. Ibid.

38. Ibid., 3.

39. Guy Geltner, "Detrusio, Penal Cloistering in the Middle Ages," *Revue Bénédictine* 118, no. 1 (2012): 89–108, quote on 91.

40. A. L. Biere develops this point further in *Masterless Men*, as does Silvia Federici in *Caliban and the Witch*.

41. "Vagabonds and Beggars Act 1494 (11 Henry VII c.2)," King's Norton, last updated August 7, 2005, accessed April 23, 2015, http://www.kingsnorton.info/time/poor_law_workhouse_timeline.htm.

42. Marx, *Capital*, 1:896–97.

43. Ibid., 897.

44. Richard Burn, *The History of the Poor Laws: With Observations* (New York: A. M. Kelley, 1973), 37.

45. "There were similar laws in France, where by the middle of the seventeenth century a kingdom of vagabonds (*royaume des truands*) had been established in Paris. Even at the beginning of the reign of Louis XVI, the Ordinance of 13 July

1777 provided that every man in good health from 16 to 60 years of age, if without means of subsistence and not practicing a trade, should be sent to the galleys. The Statute of Charles V for the Netherlands (October 1537), the first Edict of the States and Towns of Holland (10 March 1614) and the Plakaat of the United Provinces (26 June 1649) are further examples of the same kind." Marx, *Capital*, 899.

46. Geltner, *The Medieval Prison*.

47. Backman, *The Worlds of Medieval Europe*, 136.

48. Ibid., 135–36.

49. Joseph Patrick Byrne, *Encyclopedia of the Black Death* (Santa Barbara, CA: ABC-CLIO, 2012), 37–38, 90.

50. Backman, *The Worlds of Medieval Europe*, 376.

51. On the usage of early-modern identification, passport, and migrant surveillance, see Valentin Groebner, *Who Are You? Identification, Deception, and Surveillance in Early Modern Europe* (Brooklyn, NY: Zone Books, 2007).

52. Byrne, *Encyclopedia of the Black Death*, 208.

53. Burn, *The History of the Poor Laws*, 75.

54. Federici, *Caliban and the Witch*, 193.

55. For a detailed account of this practice, see ibid., 163–218.

56. For a detailed account of the crimes attributed to witches, see ibid., 166–93, quote on 171.

57. Ibid., 176.

58. Luciano Parinetto, *Streghe e politica: Dal Rinascimento italiano a Montaigne, da Bodin a Naudé* (Milan: Istituto Propaganda Libraria, 1983).

59. Lesley Byrd Simpson, *The Encomienda in New Spain: The Beginning of Spanish Mexico* (Berkeley: University of California Press, 1950), xiii.

60. Timothy Yeager, "Encomienda or Slavery? The Spanish Crown's Choice of Labor Organization in Sixteenth-Century Spanish America," *Journal of Economic History* 55, no. 4 (1995): 842.

61. Simpson, *The Encomienda in New Spain*, xi, viii.

CHAPTER 6

1. Eric Hobsbawm, "The General Crisis of the European Economy in the 17th Century," *Past and Present* 5, no. 1 (1954): 33–53.

2. "A great number of peasants were driven into vagabondage or forced to become city plebeians by the destruction of their domiciles and the devastation of their fields in addition to the general disorder." Friedrich Engels, *The Peasant War in Germany*, trans. Moissaye Olgin (New York: International Publishers, 1966), 147.

3. The innovation of modern kinopower is that it does not limit surplus motion predominantly by geography, force, or law but strictly by economic compulsion.

4. Giorgio Agamben, *The Kingdom and the Glory: For a Theological Genealogy of Economy and Government*, trans. Lorenzo Chiesa and Matteo Mandarini (Stanford, CA: Stanford University Press, 2011), 17.

5. For a detailed argument for the proletariat as a political figure of difference and minor politics, see Nicholas Thoburn, *Deleuze, Marx and Politics* (London: Routledge, 2003).

6. "Not only did many anarchists invoke nomadic themes originating in the East, but the bourgeoisie above all were quick to equate proletarians and nomads, comparing Paris to a city haunted by nomads." Gilles Deleuze and Félix Guattari, *A Thousand Plateaus: Capitalism and Schizophrenia*, trans. Brian Massumi (London: Continuum, 2008), 558n61. See also Louis Chevalier, *Labouring Classes and Dangerous Classes in Paris during the First Half of the Nineteenth Century*, trans. Frank Jellinek (London: Routledge, 1973), 362–66.

7. Goetz Briefs, *The Proletariat: A Challenge to Western Civilization* (New York: McGraw-Hill, 1937).

8. Peter Linebaugh, *The London Hanged: Crime and Civil Society in the Eighteenth Century* (London: Penguin, 1991), 122.

9. See Sidney Hook, *Marx and the Marxists: The Ambiguous Legacy* (Princeton, NJ: Van Nostrand, 1955), 13.

10. Balibar argues that we cannot define the proletariat according to the category of a fixed class or identity. See Étienne Balibar, "In Search of the Proletariat: The Notion of Class Politics in Marx," in *Masses, Classes, Ideas: Studies on Politics and Philosophy before and after Marx*, trans. J. Swenson (London: Routledge, 1994), 125–50.

11. Karl Marx, *Capital: A Critique of Political Economy*, trans. Ben Fowkes (London: Penguin, 1976), 1:781.

12. Ibid., 784.

13. Ibid., 794.

14. Ibid., 797.

15. Ibid., 799.

16. Ibid., 785.

17. Ibid., 786.

18. Karl Marx, *Collected Works of Karl Marx and Friedrich Engels, Volume 10: 1849–51* (London: Lawrence & Wishart, 1978), 73.

19. See Marx, *Capital*, 1:781–93.

20. Quoted in Richard Rubenstein, *The Age of Triage: Fear and Hope in an Overcrowded World* (Boston: Beacon Press, 1983), 36n6.

21. Enclosure figures come from Gilbert Slater, *The English Peasantry and the Enclosure of Common Fields* (New York: A. M. Kelley, 1968), 140–47; J. L. Hammond and Barbara Bradby Hammond, *The Village Labourer* (London: Longman, 1978), 17; and William E. Tate, *The Enclosure Movement* (New York: Walker, 1967), 88.

22. Tate, *The Enclosure Movement*, 88.

23. On the history of the contribution of proletarian migrants to the rise of urban industrialism, see Massimo Bacci and Carl Ipsen, *A Short History of Migration* (Cambridge, UK: Polity, 2012); and in the case of Europe specifically, see Sidney Pollard, *Peaceful Conquest: The Industrialization of Europe, 1760–1970* (Oxford: Oxford University Press, 1981), 148–53; Leslie Moch, *Moving Europeans: Migration in Western Europe since 1650* (Bloomington: Indiana University Press, 1992).

24. Marx defines this as a period of "bloody legislation" in England between 1530 and 1700. Marx, *Capital*, 1:899.

25. For detailed history of the rise of traffic created by urban migration and "the regimentation of congestion," see Lewis Mumford, *The City in History: Its Origins, Its Transformations, and Its Prospects* (New York: Harcourt, 1961), 431–45.

26. Marx, *Capital*, 1:848.

27. Ibid., 790.

28. Ibid., 786.

29. Ibid., 935.

30. Ibid., 792.

31. Ibid., 789.

32. "Some of these workers emigrate; in fact they are merely following capital, which has itself emigrated." Ibid., 794.

33. Ibid., 637.

34. Ibid., 785.

35. Ibid., 784.

36. Ibid.

37. Ibid.

38. Thomas Malthus, *An Essay on the Principle of Population* (1798; repr., Oxford: Oxford University Press, 1993), 61, viii, 26.

39. Marx, *Capital*, 1:766n6.

40. Ibid., 788.

41. This dramatic increase was spurred by a system of forced labor called "indoor relief." For further details of this survey, see Great Britain, *Abstract of the Returns Made by the Overseers of the Poor in Pursuance of an Act, Passed in the Twenty-Sixth Year of His Present Majesty's Reign, Intitled, An Act for Obliging Overseers of the Poor to Make Returns upon Oath, to Certain Questions "Specified Therein, Relative to the State of the Poor,"* 1787.

42. Marx, *Capital*, 1:520n44.

43. Rubenstein, *The Age of Triage*, 68.

44. Marx, *Capital*, 1:379n78.

45. Cited in ibid., 923.

46. Ibid.

47. Rubenstein, *The Age of Triage,* 68.

48. J. R. Poynter, *Society and Pauperism: English Ideas on Poor Relief, 1795–1834* (London: Routledge, 1969), 126.

49. Cited in Marx, *Capital,* 1:388. See also Jacob Vanderlint, *Jacob Vanderlint on Money Answers All Things* (Baltimore: Lord Baltimore Press, 1734), 242–43.

50. Marx, *Capital,* 1:388.

51. Sidney Webb and Beatrice Webb, *English Poor Law Policy* (London: Longmans, Green, 1910), 190.

52. Rubenstein, *The Age of Triage,* 72.

53. Jeremy Bentham, *Pauper Management Improved Particularly by Means of an Application of the Panopticon Principle of Construction* (London: R. Baldwin, 1812).

CHAPTER 7

1. Michel Foucault, *Discipline and Punish: The Birth of the Prison,* trans. Alan Sheridan (1977; repr., New York: Vintage Books, 1995), 210.

2. Roger Ekirch, *Bound for America: The Transportation of British Convicts to the Colonies, 1718–1775* (Oxford, UK: Clarendon Press, 1987), 1.

3. E. E. Rich, "Colonial Settlement and Its Labour Problems," in *The Cambridge History of Europe,* ed. E. E. Rich and C. H. Wilson (Cambridge: Cambridge University Press, 1967), 4:342.

4. John Hirst, "Australian Experience: The Convict Colony," in *The Oxford History of the Prison: The Practice of Punishment in Western Society,* ed. Norval Morris and David J. Rothman (New York: Oxford University Press, 1995), 266.

5. Stephen Nicholas, *Convict Workers: Reinterpreting Australia's Past* (Cambridge: Cambridge University Press, 1988), 7.

6. Hirst, "Australian Experience," 268.

7. Ibid.

8. Ibid., 272.

9. Jeremy Bentham, "Panopticon vs. New South Wales: Or the Panopticon Penitentiary System, and the Penal Colonization System, Compared," in *The Works of Jeremy Bentham* (Edinburgh: W. Tait, 1843), 4:173.

10. Nicholas, *Convict Workers,* 7.

11. James Rodway, *Guiana: British, Dutch, and French* (London: T. F. Unwin, 1912), 139–52.

12. Françoise Renaudot and Antoine Cancellieri, *L'histoire des français en Algérie, 1830–1962* (Paris: Laffont,1979), 38.

13. Nicholas, *Convict Workers,* 35.

14. Ibid., 36.

15. For a full list and detailed statistics of global penal expulsions in the nineteenth century, see ibid.

16. The forced migration of penal transport is not discussed in several important books dealing with that time period, for example, Patrick Manning, *Migration in World History* (London: Routledge, 2013); T. J. Hatton and Jeffrey G. Williamson, *The Age of Mass Migration: Causes and Economic Impact* (New York: Oxford University Press, 1998); Steven J. Gold and Stephanie J. Nawyn, *Routledge International Handbook of Migration Studies* (London: Routledge, 2013).

17. Hatton and Williamson, *The Age of Mass Migration*, 3.

18. Karl Marx, *Capital: A Critique of Political Economy*, trans. Ben Fowkes (London: Penguin, 1976), 1:899 (my italics).

19. "The choice to migrate always involved a complex balancing of costs and benefits carried out by individuals, families, and communities." Massimo Bacci and Carl Ipsen, *A Short History of Migration* (Cambridge, UK: Polity, 2012), 55. "These 'free' migrants moved voluntarily (unlike slaves) and without debt bondage (unlike indentured laborers), although they would have been constrained by social and economic circumstances." Ian Goldin, Geoffrey Cameron, and Meera Balarajan, *Exceptional People: How Migration Shaped Our World and Will Define Our Future* (Princeton, NJ: Princeton University Press, 2011), 57–58.

20. Hatton and Williamson, *The Age of Mass Migration*.

21. Bacci and Ipsen, *A Short History of Migration*, 47.

22. Ibid., 48.

23. Paul Bairoch, "The Impact of Crop Yields, Agricultural Productivity, and Transport Costs on Urban Growth between 1800 and 1910," in *Urbanization in History: A Process of Dynamic Interactions*, ed. Ad van der Woude, Akira Hayami, and Jan de Vries (Oxford: Oxford University Press, 1990), 134–51.

24. Bacci and Ipsen, *A Short History of Migration*, 49.

25. Ibid.

26. Ibid., 51.

27. Here I rely on Bacci and Ipsen, *A Short History of Migration,* for this history of emigration.

28. Robert Torrens, "A Paper on the Means of Reducing the Poor's Rates," in *The Pamphleteer* 10, no. 20 (1817), cited in Richard Rubenstein, *The Age of Triage: Fear and Hope in an Overcrowded World* (Boston: Beacon Press, 1983), 83.

29. Cited in Stanley Johnson, *A History of Emigration: From the United Kingdom to North America, 1763–1812* (New York: E. P. Dutton, 1913), 2–3.

30. Eric Hobsbawm, *The Age of Revolution: Europe 1789–1848* (London: Weidenfeld & Nicolson, 1962), 211.

31. Rubenstein, *The Age of Triage*, 82.

32. Johnson, *A History of Emigration*, 18–20.

33. Eric Hobsbawm and George F. E. Rudé, *Captain Swing* (New York: Pantheon Books, 1968), 72–80.

34. Hirst, "Australian Experience," 266.

35. T. J. Hatton and Jeffrey G. Williamson, *Global Migration and the World Economy: Two Centuries of Policy and Performance* (Boston: MIT Press, 2005).

36. Hannah Arendt, *The Origins of Totalitarianism* (New York: Harcourt, Brace, 1951), 267.

37. Ibid., 278.

38. All information cited in ibid., 279n25.

39. Ibid., 286.

40. Cited in ibid., 269n2. United States, *Nazi Conspiracy and Aggression* (Washington, DC: US Government Printing Office, 1946), 6:87.

41. David Richardson, "Involuntary Migration in the Early Modern World, 1500–1800," in *The Cambridge World History of Slavery, Volume 3: AD 1420–AD 1804,* ed. David Eltis and Stanley L. Engerman (Cambridge: Cambridge University Press, 2011), 583.

42. Herbert S. Klein, *The Atlantic Slave Trade* (Cambridge: Cambridge University Press, 1999), 140, table 6.2.

43. See Peter Linebaugh and Marcus Rediker, *The Many-Headed Hydra: Sailors, Slaves, Commoners, and the Hidden History of the Revolutionary Atlantic* (Boston: Beacon Press, 2000).

44. Cited in Ellen Meiksins Wood, *The Origin of Capitalism: A Longer View* (London: Verso, 2002), 160.

45. Ibid., 153–54.

46. Nassau Senior, *On the Third Report of the Commissioners for Inquiry into the Conditions of the Poor in Ireland* (London: House of Commons, 1837), 51:245.

47. Grosvenor Talbot Griffith, *Population Problems of the Age of Malthus* (London: A. M. Kelley, 1967).

48. See Cecil Woodham-Smith, *The Great Hunger: Ireland 1845–1849* (New York: Harper & Row, 1962), 411–12.

49. Rubenstein, *The Age of Triage,* 103.

50. Ibid., 109–10.

51. Woodham-Smith, *The Great Hunger,* 271.

52. Ibid., 123–24, 125.

53. Letter of Trevelyan to Edward B. Twistleton, September 14, 1848, quoted in Woodham-Smith, *The Great Hunger,* 371.

54. Ibid., 278–79.

55. Rubenstein, *The Age of Triage,* 119–20.

56. "Effects of Emigration on Production and Consumption," *The Economist* 2, no. 494 (February 12, 1853): 168–69.

57. Marx, *Capital,* 1:861–62.

58. Cited in Wood, *The Origin of Capitalism,* 159.

59. John Locke, *The Second Treatise of Government: An Essay concerning the True Original, Extent and End of Civil Government, and, a Letter concerning Toleration* (Oxford, UK: Blackwell, 1966), book II, sections 26, 27, 40, 43.

60. See Hagar Kotef, *Movement and the Ordering of Freedom: On Liberal Governances of Mobility* (Durham, NC: Duke University Press, 2015), 101–10.

61. See Wood, *The Origin of Capitalism,* for an account of Locke's theory in relation to the origins of capitalism.

62. Ibid., 115.

63. Locke, *Second Treatise,* book II, sec. 28.

64. Thomas Jefferson, letter to William Henry Harrison, February 27, 1803 (Library of Congress, 1803), http://images.indianahistory.org/u?/dc007,76.

CHAPTER 8

1. On the social theory of turbulence, see Lucretius, *De Rerum Natura* (Cambridge, MA: Harvard University Press, 1975); Michel Serres, *The Birth of Physics,* trans. Jack Hawkes (Manchester, UK: Clinamen Press, 2000); Gilles Deleuze and Félix Guattari, *A Thousand Plateaus: Capitalism and Schizophrenia,* trans. Brian Massumi (London: Continuum, 2008); Tim Cresswell and C. Martin, "On Turbulence: Entanglements of Disorder and Order on a Devon Beach," *Tijdschrift Voor Economische En Sociale Geografie* 103, no. 5 (2012): 516–29; Manuel De Landa, *Intensive Science and Virtual Philosophy* (London: Continuum, 2002); and Nikos Papastergiadis, *The Turbulence of Migration: Globalization, Deterritorialization, and Hybridity* (Cambridge, UK: Polity Press, 2000). "As has often been noted, the modern world is in a state of flux and turbulence. . . . While nothing is utterly random, the consequences of change are often far from predictable." Papastergiadis, *The Turbulence of Migration,* 1.

2. Henri Bergson, *Creative Evolution,* trans. Arthur Mitchell (New York: Modern Library, 1944), 9.

3. "I say to you: you still have chaos in you." Friedrich Wilhelm Nietzsche, *Thus Spoke Zarathustra: A Book for All and None,* trans. Adrian Del Caro (Cambridge: Cambridge University Press, 2006), 9.

4. For another theory of social pressure, see Yves Citton, *Renverser l'insoutenable* (Paris: Seuil, 2012), 53–119.

5. Fittingly, the English word "pressure" comes from the PIE root *per-, meaning "to strike or press."

CHAPTER 9

1. H. Barnard and Willeke Wendrich, *The Archaeology of Mobility: Old World and New World Nomadism* (Los Angeles: Cotsen Institute of Archaeology, University of California, 2008).

2. "Those who fled became, one might say, the first refugees from state power, joining others outside the state's reach." James Scott, *The Art of Not Being Governed: An Anarchist History of Upland Southeast Asia* (New Haven, CT: Yale University Press, 2009), 6.

3. See Roger Cribb, *Nomads in Archaeology* (Cambridge: Cambridge University Press, 1991).

4. We can also locate degrees of oscillation among seminomadic or highly mobile territorial peoples in Melanesian societies in the Solomon Islands. "Such are not viewed as changes in the permanent place of residence—or migration as conventionally defined—as they would in Euro-American society, but rather oscillations within the land owned by closely-related kin. To a tribesman, permanent place of residence identifies a circumstanced piece of territory but not the precise site of his household, hamlet, or village." Murray Chapman, "Tribal Mobility as Circulation: A Solomon Islands Example of Micro/Macro Linkages," *East-West Population Institute* 78 (1976): 127–42.

5. For a detailed defense of this claim, see M. P. Griaznov, *The Ancient Civilization of Southern Siberia*, trans. James Hogarth (New York: Cowles, 1969), 97–98, 131–33, cited in Gilles Deleuze and Félix Guattari, *A Thousand Plateaus: Capitalism and Schizophrenia*, trans. Brian Massumi (London: Continuum, 2008), 430.

6. Arnold Toynbee, *A Study of History* (London: Oxford University Press, 1935), 3:11.

7. In this sense nomadic peoples appear to be "profoundly settled." Hugh Brody, *The Other Side of Eden: Hunters, Farmers, and the Shaping of the World* (Vancouver, Canada: Douglas &McIntyre, 2000), 245.

8. Scott, *The Art of Not Being Governed*, 9.

9. Ibid., 9. See also Pierre Clastres, *Society against the State: Essays in Political Anthropology* (New York: Zone Books, 1989).

10. Emmanuel Laroche, *Histoire de la racine NEM- en grec ancien* (Paris: Klincksieck, 1949), 255.

11. Ibid., 116.

12. Ibn Khaldūn, *The Muqaddimah: An Introduction to History*, trans. Franz Rosenthal (Princeton, NJ: Princeton University Press, 1969), sections 8, 13.

13. Ibid., sec. 8.

14. Toynbee, *A Study of History*, 3:16, 14.

15. See Deleuze and Guattari, *A Thousand Plateaus*, 418.

CHAPTER 10

1. Daniel Snell, *Flight and Freedom in the Ancient Near East* (Leiden, Netherlands: Brill, 2001), 88–95.

2. Herodotus, *The Landmark Herodotus: The Histories*, trans. Andrea L. Purvis (New York: Pantheon Books, 2007), book II, chap. 113.

3. For an extensive analysis of the primary texts from the ancient world on the punishments for runaway slaves and refugees, see Snell, *Flight and Freedom*.

4. Aristotle, *Metaphysics*, trans. Joe Sachs (Santa Fe, NM: Green Lion Press, 1999), 1075a, 20–25.

5. Snell, *Flight and Freedom*, 58.

6. Junius Rodriguez, *Encyclopedia of Slave Resistance and Rebellion* (Westport, CT: Greenwood Press, 2007), 1:112.

7. P. J. Heather, *Empires and Barbarians: The Fall of Rome and the Birth of Europe* (New York: Oxford University Press, 2010), 212–14.

8. Strabo, *The Geography of Strabo*, trans. Horace Leonard Jones (London: W. Heinemann, 1917), book I, chap. I, sec. 17.

9. Paul Kahn and Francis Woodman Cleaves, *The Secret History of the Mongols: The Origin of Chinghis Khan*, trans. Francis Woodman Cleaves (San Francisco: North Point Press, 1984), 180.

10. Ammianus Marcellinus, *The Roman History of Ammianus Marcellinus, during the Reigns of the Emperors Constantius, Julian, Jovianus, Valentinian, and Valens*, trans. Charles Duke Yonge (London: H. G. Bohn, 1862), book XVI, chap. XII, sec. 43; book XXXI, chap. IV, sec. 6; book XVI, chap. XII, sec. 57; book XXXI, chap. III, sec. 8; book XXXI, chap. IV, sec. 9.

11. Georg Wilhelm Friedrich Hegel, *Lectures on the Philosophy of World History*, trans. Robert F. Brown and Peter Crafts Hodgson (Oxford, UK: Clarendon Press, 2011), 460.

12. Pseudo-Aristotle, *The Metaphysics Books X–XIV; Oeconomica and Magna Moralia*, trans. Hugh Tredennick and G. Cyril Armstrong (London: William Heinemann, 1969), 1.5.6.

13. "Barbaricum does not seem to have been monetised and an important part of the economy must have comprised reciprocal gift exchange." Guy Halsall, *Barbarian Migrations and the Roman West, 376–568* (Cambridge: Cambridge University Press, 2007), 124.

14. Ibid., 62.

15. "It is probably better to see this as a potentially fluid state of affairs, involving negotiation as well as force and turning on the contingencies of the current political situation, rather than envisaging (unlike, perhaps, in Ireland) a formal hierarchy of different types of king." Ibid., 125.

16. Heather, *Empires and Barbarians*, 215.

17. Halsall, *Barbarian Migrations*, 123–25.

18. Hugh Elton, *Warfare in Roman Europe, AD 350–425* (Oxford, UK: Clarendon Press, 1996), 181–92.

19. "The precise nature of this 'conspiracy' is obscure and the idea that Scots, Picts and Saxons were working in conjunction seems extremely unlikely." See Halsall, *Barbarian Migrations*, 58.

20. Ibid., 58, 177–80, 134.

21. Patrick Geary, *The Myth of Nations: The Medieval Origins of Europe* (Princeton, NJ: Princeton University Press, 2002).

22. Halsall, *Barbarian Migrations*, 129.

23. Peter Mörters, Y. Peres, Oded Schramm, and Wendelin Werner, *Brownian Motion* (Cambridge: Cambridge University Press, 2010).

24. Marcellinus, *The Roman History of Ammianus Marcellinus,* book XXXI, chap. III, sec. 8.

25. Daniel Bernoulli and Jean Bernoulli, *Hydrodynamics* (1738; repr., New York: Dover Publications, 1968).

26. Keith Bradley, "Slavery in the Roman Republic," in *The Cambridge World History of Slavery* (Cambridge: Cambridge University Press, 2011), 1:251.

27. Plutarch, *Plutarch's Lives, Volume 3* (London: Bell, 1883), "Life of Crassus," sec. VIII.

28. Ibid., sec. IX; Appianus, *The Civil Wars*, trans. John M. Carter (London: Penguin Books, 1996), book I, sec. 116.

29. Karl Marx, "Letter from Marx to Engels in Manchester Written, London, 27 February, 1861," in *Karl Marx, Frederick Engels: Collected Works* (New York: International Publishers, 1975), 41:264.

CHAPTER II

1. Norman Cohn, *The Pursuit of the Millennium: Revolutionary Millenarians and Mystical Anarchists of the Middle Ages* (New York: Oxford University Press, 1970), 105.

2. Malcolm Lambert, *Medieval Heresy: Popular Movements from the Gregorian Reform to the Reformation* (Oxford, UK: B. Blackwell, 1992), 98.

3. Silvia Federici, *Caliban and the Witch* (New York: Autonomedia, 2004), 33.

4. The history of heretical struggle against displacement, landlords, and the church is a difficult one to study since many of its original writings have been destroyed. The history of heresy is unfortunately written by its enemies.

5. Federici, *Caliban and the Witch*, 33.

6. These are the defining characteristics of pre-nineteenth-century revolt according to Charles Tilly, *Popular Contention in Great Britain, 1758–1834* (Cambridge, MA: Harvard University Press, 1995), 45.

7. Cynthia A. Bouton, "Review of History of Peasant Revolts: The Social Origins of Rebellion in Early Modern France by Yves-Marie Bercé," *Journal of Social History* 26, no. 3 (Spring 1993): 658–60. See also Yves-Marie Bercé, *Histoire des croquets* (Paris: Seuil, 1986), translated into English as *History of Peasant Revolts: The Social Origins of Rebellion in Early Modern France*, trans. Amanda Whitmore (Ithaca, NY: Cornell University Press, 1990).

8. The English words "rebellion" and "heresy" were both invented in the thirteenth century and point to a common description of vagabond counterpower. The word "heresy" comes from the Greek αἴρω (*hairein*, to seize), from the PIE root *ser-*, "to seize."

9. P. Boissonnade, *Life and Work in Medieval Europe: The Evolution of Medieval Economy from the Fifth to the Fifteenth Century*, trans. Eileen Power (New York: Harper & Row, 1964), 148.

10. Pierre Dockes, *Medieval Slavery and Liberation*, trans. Arthur Goldhammer (London: Methuen, 1982), 87.

11. R. I. Moore, *The War on Heresy: Faith and Power in Medieval Europe* (Cambridge, MA: Belknap Press of Harvard University Press, 2012), 399.

12. Gilles Deleuze and Félix Guattari, *A Thousand Plateaus: Capitalism and Schizophrenia*, trans. Brian Massumi (London: Continuum, 2008), 368.

13. David Nicholas, *Medieval Flanders* (London: Longman, 1992), 155.

14. Federici, *Caliban and the Witch*, 32.

15. Henri Pirenne, *Storia d'Europa: Dalle invasioni al 16 secolo* (Florence: Sansoni, 1956), 132.

16. Lambert, *Medieval Heresy*, 111.

17. Ibid., 117.

18. See Federici, *Caliban and the Witch*, 43.

19. Thomas More, *Three Early Modern Utopias* (Oxford: Oxford University Press, 1999), 22–23.

20. Raphael Holinshed, William Harrison, Richard Stanyhurst, John Hooker, Francis Thynne, Abraham Fleming, John Stow, and Henry Ellis, *Holinshed's Chronicles of England, Scotland, and Ireland* (London: J. Johnson, 1807), 1:186. Cited in Karl Marx, *Capital: A Critique of Political Economy*, trans. Ben Fowkes (London: Penguin, 1976), 1:898n2.

21. William Langland, *Piers Plowman* (Berkeley: University of California Press, 1979), line 5396.

22. See A. L. Beier, *Masterless Men: The Vagrancy Problem in England 1560–1640* (London: Methuen, 1985), 137–38.

23. Roger Manning, *Village Revolts: Social Protest and Popular Disturbances in England, 1509–1640* (Oxford, UK: Clarendon Press, 1988), 311.

24. Anthony Fletcher, *Tudor Rebellions* (London: Longman, 1973), 142–44.

25. Gerrard Winstanley, *The True Levellers Standard Advanced; or, The State of Community Opened, and Presented to the Sons of Men* (London: n.p., 1649).

26. Gary Snyder, "The Place, the Region, and the Commons," in *Environmental Philosophy: From Animal Rights to Radical Ecology*, ed. Michael Zimmerman (Upper Saddle River, NJ: Pearson Prentice Hall, 2005), 475.

27. Ibid.

28. Dockes, *Medieval Slavery and Liberation*, 86.

29. H. Hilton, *Bond Men Made Free: Medieval Peasant Movements and the English Rising of 1381* (New York: Viking Press, 1973), 120–21, 133.

30. Jan De Vries, *Economy of Europe in an Age of Crisis, 1600–1750* (Cambridge: Cambridge University Press, 1976), 42–43; G. Hoskins, *The Age of Plunder: King Henry's England, 1500–1547* (London: Longman, 1976), 11–12.

31. Nicholas, *Medieval Flanders*, 213–14.

32. Hilton, *Bond Men Made Free*, 128.

33. Quoted in Cohn, *The Pursuit of the Millennium*, 199.

34. Winstanley, *The True Levellers Standard*.

35. Cohn, *The Pursuit of the Millennium*, 205–22.

36. Lambert, *Medieval Heresy*, 64.

37. Federici, *Caliban and the Witch*, 34.

38. Walter Wakefield and Austin P. Evans, *Heresies of the High Middle Ages* (New York: Columbia University Press, 1969), 457.

39. Hilton, *Bond Men Made Free*, 75.

CHAPTER 12

1. Werner Sombart, *Socialism and the Social Movement* (New York: A. M. Kelley, 1968), 100; Kaethe Mengelberg, "Introduction," in *The History of the Social Movement in France, 1789–1850*, by Lorenz von Stein, trans. Kaethe Mengelberg (Totowa, NJ: Bedminster Press, 1964), 12.

2. Stein, *History of the Social Movement in France*, 68, 51, 56.

3. Ibid., 68, 76.

4. Ibid.

5. Ibid., 78–79.

6. Ibid., 93, 94.

7. Charles Tilly, *Regimes and Repertoires* (Chicago: University of Chicago Press, 2006), 56.

8. Charles Tilly, *The Contentious French* (Cambridge, MA: Belknap Press, 1986), 4.

9. These are Tilly's categories in *Popular Contention in Great Britain, 1758–1834* (Cambridge, MA: Harvard University Press, 1995), 45.

10. Sidney Tarrow, *Power in Movement: Social Movements and Contentious Politics* (Cambridge: Cambridge University Press, 1998), 55.

11. Pauline Maier, *From Resistance to Revolution: Colonial Radicals and the Development of American Opposition to Britain, 1765–1776* (New York: Knopf, 1972), 74, 75.

12. Seymour Drescher, *Capitalism and Antislavery: British Mobilization in Comparative Perspective* (New York: Oxford University Press, 1987), 78–79.

13. Tarrow, *Power in Movement,* 49.

14. It is dangerous to confuse the bourgeois revolution with the experience of the peasant and urban workers, as argued by the following authors: William Sewell, "Whatever Happened to the 'Social' in Social History?," in *Schools of Thought: Twenty-Five Years of Interpretive Social Science,* ed. J. W. Scott and D. Keates (Princeton, NJ: Princeton University Press, 2001), 209–26; William Sewell, *A Rhetoric of Bourgeois Revolution: The Abbé Sieyes and What Is the Third Estate?* (Durham, NC: Duke University Press, 1994); Olwen Hufton, *Women and the Limits of Citizenship in the French Revolution* (Toronto: University of Toronto Press, 1992); and S. Desan, "What's after Political Culture? Recent French Revolutionary Historiography," *French Historical Studies* 23, no. 1 (2000), 163–96.

15. "*Laboureurs* formed a tiny fraction of the agricultural population, however, while *gros fermiers* were rarer still. Goubert suggests that a typical village of several hundred inhabitants on the Picard plain would contain two *gros fermiers*; five or six *laboureurs*; twenty or so *haricotiers*; and between twenty and fifty households of day *laboureurs* or part-time artisans." Pierre Goubert, *Beauvais et le Beauvaisis de 1600 à 1730: Contribution à l'histoire sociale de la France du XVIIe siècle* (Paris: SEVPEN, 1960), 158, cited in Peter Jones, *The Peasantry in the French Revolution* (Cambridge: Cambridge University Press, 1988), 11.

16. John Markoff, *The Abolition of Feudalism: Peasants, Lords, and Legislators in the French Revolution* (University Park: Pennsylvania State University Press, 1996), 173.

17. Jones, *The Peasantry in the French Revolution,* 137; and Louis Chevalier, *Laboring Classes and Dangerous Classes in Paris during the First Half of the Nineteenth Century* (New York: H. Fertig, 1973).

18. Cited in Chevalier, *Laboring Classes and Dangerous Classes,* 364, 365.

19. Ibid., 361, 364.

20. Ibid., 367.

21. Honoré de Balzac, *La fille aux yeux d'or* [*The girl with the golden eyes*] (London: L. Smithers, 1896).

22. Cited in Chevalier, *Laboring Classes and Dangerous Classes,* 387.

23. Ibid., 364.

24. See ibid. for full descriptions.

25. Jacques Rancière, "Le bon temps ou la barrière des plaisirs," *Révoltes Logiques*, no. 7 (1978). Reprinted in English in *Voices of the People: The Social Life of 'La Sociale' at the End of the Second Empire*, ed. Adrian Rifkin and Roger D. Thomas (London: Routledge & Kegan Paul, 1988), 45–94, quote on 50.

26. R. Forster, *Seeds of Change, Peasants, Nobles, and Rural Revolution in 18th-Century France* (New York: Macmillan, 1975), 88–89.

27. Jean-Jacques Clère, *Les paysans de la Haute-Marne et la Révolution française: Recherches sur les structures fonçières de la communauté villageoise, 1780–1825* (Paris: Ed. du CTHS, 1988), 157.

28. Jones, *The Peasantry in the French Revolution*, 162.

29. Ibid., 155. Except in the north, where peasants banded together and collectively purchased land. See ibid., 157.

30. George Lefebvre, "La Révolution française et les paysans," in *Etudes sur la Révolution française* (Paris: Presses universitaires de France 1963), 344.

31. Georges Lefebvre, *Les paysans du nord pendant la Révolution française* (Bari, Italy: Laterza, 1959).

32. Tarrow, *Power in Movement*, 199. "A phase of heightened conflict and contention across the social system."

33. David Snow, Sarah Anne Soule, and Hanspeter Kriesi, eds., *The Blackwell Companion to Social Movements* (Malden, MA: Blackwell, 2004), 21.

34. Charles Tilly, *From Mobilization to Revolution* (Reading, UK: Addison-Wesley, 1978), 155.

35. Tarrow, *Power in Movement*, 69.

36. Benedict Anderson, *Imagined Communities: Reflections on the Origin and Spread of Nationalism* (London: Verso, 1991), 31, 34–35.

37. Alexis de Tocqueville, *Democracy in America*, ed. Brady Phillips, trans. Henry Reve (New York: Vintage, 1954), 2:517.

38. Markoff, *The Abolition of Feudalism*, 383.

39. Tarrow, *Power in Movement*, 60–62.

40. Rosabeth Moss Kanter, *Commitment and Community: Communes and Utopias in Sociological Perspective* (Cambridge, MA: Harvard University Press, 1972), 62.

41. Ian Donnachie, *Robert Owen: Social Visionary* (Edinburgh: John Donald, 2005).

42. Quoted in Alice Felt Tyler, *Freedom's Ferment: Phases of American Social History to 1860* (Minneapolis: University of Minnesota Press, 1944), 217.

43. Kanter, *Commitment and Community*, 61.

44. Karl Marx and Friedrich Engels, *The Civil War in France* (New York: International Publishers, 1940).

45. Ibid.

46. Alain Badiou, *Polemics*, trans. Cécile Winter (London: Verso, 2006), 272.

47. Mikhail Bakunin, *Bakunin on Violence: Letter to S. Nechayev, June 2 1870* (New York: Anarchist Switchboard), 19.

48. Karl Marx, "First Draft of Letter To Vera Zasulich," *Karl Marx, Frederick Engels: Collected Works* (New York: International Publishers, 1975), 24:346.

49. See Daniel Gavron, *The Kibbutz: Awakening from Utopia* (Lanham, MD: Rowman & Littlefield, 2000); Henry Near, *The Kibbutz Movement: A History* (Oxford: Published for the Littman Library by Oxford University Press, 1992).

50. See Gerald Meaker, *The Revolutionary Left in Spain, 1914–1923* (Stanford, CA: Stanford University Press, 1974).

51. Although the practice of work stoppage has documented precursors in ancient history, the strike does not become the predominant international mode of migrant resistance until the nineteenth century. See Ronald Filippelli, *Labor Conflict in the United States: An Encyclopedia* (New York: Garland Publishing, 1990).

52. Mark Traugott, *The Insurgent Barricade* (Berkeley: University of California Press, 2010), 225–42.

53. Ibid., 176–77.

54. Ibid., 175.

55. Ibid., 175–76.

56. Ibid., 12–13, quote on 13.

57. Georges Duveau, *1848: The Making of a Revolution* (New York: Pantheon Books, 1967), 174.

58. Tilly, *From Mobilization to Revolution.*

59. Tarrow, *Power in Movement,* 37–56.

CHAPTER 13

1. See John Urry, *Global Complexity* (Cambridge, UK: Polity Press, 2003); and James Rosenau, *Turbulence in World Politics: A Theory of Change and Continuity* (New York: Harvester Wheatsheaf, 1990).

2. T. J. Hatton and Jeffrey G. Williamson, *The Age of Mass Migration: Causes and Economic Impact* (New York: Oxford University Press, 1998), 27.

3. For a more detailed introduction to globalization and migration, see Saskia Sassen, *The Mobility of Labor and Capital: A Study in International Investment and Labor Flow* (Cambridge: Cambridge University Press, 1988); Saskia Sassen, *Globalization and Its Discontents: Essays on the New Mobility of People and Money* (New York: New Press, 1998); Saskia Sassen, *Sociology of Globalization* (New York: W. W. Norton, 2007); Zygmunt Bauman, *Globalization: The Human Consequences* (New York: Columbia University Press, 1998); Stephen Castles and Alastair Davidson, *Citizenship and Migration: Globalization and the Politics of Belonging* (New York: Routledge, 2000); Rachel Brickner, *Migration,*

Globalization and the State (New York: Palgrave Macmillan, 2013); and Nikos Papastergiadis, *The Turbulence of Migration: Globalization, Deterritorialization, and Hybridity* (Cambridge, UK: Polity Press, 2000).

4. In addition to Papastergiadis, Gloria Anzaldúa, and Homi Bhabha (cited in Chapter 2), others have argued that we should understand the migrant in terms of hybridity. See Amar Acheraïou, *Questioning Hybridity, Postcolonialism and Globalization* (Hampshire, UK: Palgrave Macmillan, 2011); Marwan Kraidy, *Hybridity, or the Cultural Logic of Globalization* (Philadelphia: Temple University Press, 2005).

5. For an excellent history of migration through the twentieth century, see Darshan Vigneswaran, *Territory, Migration and the Evolution of the International System* (New York: Palgrave Macmillan, 2013).

6. See Saskia Sassen, *Territory, Authority, Rights from Medieval to Global Assemblages* (Princeton, NJ: Princeton University Press, 2008); Yasemin Soysal, *Limits of Citizenship: Migrants and Postnational Membership in Europe* (Chicago: University of Chicago Press, 1994); and David Jacobson, *Rights across Borders: Immigration and the Decline of Citizenship* (Baltimore: Johns Hopkins University Press, 1996); Ruud Koopmans and Paul Statham, "Challenging the Liberal Nation State? Postnationalism, Multiculturalism, and the Collective Claims Making of Migrants and Ethnic Minorities in Britain and Germany," *American Journal of Sociology* 105 (1999): 652–96.

7. Congressional Research Service, *Mexican Migration to the United States: Policy and Trends*, June 7, 2012, http://www.fas.org/sgp/crs/row/R42560.pdf.

8. National Council for the Evaluation of Social Development Policy (CONE-VAL), *2008 Evaluation Report on Social Development Policy in Mexico*, 2012, http://issuu.com/coneval/docs/tradfucci_n_informe_de_evaluaci_n_de_la_pol_de_des.

9. David Bacon, *The Right to Stay Home: How US Policy Drives Mexican Migration* (Boston: Beacon Press, 2013), 11.

10. David Bacon, *Illegal People: How Globalization Creates Migration and Criminalizes Immigrants* (Boston: Beacon Press, 2008).

11. Octavio Paz, *The Other Mexico: Critique of the Pyramid* (New York: Grove Press, 1972), 36.

12. There is an increasing literature in this area as land grabbing increases. See Saskia Sassen, "Land Grabs Today: Feeding the Disassembling of National Territory," *Globalizations* 10, no. 1 (2013): 25–46; Borras Saturnino, Ruth Hall, Ian Scoones, Ben White, and Wendy Wolford, "Towards a Better Understanding of Global Land Grabbing: An Editorial Introduction," *Journal of Peasant Studies* 38, no. 2 (2011): 209–16; Matias E. Margulis, Nora McKeon, and Saturnino M. Borras Jr., eds., *Land Grabbing and Global Governance* (London: Routledge, 2013); Ben White, Saturnino M. Borras Jr., Ruth Hall, Ian Scoones, and Wendy Wolford, eds., *The New Enclosures* (Hoboken, NJ: Taylor & Francis, 2013).

13. On the history of the Porfiriato, see Timothy Henderson, *Beyond Borders: A History of Mexican Migration to the United States* (Malden, MA: Wiley-Blackwell, 2011), 12.

14. Ibid., 62.

15. Ibid., 46.

16. Ibid., 16.

17. Ibid.

18. Ibid., 17.

19. Karl Marx, *Capital: A Critique of Political Economy*, trans. Ben Fowkes (London: Penguin, 1990), 1:818.

20. Jeffrey Marcos Garcilazo, *"Traqueros": Mexican Railroad Workers in the United States, 1870 to 1930* (Santa Barbara: University of California Press, 1995), 374.

21. For further argument of this point, see M. W. Foley, "Privatizing the Countryside: The Mexican Peasant Movement and Neoliberal Reform," *Latin American Perspectives* 22, no. 1 (1995): 59–76, at 64.

22. Alex Penwill, "Exploitation on the Range: Migrant Guestworkers and Forced Labor," *Human Trafficking Center Blog*, May 22, 2014, http://humantraffickingcenter.org/guest-posts/h2a-visas-exploitation-migrant-herders/.

23. Henderson, *Beyond Borders*, 58–89.

24. Ibid., 62.

25. Ibid., 60.

26. J. Lewis, "Agrarian Change and Privatization of Ejido Land in Northern Mexico," *Journal of Agrarian Change* 2, no. 3 (2002): 401–19, at 403.

27. Ibid.

28. Ibid., 413, 408.

29. Jonathan Fox and Libby Haight, eds., *Subsidizing Inequality: Mexican Corn Policy since NAFTA* (Washington, DC: Woodrow Wilson International Center for Scholars/CIDE/UC Santa Cruz, 2010). Cited in Bacon, *The Right to Stay Home*, 59.

30. Francisco López Bárcenas and Mayra Montserrat Eslava Galicia, *El mineral o la vida: La legislación minera en México* (COAPI, 2011), http://desinformemonos.org/PDF/El_mineral_o_la_vida.pdf. Cited in Bacon, *The Right to Stay Home*, 45–46.

31. Bacon, *The Right to Stay Home*, 43.

32. Ibid., 132.

33. Todd Miller, "Megaprojects and Militarization: A Perfect Storm in Mexico," *NACLA Report on the Americas,* 2009, https://nacla.org/node/5830.

34. Richard Fry, "Migration and Gender," Pew Research Center, July 5, 2006, http://www.pewhispanic.org/2006/07/05/ii-migration-and-gender/.

35. Bacon, *The Right to Stay Home*, 58.

36. Ibid., 24.
37. Ibid., 239.

CHAPTER 14

1. Todd Miller, "Megaprojects and Militarization: A Perfect Storm in Mexico," *NACLA Report on the Americas,* 2009, https://nacla.org/node/5830.
2. Ibid.
3. David Bacon, *The Right to Stay Home: How US Policy Drives Mexican Migration* (Boston: Beacon Press, 2013), 56.
4. Ibid.
5. Miller, "Megaprojects and Militarization."
6. Lynn Stephen, "The Construction of Indigenous Suspects: Militarization and the Gendered and Ethnic Dynamics of Human Rights Abuses in Southern Mexico," *American Ethnologist* 26 (1999): 822–42, at 826.
7. Ibid., 828.
8. Deepa Fernandes, "Militarization Continues in Southern Mexico," *NACLA Report on the Americas* 33, no. 3 (1999): 2.
9. Stephen, "The Construction of Indigenous Suspects," 829.
10. Ibid.
11. Miller, "Megaprojects and Militarization."
12. For a detailed history of the San Andrés Accords, see Gloria Ramírez, *The Fire and the Word: A History of the Zapatista Movement* (San Francisco: City Lights Books, 2008).
13. For a history of Mexico's disenfranchisement of its indigenous people and their resistance, see Alex Khasnabish, *Zapatistas: Rebellion from the Grassroots to the Global* (Halifax, Nova Scotia: Fernwood Publishing, 2010).
14. Secure Fence Act of 2006, HR 6061, 1–2.
15. "The Obama administration claimed that it was only seeking criminals for deportation, and that participation in the program was voluntary. But when New York state and Massachusetts formally refused to participate, DHS announced that participation in Secure Communities was mandatory and implemented the program everywhere." Bacon, *The Right to Stay Home,* 175.
16. Ibid.
17. Ibid., 147.
18. Ibid., 146.
19. Joseph Nevins, *Operation Gatekeeper and Beyond: The War on "Illegals" and the Remaking of the U.S.-Mexico Boundary* (New York: Routledge, 2010), 3.
20. US Customs and Border Protection, "Border Patrol Agent Staffing by Fiscal Year (as of September 20, 2014)," http://www.cbp.gov/sites/default/files/documents/BP%20Staffing%20FY1992-FY2014_0.pdf.

21. Bill Maher, roundtable section of the HBO show *Real Time with Bill Maher*, June 21, 2013. His statement fact-checked at http://www.politifact.com/truth-o-meter/statements/2013/jul/01/bill-maher/bill-maher-said-immigration-bill-will-make-border-/.

22. "The Secretary of Homeland Security shall have the authority to waive, and shall waive, all laws such Secretary, in such Secretary's sole discretion, determines necessary to ensure expeditious construction of the barriers and roads under this section." Real ID Act, 2005, HR 418, sec. 102. In order to build the wall, the secretary of Homeland Security used the unlimited power of this act to waive more than thirty environmental regulations, including the Endangered Species Act, the National Environmental Policy Act, the Clean Water Act, the Clean Air Act, and the National Historic Preservation Act. See Richard Marosi and Nicole Gaouette, "Border Fence Will Skirt Environmental Laws," *Los Angeles Times*, April 2, 2008, http://web.archive.org/web/20080414005257/http://www.latimes.com/news/nationworld/nation/la-na-fence2apr02,0,5819252.story.

23. US Government Accountability Office, "DHS Has Faced Challenges Deploying Technology and Fencing along the Southwest Border," May 4, 2010, 10, http://www.gao.gov/assets/90/82411.pdf.

24. Daniel Wood, "Billions for a US-Mexico Border Fence, but Is It Doing any Good?," *Christian Science Monitor*, September 19, 2009, http://www.csmonitor.com/USA/2009/0919/p02s09-usgn.html.

25. Stuart Anderson, "How Many More Deaths? The Moral Case for a Temporary Worker Program," National Foundation for American Policy Brief, March 2013, http://www.nfap.com/pdf/NFAP%20Policy%20Brief%20Moral%20Case%20For%20a%20Temporary%20Worker%20Program%20March%202013.pdf.

26. Ibid.

27. *The San Diego Union* newspaper compared the perils of the task to "guerrilla warfare in Vietnam." Cited in Nevins, *Operation Gatekeeper and Beyond*, 88.

28. Both sides for and against calling Mexican migrants "barbarians" presuppose the "evil" of barbarism and the "good" of civilization. But this is a historical prejudice worthy of reconsideration: barbarism is actually a positive creative force that in many ways offers an alternative to the structural expulsion of the "empire." See Nathan Smith, "America, the Roman Empire, and 'Barbarian Invasions,'" *Open Borders*, July 26, 2012, http://openborders.info/blog/america-the-roman-empire-and-barbarian-invasions/.

29. For example, when migrant justice demonstrations sang a Spanish version of the American national anthem, "Nuestro Himno," George W. Bush responded, "I think the national anthem ought to be sung in English and I think people who want to be a citizen of this country ought to learn English, and they ought to learn to sing the national anthem in English." Mark Krikorian of

the Center for Immigration Studies responded by saying, "It's kind of an odd way for illegal immigrants to ask the American people to forgive them for their offenses—to appropriate one of our symbols and make it suit them better." Tennessee senator Lamar Alexander even introduced a resolution to, in his words, "[r]emind the country why we sing our National Anthem in English." Lloyd Vries, "Bush: Sing National Anthem In English," *CBS News*, April 28, 2006, httjp://www.cbsnews.com/news/bush-sing-national-anthem-in-english/.

30. Samuel Huntington, *Reconsidering Immigration: Is Mexico a Special Case?* (Washington, DC: Center for Immigration Studies, 2000), http://www.cis.org/ articles/2000/back1100.html; and *The Clash of Civilizations and the Remaking of World Order* (New York: Simon & Schuster, 1996).

31. Patrick Buchanan, *The Death of the West: How Dying Populations and Immigrant Invasions Imperil Our Country and Civilization* (New York: St. Martin's Press, 2002); Patrick Buchanan, *State of Emergency: the Third World Invasion and Conquest of America* (New York: St. Martin's Press, 2006).

32. "To the Romans, the German tribes were riffraff; to the Germans, the Roman side of the river was the place to be. The nearest we can come to understanding this divide may be the southern border of the United States. There the spit-and-polish troops are immigration police; the hordes, the Mexicans, Haitians, and other dispossessed people seeking illegal entry." Thomas Cahill, *How the Irish Saved Civilization: The Untold Story of Ireland's Heroic Role from the Fall of Rome to the Rise of Medieval Europe* (New York: Doubleday, 1995), 16.

33. Thomas Nail, "Child Refugees: The New Barbarians," *Pacific Standard: The Science of Society*, August 19, 2014. Republished in *The Medes*, January 15, 2015.

34. Buchanan, *State of Emergency*, 2.

35. Ibid., 3.

36. Neville Morley, *The Roman Empire: Roots of Imperialism* (London: Pluto Press, 2010).

37. Ammianus Marcellinus writes that "though they repeatedly endeavoured to calculate their numbers, at last abandoned the attempt as hopeless: and the man who would wish to ascertain the number might as well attempt to count the waves in the African sea." *Roman History* (Cambridge, MA: Harvard University Press, 1950), 31.4.6.

38. Barbarian soldiers in the Roman army were frontline fodder, and most died early in battle by the thousands. Noel Lenski, *Failure of Empire: Valens and the Roman State in the Fourth Century A.D.* (Berkeley: University of California Press, 2002), 324.

39. Ammianus, *Roman History*, 41.4.5.

40. Lenski, *Failure of Empire*, 326. "Eunapius and Zosimus lament the frenzy of Roman commanders racing to acquire sex slaves and agricultural laborers on the cheap" (Ammianus, *Roman History*, 31.4.11).

41. Ammianus, *Roman History*, 31.4.11.

42. For a detailed account of this process, see Lenski, *Failure of Empire,* chap. 7.

43. Ammianus, *Roman History*, 31.4.6.

44. "George W. Bush on Immigration," speech in Washington, D.C., June 26, 2000, http://www.ontheissues.org/celeb/George_W__Bush_Immigration.htm.

45. The DREAM Act (Development, Relief, and Education for Alien Minors) is an American legislative proposal first introduced in the Senate on August 1, 2001, S. 1291, by Dick Durbin and Orrin Hatch. The act has not passed yet. "The DREAM Act is a bipartisan bill that would provide undocumented youths who came to the United States before the age of sixteen a path toward legalization on the condition that they attend college or serve in the U.S. military for a minimum of two years while maintaining good moral character." See Raul Hinojosa Ojeda and Paule Cruz Takash, "No DREAMers Left Behind," North American Integration and Development Center, accessed April 24, 2015, http://www.immigrationpolicy.org/sites/default/files/docs/No%20DREAMers%20Left%20Behind.pdf.

46. Anderson, "How Many More Deaths?"

47. "The documents, obtained over recent months by The Times and the American Civil Liberties Union under the Freedom of Information Act, concern most of the 107 deaths in detention counted by Immigration and Customs Enforcement since October 2003, after the agency was created within the Department of Homeland Security." Nina Bernstein, "Officials Hid Truth of Immigrant Deaths in Jail," *New York Times*, January 9, 2010, http://www.nytimes.com/2010/01/10/us/10detain.html?_r=0.

48. See Morley, *The Roman Empire.*

49. Richard Taylor, *Film Propaganda: Soviet Russia and Nazi Germany* (London: Croom Helm, 1979), 175.

50. "Latinos come to the US to seek the same dreams that have inspired millions of others: they want a better life for their children. Family values do not stop at the Rio Grande. Latinos enrich our country with faith in God, a strong ethic of work, community and responsibility. We can all learn from the strength, solidarity, and values of Latinos. Immigration is not a problem to be solved, it is the sign of a successful nation. New Americans are to be welcomed as neighbors and not to be feared as strangers." "George W. Bush on Immigration."

51. The Southern Poverty Law Center, "Close to Slavery: Guestworker Programs in the United States," 2007, updated 2013 report, http://www.splcenter.org/sites/default/files/downloads/publication/SPLC-Close-to-Slavery-2013.pdf.

52. US Representative Charles Rangel, speaking on CNN's *Lou Dobbs Tonight*, January 23, 2007.

53. Quoted in Patrick Mooney and Theo J. Majka, eds., *Farmers' and Farm Workers' Movements: Social Protest in American Agriculture* (New York: Twayne Publishers, 1995), 52.

54. Fred Krissman, "Immigrant Labor Recruitment: U.S. Agribusiness and Undocumented Migration from Mexico," in *Immigration Research for a New Century: Multidisciplinary Perspectives,* ed. Nancy Foner, Rubén G. Rumbaut, and Steven J. Gold (New York: Russell Sage Foundation, 2000), 277–300.

55. See David Barboza, "Tyson Foods Indicted in Plan to Smuggle Illegal Workers," *New York Times,* December 20, 2001, http://www.nytimes.com/2001/12/20/us/tyson-foods-indicted-in-plan-to-smuggle-illegal-workers.html; and International Labor Recruitment Working Group, "The American Dream Up for Sale: A Blueprint for Ending International Labor Recruitment Abuse," February 2013, http://www.cdmigrante.org/wp-content/uploads/2013/03/The-American-Dream-Up-For-Sale.pdf. "Employers are able to exploit an essentially captive workforce, and workers are deterred from asserting their rights under U.S. law. Workers who complain routinely are blacklisted, threatened or physically intimidated by recruiters. Additionally, many internationally recruited workers face language barriers, racism, xenophobia, sexism and the pressures of poverty in both the United States and their home countries," 7.

56. Keith Cunningham-Parmeter, "Alien Language: Immigration Metaphors and the Jurisprudence of Otherness," *Fordham Law Review* 79, no. 4 (2011): 1545–98.

57. "This is a distressing evolution of the English language. In the mid-twentieth century the noun 'illegal' was used in reference to Jewish migrants in various places. By the late 1960s, it was used in quotation marks, or as a repeat reference, once illegal immigrants had already been discussed. Now it is used [in the *OED*] without drawing any special attention at all. In English, 'illegal' has become a noun." Catherine Dauvergne, *Making People Illegal: What Globalization Means for Migration and Law* (Cambridge: Cambridge University Press, 2008), 10.

58. Vagabond laws are an interesting historical case that pushes the boundary between "being" and "action." See Chapter 16 and Peter Linebaugh, *Stop, Thief! The Commons, Enclosures, and Resistance* (Oakland, CA: PM Press, 2014).

CHAPTER 15

1. Perry Anderson, *Passages from Antiquity to Feudalism* (London: NLB, 1974), 152.

2. Ibid.

3. Ibid., 413.

4. For a more detailed account of this process, see Bill Hing, *Ethical Borders: NAFTA, Globalization, and Mexican Migration* (Philadelphia: Temple University Press, 2010).

5. David Bacon, *The Right to Stay Home: How US Policy Drives Mexican Migration* (Boston: Beacon Press, 2013), 11.

6. Vandana Shiva, *Water Wars: Pollution, Profits and Privatization* (London: Pluto Press, 2002), 96.

7. Ibid.

8. See James Markusen and Steven Zahniser, *Liberalization and Incentives for Labor Migration: Theory with Applications to NAFTA* (Cambridge, MA: National Bureau of Economic Research, 1997); and David Bacon, *Illegal People: How Globalization Creates Migration and Criminalizes Immigrants* (Boston: Beacon Press, 2008).

9. Bacon, *The Right to Stay Home*, 111.

10. Human Rights Watch, "Mexico's Maquiladoras: Abuses against Women Workers," August 17, 1996, http://www.hrw.org/news/1996/08/17/mexicos-maquiladoras-abuses-against-women-workers.

11. Virginia Sole-Smith, "Sweatshops at Sea: Tightening U.S. Seafood Regulations Could Improve Human Rights in Mexico," *Utne Reader*, September–October 2010, http://www.utne.com/politics/squid-sweatshops-human-rights-seafood-mexico.aspx. See also Milah Shah, "Cons of Maquiladoras," Mount Holyoke College, accessed April 15, 2015, http://www.mtholyoke.edu/~shah20m/classweb/cons.html.

12. "Surface and groundwater supplies are threatened along the US-Mexico border due to the dumping of raw sewage, agricultural runoff, and industrial and hazardous waste pollution. . . . All streams and rivers in the border region have suffered deterioration of water quality due to the lack of adequate municipal wastewater collection and treatment systems. The current infrastructure deficit is enormous, and the added demand created by growing populations will be significant." Southwest Center for Environmental Research and Policy (SCERP), *The U.S.-Mexican Border Environment: A Road Map to a Sustainable 2020*, Border Environment Research Reports, no. 5, May 1999, http://www.scerp.org/ SCERPborder_institute.pdf.

13. All of the *colonia* statistics come from "Executive Summary Blurred Borders: Transboundary Impacts and Solutions in the San Diego-Tijuana Region," 2004, http://www.icfdn.org/publications/blurredborders/, 201.

14. Sandra Dibble, "Homeless Encampment Removed from Tijuana River," *San Diego Union-Tribune*, August 6, 2013, http://www.utsandiego.com/news/2013/aug/06/homeless-encampment-removed-from-tijuana-river/all/?print.

15. "While the Mexican government implements and encourages policies to protect Mexican migrants, such as supporting migrant shelters in Colonia Postal, it simultaneously makes use of the availability of migrant bodies by arresting them and presenting them as evidence of local police efforts to 'crack down on crime.'" Martha Escobar, "Domesticating Migration: The Gendered Criminalization of Mexican Migrants by Tijuana Police," paper presented at the annual meeting of the American Studies Association annual meeting, Hilton Baltimore, Baltimore, January 9, 2014.

16. "Texas Colonias: A Thumbnail Sketch of Conditions, Issues, Challenges and Opportunities, "Texas Secretary of State, Texas Border & Mexican Affairs, accessed April 24, 2015, http://www.sos.state.tx.us/border/colonias/faqs.shtml.

17. Emilio Godoy, "Mexico's Homeless Are Targets of 'Social Cleansing,'" Inter Press Service News Agency, November 1, 2012, http://www.ipsnews. net/2012/11/mexicos-homeless-are-targets-of-social-cleansing/.

18. Tim Cresswell, *The Tramp in America* (London: Reaktion, 2001), 56.

19. Ana Aliverti, *Crimes of Mobility: Criminal Law and the Regulation of Immigration* (Abindgon, UK: Routledge, 2013), 15, 17.

20. US Congress, *Foreign Criminals and Paupers Report to Accompany Bill H.R. 124*, Washington, DC, August 16, 1856, http://libsysdigi.library.illinois.edu/oca/Books2008-06/foreigncriminalsoounit/.

21. United States, Federal Immigration Laws between 1901–1930, "Immigration Act of February 5, 1917," http://www.illegalimmigrants.org/laws.html. "Added to the exclusion list were illiterates, persons of psychopathic inferiority, men as well as women entering for immoral purposes, alcoholics, stowaways, and vagrants."

22. Steven Bender, *Greasers & Gringos: Latinos, Law & the American Imagination* (New York: New York University Press, 2003), xiii–xv.

23. "Between 1795 and 1810, Maryland enacted vagrancy laws similar to Delaware's; required free blacks to obtain certificates of good character from local officials in order to sell products or keep hunting equipment; and allowed its courts to apprentice children of destitute or unfit black parents to white masters." Joseph Ranney, *In the Wake of Slavery: Civil War, Civil Rights, and the Reconstruction of Southern Law* (Westport, CT: Praeger Publishers, 2006), 17.

24. "City ordinances frequently serve as a prominent tool to criminalize homelessness. Of the 224 cities surveyed for our report: 28% prohibit 'camping' in particular public places in the city and 16% had city-wide prohibitions on 'camping.' 27% prohibit sitting/lying in certain public places. 39% prohibit loitering in particular public areas and 16% prohibit loitering city-wide. 43% prohibit begging in particular public places; 45% prohibit aggressive panhandling and 21% have city-wide prohibitions on begging." National Coalition for the Homeless and National Law Center on Homelessness & Poverty, *A Dream Denied: The Criminalization of Homelessness in U.S. Cities*, January 2006, http://www.nationalhomeless.org/publications/crimreport/report.pdf.

25. Arizona SB 1070, sec. 2, 2010, http://www.azleg.gov/legtext/49leg/2r/bills/sb1070s.pdf.

26. "Jeff Duncan, South Carolina Rep, Compares Undocumented Immigrants to Vagrants, Animals," *Huffington Post*, November 2, 2011, http://www.huffingtonpost.com/2011/11/02/jeff-duncan-south-carolina-immigrants_n_1071695.html.

27. The point here is not simply a normative one: "[W]e should reject Duncan's usage of the word animal and vagrant and affirm that migrants are human too." Duncan's comment is actually an accurate description of the way in which migrants are viewed by many US lawmakers, laws, and political representatives (not to mention the anti-immigrant base who continues to support this sort of criminalization).

28. Bacon, *The Right to Stay Home*, 148.

29. Ibid., 158.

30. Ibid., 193.

31. See Ronald Mize and Alicia Swords, *Consuming Mexican Labor: From the Bracero Program to NAFTA* (Toronto: University of Toronto Press, 2011).

32. See Bacon, *The Right to Stay Home*, 148–93.

33. The Southern Poverty Law Center, "Close to Slavery: Guestworker Programs in the United States," 2007, updated 2013 report, http://www.splcenter.org/sites/default/files/downloads/publication/SPLC-Close-to-Slavery-2013.pdf.

34. Peter Nyers, "Community without Status: Non-status Migrants and Cities of Refuge," in *Renegotiating Community: Interdisciplinary Perspectives, Global Contexts*, ed. Diana Brydon and William Coleman (Vancouver: University of British Columbia Press, 2008), 123–38, quote on 134.

35. Bacon, *The Right to Stay Home*, 143.

36. Department of Homeland Security, Office of Inspector General, "Immigration and Customs Enforcement's Tracking and Transfers of Detainees," March 2009, http://www.oig.dhs.gov/assets/Mgmt?OIT_09-41_Mar09.pdf, 2.

37. These statistics are all from Associated Press, "Immigrants Face Long Detention, Few Rights: Many Detainees Spend Months or Years in US Detention Centers," NBC News, March 15, 2009, http://www.nbcnews.com/id/29706177/#.VQ5FF-FcoQh.

38. Bacon, *The Right to Stay Home*, 145.

CHAPTER 16

1. Philip Russell, *The History of Mexico: From Pre-Conquest to Present* (New York: Routledge, 2010), 457.

2. Ibid.

3. Ibid., 457, 440, 462.

4. Cited in ibid., 463. See CDIA (Centro de Investigaciones Agrarias), *Estructura agraria y desarrollo agrícola en México* (Mexico City: Fondo de Cultura Económica, 1974), 1028, 1042.

5. "Early 1960s legislation forced foreign mining companies to sell 51 percent of their capital to Mexicans and stipulated that new mining concessions would

only be granted to firms with at least 66 percent Mexican capital." Russell, *The History of Mexico,* 464.

6. Ibid.

7. Cited in ibid., 506.

8. Cited in ibid., 493.

9. See ibid., 490–506.

10. Cited in ibid., 506.

11. See Joseph Schumpeter, *Capitalism, Socialism, and Democracy* (New York: Harper, 1950).

12. Ibid., 542–45.

13. Cited in ibid., 543.

14. Cited in ibid., 545. See also Marko Voljc and Joost Draaisma, "Privatization and Economic Stabilization in Mexico," *Columbia Journal of World Business* 28 (Spring 1993): 122–34, at 126.

15. Cited in Russell, *The History of Mexico,* 508.

16. Ibid., 556.

17. Richard H. K. Vietor and Alexander Veytsman, "American Outsourcing," Harvard Business School Case 705-037, April 2005 (revised February 2007).

18. D'Vera Cohn, Ana Gonzalez-Barrera, and Danielle Cuddington, "Remittances to Latin America Recover—but Not to Mexico," Pew Hispanic Center, November 15, 2013, http://www.pewhispanic.org/2013/11/15/remittances-to-latin-america-recover-but-not-to-mexico/.

19. Cited in David Bacon, *The Right to Stay Home: How US Policy Drives Mexican Migration* (Boston: Beacon Press, 2013), 19.

20. Cited in ibid., 19–20.

21. See Francisco Balderrama and Raymond Rodriguez, *Decade of Betrayal: Mexican Repatriation in the 1930s* (Albuquerque: University of New Mexico Press, 1995).

22. Terms like "bracero," meaning "manual laborer" (from *brazo,* meaning "arm"), or terms with the same root have been used throughout history to describe the temporary migrant laborer. In the thirteenth century in Southern France, the *brassien* lived entirely by selling the strength of their arms (*bras*) and hiring themselves out to richer peasants or landed gentry.

23. As the November 1960 CBS documentary *Harvest of Shame* argued. Edward Murrow and Dan Rather, *Harvest of Shame* (New York: Docudrama, 2005).

24. Philip Martin, "The Bracero Program: Was It a Failure?," History News Network, accessed April 24, 2015, http://historynewsnetwork.org/article/27336.

25. The Pew Hispanic Center, "Modes of Entry for the Unauthorized Migrant Population," *Fact Sheet,* May 22, 2006, http://pewhispanic.org/files/factsheets/19.pdf.

CHAPTER 17

1. Several other authors have also pointed out this connection. See Tim Cresswell, "Towards a Politics of Mobility," *Environment and Planning D: Society and Space* 28, no. 1 (2010): 17–31; Patricia Tuitt, *False Images: Law's Construction of the Refugee* (London: Pluto Press, 1996), 67–79; A. White, "Geographies of Asylum, Legal Knowledge and Legal Practices," *Political Geography* 21, no. 8 (2002): 1055–73.

2. California Proposition 187 was passed in November 1994, but in 1999 a federal court found the law unconstitutional and ruled against it.

3. Otto Santa Ana, *Brown Tide Rising: Metaphors of Latinos in Contemporary American Public Discourse* (Austin: University of Texas Press, 2002), 69, 76.

4. Ibid., 75.

5. Thomas Nail, "Child Refugees: The New Barbarians," *Pacific Standard: The Science of Society*, August 19, 2014. Republished in *The Medes*, January 15, 2015.

6. Keith Cunningham-Parmeter, "Alien Language: Immigration Metaphors and the Jurisprudence of Otherness," *Fordham Law Review* 79, no. 4 (2011): 1545–98.

7. Ibid., 1581.

8. On the concept of social change as pressure, see Yves Citton, *Renverser l'insoutenable* (Paris: Seuil, 2012), 53–118.

9. "Humane Borders is committed to maintaining water and first aid stations throughout the Sonora desert, and has utilized Geographic Information Systems (GIS) and other locational technologies to augment these practices." J. Walsh, "Remapping the Border: Geospatial Technologies and Border Activism," *Environment and Planning D: Society and Space* 31, no. 6 (2013): 969–87, quote on 970.

10. See Maria Boletsi, *Barbarism and Its Discontents* (Stanford, CA: Stanford University Press, 2013), 127–38.

11. Walter Benjamin, "Erfahrung und Armut," in *Gesammelte Schriften, Volume 2*, ed. Rolf Tiedemann and Hermann Schweppenhäuser (Frankfurt am Main: Suhrkamp, 1972), 213–19, quote on 215.

12. "Problem: where are the barbarians of the twentieth century? Obviously they will come into view and consolidate themselves only after tremendous socialist crises." Friedrich Wilhelm Nietzsche, *The Will to Power*, ed. R. J. Hollingdale, trans. Walter Arnold Kaufmann (New York: Vintage Books, 1968), 465.

13. Ibid., 487.

14. Ernest Coeurderoy and Octave Vauthier, *La barrière du combat* (Brussels: Impr. Labroue, 1852); Ernest Coeurderoy, *De la révolution dans l'homme et dans la société* (Brussels: Impr. Labroue, 1852).

15. Joseph Déjacque, *L'Humanisphère* (Brussels: Administration, 1899), working translation by Shawn P. Wilbur at http://libertarian-labyrinth.blogspot.com/2012/10/joseph-dejacque-humanisphere-part-iii.html.

16. Michael Hardt and Antonio Negri, *Empire* (Cambridge, MA: Harvard University Press, 2000), 20.

17. Crisso and Odoteo, *Barbarians: The Disordered Insurgence*, trans. Wolfi Landstreicher (Sacramento, CA: Black Powder Press, 2006), 82.

18. Ibid., 76.

19. John Holloway and Eloína Peláez, eds., *Zapatista! Reinventing Revolution in Mexico* (London: Pluto Press, 1998), 1.

20. Subcomandante Insurgente Marcos, *Ya Basta! Ten Years of the Zapatista Uprising*, ed. Žiga Vodovnik (Oakland, CA: AK Press, 2004), 208.

21. Thomas Nail, *Returning to Revolution: Deleuze, Guattari and Zapatismo* (Edinburgh: Edinburgh University Press, 2012).

22. Marcos, *Ya Basta!*, 197.

23. For a collection of popular references to migrants as "invaders," see Ediberto Román, "The Alien Invasion?," *Houston Law Review* 45, no. 841 (2008): 872–81.

24. Chief Justice Warren E. Burger, 1975. Cited in Cunningham-Parmeter, "Alien Language," 1546. United States v. Ortiz, 422 U.S. 891, 904 (1975) (Burger, J., concurring) (quoting United States v. Baca, 368 F. Supp. 398, 402–08 [S.D. Cal. 1973]).

25. Cunningham-Parmeter, "Alien Language," 1583.

26. Bob Miller, "'No Papers, No Fear': Undocumented Immigrants Declare Themselves on Bus Tour," NBC News, August 17, 2012, http://usnews.nbc-news.com/_news/2012/08/17/13333450-no-papers-no-fear-undocumented-immigrants-declare-themselves-on-bus-tour?lite.

27. David Bacon, *The Right to Stay Home: How US Policy Drives Mexican Migration* (Boston: Beacon Press, 2013), 98–112.

28. Ibid., 104.

29. The following events are all discussed at length in ibid.

30. Ibid., 122–29.

31. Hardt and Negri, *Empire*, 207.

32. Ibid., 205.

33. Ilyce Glink and Samuel J. Tamkin, "Is the Foreclosure Crisis Over? Evidence Points Both Ways," *Chicago Tribune*, September 29, 2013, http://articles.chicagotribune.com/2013-09-29/marketplace/sns-201305312000--tms--realest-mctnig-a20130607-20130607_1_foreclosure-crisis-housing-crisis-housing-market.

Index

The authorized representative in the EU for product safety and compliance is:
Mare Nostrum Group
B.V Doelen 72
4831 GR Breda
The Netherlands

www.ingramcontent.com/pod-product-compliance
Lightning Source LLC
Chambersburg PA
CBHW020829270326
41928CB00006B/471